OFFICIAL PROCEEDINGS

OF THE

NATIONAL

DEMOCRATIC CONVENTION,

HELD AT

NEW YORK, JULY 4—9, 1868.

REPORTED BY GEORGE WAKEMAN,
OFFICIAL REPORTER OF THE CONVENTION.

BOSTON:
ROCKWELL & ROLLINS, PRINTERS,
122 WASHINGTON STREET.
1868.

NATIONAL DEMOCRATIC CONVENTION.

NEW YORK, Saturday, July 4th, 1868.

THE National Democratic Convention, to nominate candidates for the office of President and Vice-President of the United States, assembled at Tammany Hall, in the City of New York, at 12 M., July 4th, Independence Day, pursuant to the call of the National Democratic Executive Committee.

The Hon. AUGUST BELMONT, Chairman of the National Democratic Committee, appeared upon the platform in the performance of his duty of calling the Convention to order, and was greeted with loud cheering. When order was completely restored, he spoke as follows, —

Speech of the Hon. August Belmont.

GENTLEMEN OF THE CONVENTION, — It is my privilege to-day to welcome you here in this hall, constructed with so much artistic taste and tendered to you by the time-honored society of Tammany. (Loud cheers.) I welcome you to this magnificent temple, erected to the Goddess of Liberty by her stanchest defenders and most fervent worshippers. (Applause.) I welcome you to this good city of New York, the bulwark of Democracy (Great applause), which has rolled back the surging waves of Radicalism through all the storms of the last eight years; and I welcome you, gentlemen, to our Empire State, which last fall redeemed herself from Republican misrule by a majority of nearly 50,000 votes, and which claims the right to lead the vanguard of victory in the great battle to be fought next November for the preservation of our institutions, our laws, and our liberties. (Great cheering.)

It is a most auspicious omen that we meet under such circumstances, and are surrounded by such associations, and I share your own confident hope of the overwhelming success of the ticket and the platform which will be the result of your deliberations. (Applause.) For it is to the American people that our appeal lies. Their final judgment will be just. The American people will no longer remain deaf to the teachings of the past. They will remember that it was under successive Democratic administrations, based upon our national principles, the principles of constitutional liberty, that our country rose to a prosperity and greatness unsurpassed in the annals of history;

they will remember the days when North and South marched shoulder to shoulder together in the conquest of Mexico, which gave us our golden empire on the Pacific; our California and our Oregon, now the strongholds of a triumphant Democracy (Cheers); they will remember the days when peace and plenty reigned over the whole Union, when we had no national debt to crush the energies of the people, when the Federal tax-gatherer was unknown throughout the vast extent of the land, and when the credit of the United States stood as high in the money marts of the world as that of any other government (Applause); and they will remember, with a wise sorrow, that, with the downfall of the Democratic party, in 1860, came that fearful civil war which has brought mourning and desolation into every household; has cost the loss of a million of American citizens, and has left us with a national debt the burden of which drains the resources, cripples the industry, and impoverishes the labor of the country. (Applause.) They will remember that, after the fratricidal strife was over, when the bravery of our army and navy and the sacrifices of the people had restored the Union and vindicated the supremacy of the law; when the victor and the vanquished were equally ready to bury the past and to hold out the hand of brotherhood and good-will across the graves of their fallen comrades, — it was again the defeat of the Democratic candidates in 1864 which prevented this consummation so devoutly wished for by all. Instead of restoring the Southern States to their constitutional rights, — instead of trying to wipe out the miseries of the past by a magnanimous policy, dictated alike by humanity and sound statesmanship, and so ardently prayed for by the generous heart of the American people, — the Radicals in Congress, elected in an evil hour, have placed the iron heel of the conqueror upon the South. Austria did not dare to fasten upon vanquished Hungary, nor Russia to impose upon conquered Poland, the ruthless tyranny now inflicted by Congress upon the Southern States. (Loud applause.) Military satraps are invested with dictatorial power, overriding the decisions of the courts, and assuming the functions of the civil authorities; the whole populations are disfranchised or forced to submit to test oaths alike revolting to justice and civilization; and a debased and ignorant race, just emerged from servitude, is raised unto power to control the destinies of that fair portion of our common country. (Applause.) These men, elected to be legislators, and legislators only, trampling the Constitution under their feet, have usurped the functions of the Executive and the Judiciary, and it is impossible to doubt, after the events of the past few months, and the circumstances of the impeachment trial, that they will not shrink from an attempt hereafter to subvert the Senate of the United States, which alone stood between them and their victim, and which had virtue enough left not to allow the American name to be utterly disgraced, and justice to be dragged in the dust. (Cheers.) In order to carry out this nefarious programme, our army and navy are kept in times of profound peace on a scale which involves a yearly expenditure of from one to two hundred millions; prevents the reduction of our national debt, and imposes upon our people a system of the most exorbitant and unequal taxation, with a vicious, irredeemable, and depreciated currency. (Applause.) And now this same party, which has brought all these evils upon the country, comes again before the American people, asking for their suffrages; and whom has it chosen for its candidate? *The General commanding the Armies of the United States.*

Can there be any doubt left as to the designs of the Radicals, if they should be able to keep their hold on the reins of government? *They intend Congressional usurpation of all the branches and functions of the Government, to be enforced by the bayonets of a military despotism!* (Loud applause.) It is impossible that a free and intelligent people can longer submit to such a state of things. They will not calmly stand by to see their liberties subverted, the prosperity and greatness of their country undermined, and the institutions bequeathed to them by the fathers of the Republic wrested from them. (Cheers.) They must see that the conservative and national principles of a liberal and progressive Democracy are the only safeguards of the Republic. Gentlemen of the Convention: Your country looks to you to stay this tide of *disorganization, violence, and despotism.* It will not look in vain, when next November the roll shall be called, and when State after State shall respond, by rallying around the broad banner of Democracy, on which, in the future, as in the past, will be inscribed our undying motto: "*The Union, the Constitution, and the Laws!*"

Mr. BELMONT closed amid enthusiastic and long-continued cheering. When the applause had subsided, Mr. Belmont resumed, —

GENTLEMEN, — I have the honor to nominate, as temporary Chairman of this Convention, the Hon. Henry L. Palmer, of Wisconsin. The nomination was received with loud cheers. Mr. Palmer, on coming forward, was received with applause, and spoke as follows, —

Speech of the Temporary Chairman.

GENTLEMEN OF THE CONVENTION, — Permit me to return to you my most sincere acknowledgments for the high compliment you have conferred upon my State, and the great honor you have chosen to bestow upon me, in the choice you have made of a temporary presiding officer of this Convention. Permit me to assure you, gentlemen, that, during the brief period I shall have occasion to discharge the duties of the chair, I shall bring to bear such ability as I may possess to discharge those duties with perfect fairness to all the States, and to all the delegates. I do not regard myself competent, and if I did, I should not regard it as my duty, in occupying the chair temporarily, to enter into any general discussion of the political situation of the day, or to advise or seek to instruct this Convention in regard to the performance of its labors. I may, however, be permitted to congratulate you, and to congratulate our country at large, that, on this bright and beautiful anniversary of our nation's birth, once more a Convention of the Democracy of this country is assembled in which all the States are represented (Enthusiastic cheering; many of the audience rising and waving their handkerchiefs), and in which delegates from the East, and from the West, and from the North, and from the South, all come here and unite together to perform a great work for our common country. (Long-continued applause.) And permit me to express the hope that this fact may be an omen of a unity of sentiment in this Convention which shall enable you to produce such a work as will commend itself to the approval of the people of our whole country, and thus wrest it from the hands which seek its destruction. (Loud applause.)

Again thanking you, gentlemen, for the compliment you have chosen to pay me, I have the pleasure of presenting to the Convention the Rev. Dr. Morgan, of New York.

Rev. Dr. MORGAN, the Rector of St. Thomas's Church, New York, then offered an impressive prayer as follows, the whole Convention rising, —

Prayer.

O Lord, who art the blessed and only Potentate, the King of Kings, and Lord of Lords, the Almighty Ruler of Nations, we adore and magnify Thy glorious name for all the great things which Thou hast done for us. We render Thee thanks for the goodly heritage which Thou hast given us; for the civil and religious privileges which we enjoy, and for the multiplied manifestations of Thy favor toward us. Grant that we may show forth our thankfulness for these, Thy mercies, by living in reverence of Thy Almighty power and dominion, in humble reliance on Thy goodness and mercy, and in holy obedience to Thy righteous laws. Preserve, we beseech Thee, to our country, the blessings of peace; restore them to nations deprived of them, and secure them to all the people of the earth. May the Kingdom of the Prince of Peace come, and, reigning in the hearts and lives of men, unite them in holy fellowship, that so their only strife may be, who shall show forth with most humble and holy fervor the praises of Him who both loved them and made them kings and priests unto God. We implore Thy blessing on all in legislative, judicial, and executive authority, that they may have grace, wisdom, and understanding to discharge their duties as most effectually to promote Thy glory, the interests of true religion and virtue, and the peace, good order, and welfare of the nation. Especially do we pray that the deliberations of this Convention may be ordained and settled by Thy governance upon the best and surest foundation; that peace and happiness, truth and justice, religion and piety may be established among us for all generations. Give to its officers wisdom, and to its members a sound mind; and may all their doings tend to Thy glory, and to the safety, honor, and welfare of thy people. Continue, O Lord, to prosper our institutions for the promotion of sound learning, the diffusion of virtuous education, the advancement of Christian truth, and for the purity and prosperity of Thy Church. Change, we beseech Thee, every evil heart of unbelief, and shed the quickening influences of Thy Holy Spirit on all the people of this land. Save us from the guilt of abusing the blessings of prosperity to luxury and licentiousness, to irreligion and vice, lest we provoke Thee, in just judgment, to visit our offences with a rod, and our sins with scourges. O Almighty God, who hast never failed those who put their trust in Thee, imprint on our hearts, we beseech Thee, a deep and habitual sense of this great truth, that the only security for the continuance of the blessings which we enjoy consists in our acknowledgment of Thy sovereign and gracious Providence, and in humble and holy submission to the Gospel of Thy Son, Jesus Christ, to whom all power is given in heaven and on earth, and who is one with the Father, and the Holy Ghost, in the eternal Godhead, — our Mediator, and Redeemer. Amen.

The Rules for the Temporary Organization.

General MCCOOK, of Ohio. — Mr. Chairman, I move for the adoption by the Convention, before any other business is proceeded with, a resolution which I presume will meet with unanimous concurrence.

Resolved, That, until the Convention shall otherwise provide, the rules of the House of Representatives shall govern the deliberations of this body.

The motion was seconded.

Mr. ERASTUS BROOKS, of New York. — Mr. Chairman, there are many gentlemen in the Convention who do not recognize the rules of the present House of Representatives. (Cheers.) I trust the gentleman will accept as an amendment, that the rules which govern deliberative bodies shall be the rules of this Convention until otherwise ordered. (Applause.)

General McCOOK. — I would gladly accept the amendment of the gentleman on my right, but he does me great injustice if he thinks I would move the adoption of the rules of the present House, if I did not know that they had not dared to change one of the time-honored rules that were established under Democratic auspices. (Applause.) It is best, in my opinion, that we should adopt, for the present, the rules of the House of Representatives, for reasons which, I think, every gentleman who has taken part in National Conventions will appreciate upon reflection. I cannot, therefore, accept the amendment of the gentleman on my right (Mr. Brooks).

Gov. RICHARDSON, of Illinois. — I agree with the gentleman from Ohio, that we should adopt the rules of the House of Representatives, but I have a single suggestion to make. I do not know whether this Radical Congress have overthrown any of the important rules of the House of Representatives, but they have done so much damage, so much mischief, so much outrage, and so much of wrong, that they may have violated some of these rules. I therefore ask my friend from Ohio to go back and accept the rules as they existed in 1860, before these Radical assaults had been made upon the time-honored usages of our country. (Applause.)

Mr. FRANCIS KERNAN, of Oneida, N. Y. — Mr. Chairman, I would submit to our friends that there is a better rule to govern our action than proposed by either of the gentlemen, — one time-honored, one that has always been satisfactory to Democrats. I therefore, sir, suggest and move as an amendment that, until otherwise ordered, we adopt as the rules to govern our deliberations, the rules which have governed Democratic Conventions heretofore. (Applause.) These, sir, we know have not been changed; these we know have not been tampered with by Radicals, and they were found wise and satisfactory. I move, as an amendment to the amendment of the gentleman from New York, that we adopt the rules of the Convention of 1864. (Applause.)

The CHAIRMAN. — The Chair requests that, until he becomes more familiar with the delegates, each gentleman, as he rises in his seat, will announce his name.

Mr. S. S. COX. — Mr. Chairman, I was about to say almost what has been said by the gentleman from New York. The rules which have been adopted heretofore by the National Conventions, as in 1860, were the rules of the House of Representatives (Applause); but the House of Representatives from time to time have changed these rules. I have a copy here of the rules adopted by the last Democratic National Convention. I hope my friend from Ohio will accept this as an amendment to his resolution upon the subject, —

Resolved, That the rules of the last Democratic Convention govern this body until otherwise ordered.

I move that, sir, as an amendment.

General McCOOK. — I shall be very happy to accept the amendment made by the gentleman from Illinois (Mr. Richardson), that we adopt the rules of the House of Representatives as they existed in 1860. That preserves us from any erroneous rules with which persons on this floor are not acquainted; but I cannot accept the amendment of the gentleman from New York, seconded by the gentleman from New York, whose face is quite familiar to people from Ohio (Mr. Cox). I accept the amendment of the gentleman from Illinois (Mr. Richardson).

Mr. REEVE, of Indiana. — If this motion would directly or indirectly abrogate the two-thirds rule, then I warn gentlemen to be careful before they vote.

The CHAIRMAN. — The Chair will state the position of the question as he understands it. The gentleman from Ohio offered a resolution which provides for the adoption of the rules of the House of Representatives to govern the Convention until otherwise ordered. The gentleman from New York (Mr. Brooks) proposes an amendment, which the Chair does not understand has been withdrawn.

Mr. ERASTUS BROOKS, of New York. — I withdraw the amendment, and accept the amendment moved by Mr. Cox, of New York. (Applause.)

The CHAIRMAN.—The Chair understands, the amendment of the gentleman from New York being withdrawn, that the amendment of the gentleman from Illinois (Mr. Richardson) will be in order.

A VOICE. — It has been accepted by the mover.

General McCOOK. — I accept the amendment of Mr. Richardson.

The CHAIRMAN. — The question will then recur upon the amendment offered by the gentleman from New York. Is the Convention ready for the question?

Mr. KERNAN, of New York. — I desire to inquire of the mover whether, if we adopt his motion, we do not abolish, without any consideration, the two-thirds rule, which has prevailed generally in Democratic Conventions?

General McCOOK. — If the two-thirds rule ever applied in a Democratic Convention, except on a vote on the nomination for President, the delegates from Ohio hear it now for the first time.

Mr. KERNAN. — We desired to know what was the understanding.

General McCOOK. — This resolution provides for the temporary organization and government of the Convention, until it shall otherwise provide, which will be done by a Committee on Rules and on Permanent Organization Monday morning.

Mr. RICHARDSON. — There is no difficulty about this question if we understand ourselves. We all agree that this is to govern us while we are in temporary existence. The Committee on Permanent Organization considers the question referred to by the gentlemen from New York, and we are cut off from nothing. We are doing nothing more than we have done at every Democratic Convention for the last twenty-four years.

Mr. STEELE, of California. — I rise to ask whether the amendment which we are asked to vote for at the present time is the amendment offered by the gentleman from New York, that the rules of the last Convention are to govern us until the permanent organization of this Convention?

The CHAIRMAN. — The resolution of the gentleman from Ohio, as it now stands, is as follows, —

Resolved, — That, until the Convention shall otherwise provide, the rules of the House of Representatives, prior to 1860, shall be the rules to govern this Convention.

The amendment proposed is to strike out all after the word "Resolved," and insert the following, — "That the rules of the last National Democratic Convention govern this body until otherwise directed."

Cries, "Question!" "question!"

The amendment prevailed and the resolution as amended was adopted.

The CHAIRMAN. — Permit me to suggest to the Convention, that the National Executive Committee have suggested the name of Mr. E. O. Perrin, of New York, as temporary Secretary of the Convention. I will put the question upon his appointment.

The appointment was agreed to.

Mr. J. M. TOWER was selected as Assistant Secretary.

Mr. HIESTER CLYMER, of Pa. — I beg leave to offer the following resolution, —

Resolved, that a committee of one from each State be selected by the respective delegations whose duty it shall be to select permanent officers for this Convention.

Mr. JOHN A. GREEN, of New York. — I rise to a point of order. I think it is proper that the States be called in their order, and that the names and credentials of delegates be presented by the chairmen of delegations before further proceedings are taken.

The CHAIRMAN. — The Chair desires to say to the Convention that the temporary organization has been effected, and that thus far that is all that has been done except to adopt the rules to govern this temporary organization. The call under which this Convention is assembled will now be read by the Secretary, if there is no objection, before entertaining the resolution offered by the gentleman from Pennsylvania.

The Secretary then read the call, as follows, —

Call for the Convention.

The National Democratic Committee, by virtue of the authority conferred upon them by the last National Democratic Convention, at a meeting held this day, at Washington, D. C., voted to hold the next Convention for the purpose of nominating candidates for President and Vice-President of the United States, on the 4th day of July, 1868, at 12 o'clock M., in the City of New York.

The basis of representation, as fixed by the last Democratic Convention, is double the number of Senators and Representatives in Congress in each State under the last apportionment.

Each State is invited to send delegates accordingly.

S. R. LYMAN,	JOSIAH MINOT,	H. B. SMITH,
WM. M. CONVERSE,	GIDEON BRADFORD,	W. G. STEEL,
W. A. GAILBRAITH,	JOHN A. NICHOLSON,	ODIN BOWIE,
JAMES GUTHRIE,	L. S. TRIMBLE,	RUFUS P. RANNEY,
W. E. NIBLACK,	WILBER F. STOREY,	W. L. BANCROFT,
LEWIS V. BOGY,	GEORGE H. PAUL,	D. O. FINCH,
ISAAC E. EATON,	THOMAS HAYNES,	WILLIAM McMILLAN,
WILLIAM AIKEN,	ABSALOM H. CHAPPELL,	GEORGE A. HOUSTON,
JOSEPH A. ROZIER,	A. B. GREENWOOD,	JOHN W. LEFTWICH,
THOMAS SWEENEY,	JOHN PATRICK,	JAMES W. McCOCKLE,
W. L. SHARKEY,	JOHN HANCOCK,	JOHN H. McKINNEY,

FREDERICK O. PRINCE, *Secretary.*   AUGUST BELMONT, *Chairman.*

WASHINGTON, February 22, 1868.

Mr. GREEN, of New York. — I move that the States be called in their order, and the chairman of each delegation hand in the names of delegates.

The CHAIRMAN. — The gentleman from Pennsylvania (Mr. Clymer) offered a resolution.

Mr. CLYMER. — I will say that if it is the express desire of the Convention that the roll of States be called, I will withdraw my resolution temporarily. I offered it after consultation with the members of the National Committee, who suggested that the proper time to offer it would be after the election of the temporary Chairman and Secretary. I did so in obedience to their suggestion.

Mr. STUART, of Michigan. — I will trouble this Convention but a moment. The common practice is to appoint a Committee on Credentials. The chairman of that committee announces when they will meet. Each delegation presents to that chairman its credentials. That is short and easy, and does not occupy the time of the Convention. The motion that was made to appoint a committee to recommend a permanent organization was in order; one for the Committee on Credentials will also be in order, and we will save hours if we take that course.

Mr. CLYMER, of Pennsylvania. — The only precedent we have in this matter is the action at Charleston, where the seats of Illinois and New York were contested. The motion for a Committee on Permanent Organization was made at that time by General McCook, of Ohio. An attempt was made to amend the motion in various forms, and the final action was that a Committee on Organization and a Committee on Credentials were appointed by the same resolution. I have not heard that there are any contested seats at this time in this Convention. I believe that there is no discord in the Democratic party (Cheers), and think no committee absolutely necessary on credentials, and therefore I offered but a single resolution. If any gentleman desires so to amend it as to embrace a Committee on Credentials I shall have no objection.

Mr. STUART. — I move that amendment.

Mr. CLYMER. — I accept the amendment.

The CHAIRMAN. — The Chair understood the gentleman from Pennsylvania to withdraw his resolution.

Mr. CLYMER. — Temporarily.

The CHAIRMAN. — Temporarily, to allow the motion of the gentleman from New York (Mr. Green) to be entertained. That motion is now the pending question. It is that the roll of States be called by the Secretary.

Mr. GREEN. — I beg leave to explain. My motion was that the roll of States be called, and that the chairman of the delegation from each State hand in to the Secretary a list of the delegates from that State; not that the roll of delegates be called, because that would take too much time.

The CHAIRMAN. — So the Chair understood. Is the Convention ready for the question?

Cries — "Question!" "question!"

Mr. CLYMER. — I do not conceive that there is any list of delegates.

The CHAIRMAN. — The list of States is what is meant.

Mr. RICHARDSON, of Illinois. — In order to get rid of that question, for which there is no necessity, I move to lay it on the table.

The motion to lay it on the table was seconded and prevailed.

Mr. CLYMER. — I beg leave to renew my motion.

The Secretary read the resolution offered by Mr. CLYMER (as amended) as follows, —

Resolved, That a committee of one from each State be selected by the respective delegations, whose duty it shall be to select permanent officers of this Convention, and one also from each State upon credentials.

A DELEGATE from Montana. — I desire to add a slight amendment to the resolution, so that it may read " each State and Territory."

Mr. STEELE, of California, moved as an amendment to Mr. Clymer's resolution, the following, —

Resolved, That a committee of one from each State and Territory represented be appointed by the several delegations, to constitute a Committee on Credentials, and upon Permanent Organization to nominate permanent officers of the Convention, and upon the order of business, with instructions to report at the reassembling of the Convention on Monday, the 6th instant.

The Chairman announced the question to be on the amendment.

Mr. CLYMER. — One moment. It may be possible that if a Committee on Organization be appointed at this session, and if it be the pleasure of the Convention to have another session at a later hour this day, it may be able to report officers for permanent organization, and thereby save much valuable time to many gentlemen from distant portions of the Union. (Applause.) Therefore I do not desire the amendment to prevail, because it would bind the Convention not to assemble again, or at least not to organize permanently until Monday next. I trust that the gentleman from California will not press the adoption of the amendment. This is the only material difference between his amendment and the resolution offered by myself; his contemplates only one committee to perform both duties. I have no objection to that; but I have objections to wasting the time of the delegates until the committee reports.

A DELEGATE. — I would ask whether that resolution contemplates Territorial representation, either in the committees or in the permanent organization of the Convention?

The CHAIRMAN. — It does.

The same DELEGATE. — Then I am opposed to it.

Mr. STEELE. — As I offered that amendment, I desire to say a few words in regard to it. In the first place, if you have a committee organized now for the purpose of a permanent organization, they will have no advice whatever as to who are the delegates to this Convention from the various States. They must have legal information of that fact before they can advance intelligently to the important business which will come before the Convention. We must know that the men who are here upon this floor are elected to seats in this Convention from the States within the Union. There is another proposition. Although the Territories of the North-west are not entitled to vote upon the Presidential question, yet their people are subject to the government of the United States, and they should be represented here in the making of the nominations to be voted upon by the States; and they should be permitted to advise here with the people of the States, so that officers may be selected for the administration of the government who will be agreeable to them as well as to the States. It is true that they cannot participate with us in the election; but they have as vital an interest in the ultimate decision of the great questions of this contest as have the citizens of any other part of the country; and, therefore, I say that their representatives should have seats upon this floor.

Mr. THOMAS B. BRADFORD, of Delaware. — I move that the amendment offered by the gentleman from California be laid upon the table.

Mr. CLYMER. — That will carry the original resolution with it. I hope that gentleman will consider its effect. I hope it will be voted down instead of being tabled.

Mr. RICHARD D. RICE, of Maine. — Will you be kind enough to state the effect of that resolution?

The CHAIRMAN. — The gentleman from California (Mr. Steele) proposes to amend the resolution of the gentleman from Pennsylvania (Mr. Clymer). The gentleman from Delaware moves to lay that on the table. If that motion prevails both the amendment and the resolution will be laid on the table.

Mr. BRADFORD. — I withdraw the motion to lay on the table.

Mr. BERNARD SCHWARTZ, of Missouri. — I move to strike out that part of the resolution fixing the time that the report shall be made on Monday, and insert instead, to report at three o'clock this afternoon to this Convention.

Mr. STEELE. — I accept the amendment.

A DELEGATE FROM NEW JERSEY. — Will the Chairman state the question again?

The CHAIRMAN. — The question will now be upon the amendment proposed by the gentleman from California, as it has been modified, providing that the committee report this afternoon at three o'clock.

The amendment of the gentleman from California was lost, and the question recurred on Mr. Clymer's resolution.

Mr. W. B. MACHEN, of Kentucky. — I ask for a reading of the resolution.

The resolution was read.

Mr. CLYMER, of Pennsylvania. — I wish to accept the amendment which was proposed, so that the resolution will read " each State and Territory." I propose to accept it for the purpose of gratifying our friends from the extreme West.

Mr. J. M. CAVANAUGH, of Montana, said he represented the Territory of Montana as a delegate. There were no more earnest or zealous people for the cause of Democracy in the land than the people of Montana. It was true, they had no vote in the Electoral College. But they had hearts and voices and influence, and they would do, and he would do, in his feeble way, as much for the ticket to be named by this Convention as any others in the country. He urged that no invidious distinction should be made in the Convention between a State and a Territory.

Mr. STANTON, of Kentucky, moved the previous question, which prevailed.

The question recurring on the adoption of the resolution, it was again read.

General McCOOK, of Illinois. — Mr. Chairman, I rise to a point of order, and my point of order is this: that this is a Convention of States, and not of Territories. They were not included in the call, and it is the first time in a Democratic Convention in which there has ever been heard a talk of the admission of delegates, except from the sovereign States of the Union.

Mr. GEORGE W. BREWER, of Pennsylvania. — I rise to a point of order- This Convention has, by resolution, adopted the rules that regulated the Convention of 1860. These rules are now the law of this body. By the rules and regulations of that Convention, the Territories are not to be represented upon the floor by delegates to the Convention.

The vote was then taken on the resolution of Mr. CLYMER, as modified to include Territories, and it was declared in the negative.

A division being called for, the Chair directed the roll of States to be called, and the chairman of each delegation to announce the vote of his State.

The roll of States was then called with the following result, —

Alabama	Nay	Mississippi	Nay
California	Aye	Nebraska	Aye
Connecticut	Nay	Nevada	Aye
Delaware	Nay	New Hampshire	Aye
Florida	Nay	New Jersey	Aye
Georgia	Aye	New York	Nay
Illinois	Nay	North Carolina	Nay
Iowa	Aye	Ohio	Aye
Kansas, equally divided		Oregon	Nay
Maine	Nay	Pennsylvania	Aye
Maryland	Aye	Rhode Island	Nay
Massachusetts	Aye	Texas	Aye
Michigan	Nay	West Virginia	Nay
Missouri	Aye	Wisconsin	Nay
Minnesota	Aye		

On the call of Illinois, Mr. RICHARDSON said, — The State of Illinois gives her vote as a unit, nay.

Mr. DOWDALL, of Illinois. — I wish to say that thirteen of our delegation desire to vote aye upon that resolution.

Mr. RICHARDSON. — The State of Illinois required her delegation in this Convention to vote as a unit, and in compliance with that resolution I cast the vote of Illinois nay.

Mr. DOWDALL. — We were requested to vote as a unit for a candidate for President, but for nothing else; and the delegates believe that they have a right to vote on all other questions as they prefer. In our State Convention we were instructed to cast our vote as a unit for Mr. Pendleton for President, and for no one else: we are prepared to do that; but we are not instructed to act as a unit in any other matters. There are thirteen of our delegation that desire the admission of delegates from the Territories, and we wish to vote as we think is right and proper, and not according to the notions of our chairman.

Mr. RICHARDSON. — I have cast the vote of two-thirds of our delegation. Our instructions were to cast the vote of the delegation as a unit; I have carried out that instruction, and intend to carry out that instruction. I am instructed by a decided majority of our delegation to cast the vote as I have.

A DELEGATE from Illinois. — Mr. Chairman, I have but a word to say : We may as well settle this difference at this point as at any other. The difficulty arises from a mere difference of opinion as to how far our instructions go. On the question of voting for President we have no difference of opinion. On that question we shall vote at all times as we are instructed, — as a *unit*. On other questions a portion of our delegation believe that we have a right to vote without any instructions whatever. It is for the President of the Convention, having this resolution before him, and knowing our status in regard to it, to determine this difference of opinion between us. My own opinion is that we have a right to vote as we see fit on this question, — each delegate being responsible for his own vote. I desire to vote aye.

Mr. DOWDALL. — I desire to vote aye, and was informed that thirteen of our delegates desired to vote the same way. If I am wrongly informed I withdraw my objection.

The Chair then announced the vote as follows: Ayes, 106; nays, 184.

Mr. CLYMER, of Pennsylvania, offered the following, —

Resolved, That there now shall be two committees appointed, each committee to consist of one delegate from each State, to be selected by the respective delegates thereof; one committee to act as a Committee on Permanent Organization, and the other as a Committee on Credentials.

The resolution was adopted.

Mr. CLYMER.—I move the call of the roll of States for the purpose of having the gentlemen selected on the committees announced.

The CHAIRMAN.—The Secretary will call the roll of States, and the chairman of each delegation will please announce and pass up the names of the delegates selected for members of the Committees on Permanent Organization and on Credentials.

The Committee on Credentials.

The roll of delegates was then called, and the following gentlemen were selected as a Committee on Credentials, —

Alabama — W. H. Barnes.
Arkansas — E. C. Boudinot.
California — A. Jacoby.
Connecticut — M. Bulkley.
Delaware — C. W. Wright.
Florida — A. Hewling.
Georgia — E. H. Pottle.
Illinois — T. A. Hoyne.
Indiana — Charles H. Reeve.
Iowa — J. D. Test.
Kansas — W. Shannon, Jr.
Kentucky — J. B. McCreary.
Louisiana — D. D. Laponte.
Maine — I. T. Drew.
Maryland — G. F. Maddox.
Massachusetts — George W. Gill.
Michigan — B. G. Stout.
Minnesota — W. A. Gorman.
Mississippi — P. M. Brown.
Missouri — S. L. Sawyer.
Nebraska — John Black.
Nevada — J. E. Doyle.
New Hampshire — J. Proctor.
New Jersey — J. R. Mullaney.
New York — J. A. Hardenburgh.
North Carolina — Gen. W. R. Cox.
Ohio — W. Griswold.
Oregon — O. Joynt.
Pennsylvania — Gen. W. H. Miller.
Rhode Island — W. Hale.
South Carolina — W. D. Simpson.
Tennessee — J. F. House.
Texas — H. Boughton.
Vermont — W. Brigham.
Virginia — George Blow.
West Virginia — J. J. Davis.
Wisconsin — S. A. Pease.

The Committee on Organization.

The following gentlemen were selected a Committee on Organization,—

Alabama — J. H. Clauton.
Arkansas — J. S. Dunham.
California — E. Steele.
Connecticut — J. A. Hovey.
Delaware — C. Beasten.
Florida — A. J. Seeler.
Georgia — C. Peeples.
Illinois — W. R. Morrison.
Indiana — S. A. Buskirk.
Iowa — W. F. Braman.
Kansas — T. P. Fenlon.
Kentucky — W. B. Machen.
Louisiana — G. W. McCramie.
Maine — J. E. Madigan.
Maryland — A. R. Syester.
Massachusetts — John R. Briggs.
Michigan — John Moore.
Minnesota — E. A. McMahon.
Mississippi — B. Matthews.
Missouri — W. H. D. Hunter.
Nebraska — G. L. Miller.
Nevada — G. G. Berry.
New Hampshire — I. Adams.
New Jersey — Henry S. Little.
New York — General J. A. Green, Jr.
North Carolina — W. N. R. Smith.
Ohio — F. C. LeBlond.
Oregon — N. M. Bell.
Pennsylvania — H. Clymer.
Rhode Island — L. Pierce.
South Carolina — Carlos Tracey.
Tennessee — General W. B. Bate.
Texas — J. M. Burroughs.
Vermont — J. D. Deavitt.
Virginia — J. A. Barbour.
West Virginia — H. S. Walker.
Wisconsin — S. Clark.

Mr. WING, of New York. — I move the adoption of the following resolution, —

Resolved, That the two committees just appointed be instructed to report at five o'clock this evening; and that this Convention stand adjourn until that hour, when adjourned.

Applause.

Mr. CLYMER. — I move to insert seven o'clock this evening.

Mr. REED, of Pennsylvania. — I move to strike out seven o'clock, and insert six o'clock.

The question was taken on the amendment to insert six o'clock, which was lost. The question was then taken on the amendment to insert seven o'clock, which prevailed.

The resolution as amended was adopted.

Mr. KERR, of Pennsylvania. — I now move that on the reassembling of this Convention, the Secretary be directed to read the Declaration of Independence. We are the disciples of the man who wrote that instrument ninety-two years ago, at a time, sir, when we were colonies. Now we are a great people, and we ought to teach a lesson of our reverence for the charter of our liberties, and rebuke the Republican party in power for its tyranny and oppression.

The motion prevailed.

Mr. H. C. MURPHY, of New York, offered the following resolution, —

Resolved, That a committee of one delegate, from each State, to be selected by the delegation thereof, be appointed to report resolutions, and that all resolutions in relation to the platform of the Democratic party be referred to said committee without debate.

Mr. W. W. EATON, of Connecticut. — I think that the resolutions ought to be read in the hearing of the Convention, — not debated, but read. With that amendment, I have no objection to the motion; but every resolution that is to form a part of the platform of the great National Democratic party ought to be read in the hearing of the Convention.

Mr. MURPHY. — I perfectly concur with the gentleman from Connecticut, and I think a fair construction of the resolution contemplates the reading, but not the debating, of resolutions.

The resolution was adopted.

The Secretary then received from the chairman of the different delegations the names of the Committee on Resolutions and Platform, as follows, —

The Committee on Resolutions.

Alabama — Charles C. Langdon.
Arkansas — W. H. Garland.
California — A. H. Rose.
Connecticut — T. E. Doolittle.
Delaware — James A. Bayard.
Florida — W. McCall.
Georgia — Henry S. Fitch.
Illinois — Wm. J. Allan.
Indiana — J. E. Macdonald.
Iowa — J. H. O'Neill.
Kansas — Geo. W. Glick.
Kentucky — Wm. Preston.
Louisiana — J. B. Eustis.
Maine — R. D. Rice.
Maryland — Stephenson Archer.
Massachusetts — Edward Avery.
Michigan — Charles E. Stuart.
Minnesota — J. J. Green.
Mississippi — E. Barksdale.
Missouri — Charles A. Mansur.
Nebraska — Charles F. Porter.
Nevada — J. A. St. Clair.
New Hampshire — J. M. Campbell.
New Jersey — Jacob R. Wortendyke.
New York — Henry C. Murphy.
North Carolina — R. Strange.
Ohio — William J. Gilmore.
Oregon — R. D. Fitch.
Pennsylvania — F. W. Hughes.
Rhode Island — Thomas Steere.
South Carolina — Wade Hampton.
Tennessee — E. Cooper.
Texas — Geo. W. Smith.
Vermont — Charles M. Davenport.
Virginia — T. A. Bocock.
West Virginia — John J. Davis.
Wisconsin — James A. Mallory.

Mr. REEVE, of Indiana, offered the following resolution, —

Resolved, That the Committee on Permanent Organization be required to include a Sergeant-at-Arms as one of the officers of the Convention proper, to be selected by the Convention.

Mr. BREWER, of Pennsylvania, moved an amendment, as follows, —

Resolved, That the committee appointed to report officers for the permanent organization, be instructed to report rules for the government of this Convention.

Mr. REEVE. — In presenting my resolution to include the Sergeant-at-Arms, I wish to make this remark : I am informed, and believe it to be true, that the Sergeant-at-Arms of this body has been appointed by the National Executive Committee, with power to select his subordinates. That is all very well for a temporary organization, but, with all due respect to the Chairman of the Executive Committee, I think that that is a patronage which belongs to the Convention, and not to any one man, or set of men, to be distributed by them without the consent of the Convention.

The question was upon the amendment offered by Mr. BREWER, which prevailed.

The original resolution offered by Mr. REEVE was then adopted as amended.

Mr. EMERY, of Maine, inquired what provision had been made for the accommodation of spectators at the next session.

Mr. C. H. REEVE, of Indiana, offered the following resolution, —

Resolved, That a committee of one from each State be appointed, to be selected by the chairman of each delegation, whose duty it shall be to inquire into the admission of visitors to the Convention, the distribution of tickets therefor, and the other legitimate matters connected with the occupation of the hall, for the convenience of delegates, and report by resolution or otherwise, for the action of this Convention.

Mr. AUGUST BELMONT. — Mr. Chairman, each delegate has had his allotment of tickets to be distributed to as many spectators as the hall will hold. The tickets will be given out in this manner for each day of the Convention. It is the way this matter has been arranged at three former Conventions, where I was on the committee, and it is the first time that fault has been found with the action of the committee, if this resolution is dictated by such a feeling. I move that the resolution be laid on the table.

Mr. C. H. REEVE, of Indiana. — I know the motion is not debatable, but I wish to ask, if this motion prevails, if it is the final disposition of it?

The CHAIRMAN. — It is.

The motion to table prevailed.

The CHAIRMAN. — The Chair has received a telegram, which the Secretary will read to the Convention.

The despatch was read, as follows, —

Please announce to the Convention that the Democratic Association of Philadelphia, now assembled, promises the electoral vote of Pennsylvania to the nominee of the Convention. (Loud cheers.)

Mr. E. STEELE, of California, presented the following resolutions, which were referred to the Committee on Resolutions, —

Whereas, The history of our country for the last few months has developed one or more glaring defects in the Constitution of these United States, — features that in themselves by a simple administration in honesty, truth, and the spirit in which they were enacted, could work no wrong, — which when subject to the interpretation of a corrupt political body, working under the control of ambitious and unscrupulous leaders, whose only aim is at any hazard to perpetuate their own power, can, and may be used as a fearful engine for the purpose of smothering political freedom and integrity; and

Whereas, But for the stern and unflinching integrity of the President of the United States, Andrew Johnson, and of his faithful Cabinet advisers (excepting always therefrom Edwin M. Stanton), the political control of the nation would have been usurped by the congressional majority of the Republican party and a Dictatorship and Privy Council in perpetuity would have been established in lieu of our free representative Democratic government; and

Whereas, The ambitious leaders of the dominant party in Congress have endeavored through the form, but in total disregard of the spirit, of constitutional law, by party regulations and discipline, to remove the obstacle to their ambition, by the form of impeachment for high crimes and misdemeanors in office, themselves the prosecutors, the judges, and jurors, upon specifications showing only an honest disregard of that high functionary of party usages, rules, and domination, where the safety of the country, the liberties of the people, and the unity, permanency, and prosperity of the nation was concerned; and

Whereas, The result has shown, in the narrow escape of the honored Chief Magistrate from machinations of his and the nation's determined and unrelenting enemies, the fearful vortex into which our country is liable to be plunged by vesting in any political body judicial functions; and

Whereas, Of the large majority of Republican Senators constituting the Senate of the United States, there were found only Fessenden, Trumbull, Fowler, Grimes, Patterson, Ross, Van Winkle, and Henderson, the honorable and ever-to-be-honored few whose intelligence, integrity, and patriotism enabled them to rise above the tempest of howling and vindictive partisans, and dare to decide the right, and brave the detractions and misrepresentations of the thousand-tongued venal, subsidized party press; and

Whereas, The hair-breadth escape of the nation from foundering upon that, to a free government, dangerous rock, ambition, — one vote only being wanting to crush out the last vestige of a representative government, proves the necessity of changing the watch in that the darkest hour that can fall upon a nation, and placing upon that post other and more reliable guardians of the liberties of the people, — guardians who can have no interest other than in common with all worthy citizens, and that the supremacy of the right and suppression of wrong; — therefore,

Resolved, That it be established as one of the fundamental principles of the Democratic party, that the Constitution of the United States ought to be amended by striking out all of that paragraph of Article one (1), Section (3) three, of the Constitution, that reads as follows: "The Senate shall have the sole power to try all impeachments; when sitting for that purpose they shall be on oath or affirmation. When the President of the United States is tried the Chief-Justice shall preside, and no person shall be convicted without the concurrence of two-thirds of the members present;" and inserting an amendment to Article three (3), Section two (2), by vesting in the Judiciary the sole right to try all impeachments, and creating a Court therefor, to consist of the Chief-Justice of the United States, who shall be the presiding officer, and decide all questions of admissibility of evidence, subject to an appeal to the body of the Court in form as they may determine, except when the Chief-Justice is himself on trial, in which case the Court shall designate one of the Circuit Judges to act as presiding officer. The Circuit Judges of the United States and the Chief-Justices of the Supreme Courts of each of the States of the United States that ever have been recognized as States composing the great republic of the United States; *Provided*, That the said Court may consist of any number of said Judges not less than two-thirds of those entitled to sit therein; *And provided further*, That no conviction shall be had unless upon the concurrence of two-thirds of all the members entitled to sit in judgment in said Court, and that no member of said Court shall be entitled to vote upon any question of impeachment, during the trial of which he shall not have attended and listened to the evidence as offered by the parties, nor in a case in which he shall have formed or expressed an unqualified opinion of the guilt or innocence of the party accused, or to which he shall be a party defendant; — or, by some other detail, to so amend the Constitution as to separate all judicial functions from the political and law-making power.

Mr. A. T. WHITTLESEY, of Indiana. — I move that this Convention do now adjourn.

Mr. ERASTUS BROOKS, of New York. — In behalf of the New York delegation, as well as in behalf of the city of New York, I rise to make a privileged motion, and that is, to reconsider the motion which was adopted some time ago, that this Convention reconvene at seven o'clock this evening. Warm as it is in this mid-day weather, when the gas is lighted in this hall the atmosphere here will be still more oppressive.

Mr. A. T. WHITTLESEY, of Indiana. — I rise to a point of order. A motion to adjourn was made. I made it myself, and I have not withdrawn it.

The motion to adjourn was lost.

Mr. BROOKS. — I will say, sir, that we are at the close of the week, and that to-morrow is the Sabbath. This being the national anniversary, the city of New York has made great preparations for a proper celebration of the day, at its close; and I hope that the display of fireworks which has been prepared for this evening will be attended by a large number of our fellow-citizens of other States who are in the city. I trust that the resolution for meeting this evening may be reconsidered, and that we reconvene in this place on Monday next, at ten o'clock, to complete our deliberations. I therefore make that motion.

Mr. BRADFORD. — I trust that the motion will be adopted as a matter of courtesy to the citizens of New York.

Mr. MCCLELLAND, of Michigan. — Mr. Chairman, there are many of us who have come from a great distance to attend this Convention, and have come because of the great importance of the occasion. We are anxious to complete our labors and to return to our homes, and that anxiety compels us to resist this motion, inasmuch as we believe that we can effect our organization to-day, and come in on Monday, and on Monday or Tuesday, in all probability, gloriously close the proceedings of this Convention. I therefore move to lay the motion to reconsider on the table.

The motion to table did not prevail.

Mr. BROOKS, of New York, moved the previous question on the motion to reconsider.

The previous question was ordered, and the motion of Mr. Brooks to reconsider prevailed.

Mr. BROOKS, of New York. — Mr. Chairman, I move that when this Convention adjourn, it adjourn to meet at ten o'clock on Monday morning. (Applause.)

The motion prevailed.

Mr. MCLEAN, of Ohio, offered the following, —

Resolved, That the alternates to this Convention, the editors present, and the delegates to the Soldiers' and Sailors' Convention, be invited to seats in the hall during the session of the Convention.

The resolution was adopted.

Mr. FAULKNER, of New York. — It has been ordered by this Convention, as I understand it, that the Declaration of Independence shall be read this evening. If, sir, this Convention shall adjourn until Monday, we shall not be able to have that resolution carried into effect. I am unwilling, after this Convention has made a point of the reading of the Declaration of Independence before this body, to have it omitted. (Applause.) I move you, sir, that the Secretary be instructed to read the Declaration of Independence now.

The motion prevailed.

A DELEGATE. — Is there any military commander here who is likely to arrest the Secretary for disloyalty for reading the Declaration of Independence?

The CHAIRMAN. — I suppose no such person exists in the Empire State.

The Secretary then read the Declaration of Independence, which was received with cheers.

On motion the Convention then adjourned till Monday at ten o'clock, A. M.

SECOND DAY.

July 6, 1868.

The Convention was called to order by Hon. H. L. PALMER, the temporary President, at 10½ o'clock.

The CHAIRMAN. — Gentlemen of the Convention, I have the pleasure of introducing to you Rev. WILLIAM QUINN, of New York, who will open our proceedings with prayer.

Prayer.

Rev. Mr. QUINN then offered the following prayer, —

O, Almighty and Eternal God, Creator of heaven and earth, and of all things therein, who art infinite knowledge and infinite wisdom, and by whom just laws are administered, assist those in high authority on earth, that wholesome laws may be enacted, and that they may be administered with clemency and mercy, restraining vice, encouraging the practice of good works. We pray Thee, also, Almighty God, that our brethren and fellow-citizens throughout the United States may be blessed in the knowledge and sanctified in the observance of Thy holy law; that they may be united together more and more in union and in the enjoyment of that peace which the world cannot give; and that, after enjoying the things of this life, they may become partakers of joys that are eternal. We pray Thee, also, O God, for those who are now here assembled in Convention from the different and most remote parts of our country, that their deliberations may be conducted in the spirit of harmony, of peace, of charity, and may have reference chiefly to the public good and well-being of society, — to the peace, and happiness, and prosperity of our beloved land. We pray Thee, also, Almighty God, that these, Thy children, who are now assembled, whilst devoting their best faculties to these great and exalted interests, may not be unmindful of Thy presence or of the high responsibilities that they owe Thee. These, O Almighty God, and other precious gifts and blessings, we pray thee to shower down upon us this day, and always through the merits of Thy beloved Son, our Lord and Saviour, Jesus Christ, who reigneth with Thee in the unity of the Holy Ghost, world without end.

The Chairman announced the next business in order to be the reading of the journal of Saturday's proceedings.

Mr. TILDEN, of New York. — To expedite the business of the Convention, I move that the reading of the journal be dispensed with.

The motion prevailed.

Mr. RICHARDSON, of Illinois. — I hold in my hand a communication from a distinguished citizen of Illinois, which I desire to have referred to the Committee on Resolutions.

It was so referred.

Mr. G. W. MORGAN, of Ohio. — I move that the courtesies of this Convention be extended to the members of the National Workingmen's Association, and that they be invited to accept seats on this floor.

The motion prevailed.

The Permanent Organization.

Mr. CLYMER, of Pennsylvania, from the Committee on Organization, submitted the following report of officers of the Convention, —

For President.
HON. HORATIO SEYMOUR, OF NEW YORK.

For Vice-Presidents and Secretaries.

Vice-President.		Secretary.
	ALABAMA.	
Reuben Chapman.		William M. Lowe.
	ARKANSAS.	
B. D. Turner.		John W. Wright.
	CALIFORNIA.	
A. H. Rose.		M. G. Gillette.
	CONNECTICUT.	
Henry A. Mitchell.		George D. Hastings.
	DELAWARE.	
George W. Cummins.		Custis W. Wright.
	FLORIDA.	
Thomas Randall.		C. H. Smith.
	GEORGIA.	
A. R. Wright.		William A. Reid.
	ILLINOIS.	
D. M. Woodson.		W. T. Dowdell.
	INDIANA.	
James A. Cravens.		W. R. Bowes.
	IOWA.	
Wm. McClintock.		P. H. Bousquet.
	KANSAS.	
Andrew J. Mead.		Isaac Sharp.
	KENTUCKY.	
Lucius Desha.		Hart Gibson.
	LOUISIANA.	
Louis St. Martin.		J. H. Kennard.
	MAINE.	
Isaac Reid.		J. A. Linscott.
	MASSACHUSETTS.	
Peter Harvey.		Charles G. Clark.
	MICHIGAN.	
A. N. Hart.		Frederick V. Smith.
	MARYLAND.	
George R. Dennis.		Outerbridge Horsey.
	MISSISSIPPI.	
E. C. Walthall.		Felix Labauve.
	MINNESOTA.	
Winthrop Young.		Isaac Staples.

OFFICIAL PROCEEDINGS OF THE

Vice-President.		Secretary.
	MISSOURI.	
Thomas L. Price.		A. J. Reid.
	NEBRASKA.	
George N. Crawford.		Peter Smith.
	NEVADA.	
D. E. Buell.		George H. Willard.
	NEW HAMPSHIRE.	
George H. Pierce.		Albert R. Hatch.
	NEW JERSEY.	
Francis S. Lathrop.		Charles E. Hendrickson.
	NEW YORK.	
Wm. M. Tweed.		Henry A. Richmond.
	NORTH CAROLINA.	
Bedford Brown.		R. B. Haywood.
	OHIO.	
Edson B. Olds.		John Hamilton.
	OREGON.	
E. L. Bristow.		A. D. Fitch.
	PENNSYLVANIA.	
John L. Dawson.		W. M. Reilly.
	RHODE ISLAND.	
Amasa Sprague.		E. B. Bronson.
	SOUTH CAROLINA.	
B. F. Perry.		William S. Mullins.
	TENNESSEE.	
A. O. P. Nicholson.		Joseph H. Thompson.
	TEXAS.	
Ashbell Smith.		D. A. Veitch.
	VERMONT.	
Henry Keyes.		George H. Simmons.
	VIRGINIA.	
Robert Y. Conrad.		William D. Coleman.
	WEST VIRGINIA.	
Joseph W. Gallaher.		Carlos A. Sperry.
	WISCONSIN.	
Nelson Dewey.		G. T. Thorn.

For Reading Secretaries.
E. O. Perrin, of New York.
Moses M. Strong, of Wisconsin.
V. A. Gaskill, of Georgia.
F. M. Hutchinson, of Pennsylvania.
Robert P. Tansey, of Illinois.

For Sergeant-at-Arms.
Edward A. Moore, of New York.

The Committee recommend that the rules and regulations of the National Democratic Convention of 1864 be adopted by this Convention for the government of its proceedings.

W. R. MORRISON, *Secretary.*   HIESTER CLYMER, *Chairman.*

At the reading of Governor Seymour's name, the Convention rose and gave cheer after cheer.

General McCook, of Ohio. — I move the acceptance of the report and the discharge of the committee.

Mr. White, of Maryland. — I desire to ask the chairman of the committee whether the adoption of their report will require for the nomination of the candidates for President and Vice-President two-thirds of all the votes in the Electoral College, or whether two-thirds of the votes cast in this Convention will be sufficient to nominate the candidates? The reason I make this interrogatory is this: I observed, on Saturday last, that some of the States represented on this floor cast no votes on the questions which arose in our temporary organization. When we come to vote for candidates for President and Vice-President, the same States may withhold their votes, and consequently it will take a much larger vote to make two-thirds of the votes of the Electoral College, than if the rule applied only to the votes cast in this Convention. In 1832, the rule was, that it required two-thirds of the votes cast in the Convention; but, if I remember correctly, at Charleston the rule was qualified so as to require two-thirds of all the votes cast in the Electoral College. I want to know, therefore, so that we can vote intelligently, whether, if we adopt in their entirety the rules of the Chicago Convention in 1864, the candidates must receive two-thirds of the Electoral vote, or only two thirds of the votes cast in the Convention?

The Chairman. — The Chair is of opinion that the merits of the report are not now under consideration. The question is whether the report shall be accepted and the committee discharged.

The question was put on accepting the report, and discharging the committee, and it prevailed.

The Chairman announced the question to be upon the adoption of the report of the Committee on Organization.

A Delegate from Wisconsin. — Before the vote is taken, I desire to say that we can see nothing and hear nothing. Will the Chair have the goodness to request that everybody be kept in their seats?

The Chairman. — The Chair will direct the Sergeant-at-Arms to see that the aisles be kept clear, that the members of the Convention remain in their seats, and that order is preserved.

The question was put on the adoption of the report of the Committee on Organization, and it was declared carried.

Mr. H. C. Murphy, of New York. — I am requested by the Committee on Resolutions to ask permission of this body to sit during its meetings.

A Delegate. — I move that the Committee on Resolutions have leave to sit during the session of the Convention.

The motion prevailed.

The Chairman appointed Governor Bigler, of Pennsylvania, and Governor Hammond of South Carolina, a Committee to escort Governor Seymour, the permanent President of the Convention, to the chair.

The committee, amid great applause, performed the duty.

The CHAIRMAN. — I introduce to you the President-elect, Hon. Horatio Seymour, of New York.

Governor Seymour, upon reaching the platform, in company with the gentlemen appointed to conduct him to the chair, was received with the wildest enthusiasm. The whole Convention rose, and greeted him with long-continued cheering and waving of handkerchiefs. The spectators in the galleries, also, and the ladies at the sides of the platform, manifested their enthusiasm.

Governor Seymour then came forward, and, when quiet was restored, spoke as follows, —

Speech of Hon. Horatio Seymour.

GENTLEMEN OF THE CONVENTION, — I thank you for the honor you have done me in making me your presiding officer. (Cheers.) This Convention is made up of a large number of delegates from all parts of our broad land. To a great degree we are strangers to each other, and view the subjects which agitate our country from different stand-points. We cannot, at once, learn each other's modes of thought, or grasp all the facts which bear upon the minds of others. Yet our session must be brief, and we are forced to act without delay upon questions of an exciting character and of deep import to our country. (Applause.) To maintain order, to restrain all exhibitions of passion, to drive out of our minds all unkind suspicions is, at this time, a great duty. (Cheers.) I rely upon your sense of this duty, and not upon my own ability, to sustain me in the station in which I am placed by your kind partiality. We never met under greater responsibilities than those which now weigh upon us. (Applause.) It is not a mere party triumph which we seek. We are trying to save our country from the dangers which overhang it. (Cheers.) We wish to lift off the perplexities and the shackles which, in the shape of bad laws and of crushing taxation, now paralyze the business and labor of our land. (Loud cheers.) We hope, too, that we can give order, prosperity, and happiness to those sections of our country which suffer so deeply to-day in their homes and in all the fields of their industry from the unhappy events of the last eight years. I trust that our actions will show that we are governed by an earnest purpose to help all classes of our citizens. Avoiding harsh invectives against men, we should keep the public mind fixed upon the questions which must now be met and solved. (Cheers.) Let us leave the past to the calm judgment of the future and confront the perils of the day. (Cheers.) We are forced to meet the assertions of the resolutions put forth by the late Republican Convention. I aver there is not in this body one man who has it in his heart to excite so much of angry feeling against the Republican party, as must be stirred up in the minds of those who read these declarations in the light of recent events, and in view of the condition of our country. (Applause.) In the first place, they congratulate the perplexed man of business, the burdened tax-payer, the laborer whose hours of toil are lengthened out by the growing cost of the necessaries of life, upon the success of that reconstruction policy which has brought all these evils upon them by the cost of its military despotism, and the corruption of its bureau agencies. In one resolution they "*denounce all forms of repudiation as a national crime.*" Then why did they put upon the statute books of the nation the laws which invite the citizens who borrow coin to force their creditor to take debased paper, and thus wrong him of a large share of his claim in violation of the most solemn compact? (Cheers.) If repudiation is a national crime, is it no crime to invite all the citizens of this country thus to repudiate their individual promises? (Applause.) Was it not a crime to force the creditors of this and other States to take a currency at times worth no more than forty cents on the dollar, in repayment for the sterling coin they gave to build roads and canals which yield such ample returns of wealth and prosperity? (Applause.) Again they say, "*It is due to the laborer of the nation that taxation should be equalized.*" Then why did they make taxation unequal? Beyond the injustice of making one class of citizens pay for another their share of the cost of schools, of roads, of the local laws which protect their lives and property, it was an unwise and hurtful thing. (Cheers.) It sunk the credit of the country, as unusual terms are always hurtful to the credit of the borrower. They also declare, "*The best policy to diminish our burden of debt is to improve our credit, that capitalists will seek to loan us money at lower rates of interest than we now pay, and we must continue to pay, so long as repudiation, partial or total, open or covert, is threatened or suspected.*" Then why have they used full five hundred millions of the taxes drawn from the people of this country to uphold a despotic military authority, and to crush out the life of the States, when, if this money had been used to pay our debts, capitalists would now seek to lend us money at lower rates of interest? (Cheers.) But for this "covert repudiation" our national credit would not be tainted in the markets of the world. Again, they declare, "Of all who were faithful in the trials of the late war, there were none entitled to more especial honor than the brave soldiers and seamen who endured the hardships of campaign and cruise, and imperilled their lives in the service of the country; the bounties and pensions provided by the laws of these brave defenders of the nation are obligations never to be forgotten; the widows and orphans of the gallant dead are the wards of the people, — a sacred legacy bequeathed to the nation's protecting care. How have these sacred duties been performed? They pay to the maimed man, to the widow, or the orphan, a currency which they have sunk one-quarter below its rightful value by their policy of hate, of waste, and of military despotism. The pittance paid to the wounded soldiers is pinched down twenty-five per cent. below the value of that coin which he had a right to expect. (Loud cheering.) Is there no covert repudiation in this? (Applause.) Again they say, "*Foreign immigration, which has added so much to the wealth, development, and resources and increase of power of this Republic, the asylum of the oppressed of all nations, should be fostered and encouraged by a liberal and just policy.*" Is this foreign immigration fostered by a policy which, in cruel mockery of laws just passed, declaring eight hours to be a legal day's labor, by the cost of government and of swarms of officials, so swells the costs of living that men must toil on to meet the exactions? (Cheers.) The time was when we could not only invite the European to share with us the material blessings of our great country; but more than that, — we could tell those who fled from oppression that we lived under a government of laws administered by the Judiciary, which kept the bayonet and the sword in due subordination. (Cheers.) We could point to a written constitution which not only marked out the powers of government, but with anxious care secured to the humblest men the rights of property, of persons, and of conscience. Is immigration encouraged by trampling that Constitution in the dust; treating it with contempt; shackling the Judiciary; insulting the Executive, and giving all the world to understand that the great guaranties of political and social rights are destroyed? (Great applause.) But the crowning indictment against the follies and crimes of those in power is in these words: " That we recognize the great principles laid down in the immortal Declaration of Independence as the true foundation of Democratic government, and we hail with gladness every effort towards making these principles a living reality on every inch of American soil." If within the limits of ten States of this Union, an American citizen, stung by a sense of his wrongs, should publicly and truthfully denounce the men in power because, in the very language of this Declaration of Independence, " *They have erected a multitude of new offices, and sent forth swarms of officers to harass our people and eat out their substance,*" he would, in all human probability, be dragged to a prison. Or if, in the indignant language of our fathers, he should exclaim, " *They have affected to render the military independent of, and superior to, the civil power; they have abolished the free system of English laws, and established herein an arbitrary government*" — for the offence of asserting these principles he would be tried and punished by a military tribunal. (Great cheering.) Having declared that the principles of the Declaration of Independence should be made a "*living reality on every inch of American soil,*" they put in nomination a military chieftain who stands at the head of that system of despotisms that crushes beneath its feet the greatest principles of the Declaration of Independence. (Cheers.) To-day, in some States, it is held by military orders to be a crime to speak out the indignation and contempt which burn within the bosoms of patriotic men. If to-morrow a military order should be put forth in that State where the ashes of Washington are entombed, that it should be an offence to declare that the military should ever be subordinate to the civil authority, — to speak out the sentiment that it was a disgrace to our country to let the hordes of officials eat up the substance of the people, — he who uttered these words would be dragged to prison from the very grave where lie the remains of the author of the Declaration of Independence — (Loud cheers) — from this outrage there could be no appeal to the courts; and the Republican candidate for the presidency has accepted a position which makes the rights and liberties of a large share of our people dependent upon his will. (Applause.) In view of these things, can there be one man in this Convention who can let a personal ambition, a passion, a prejudice, turn him aside one hair's breadth in his efforts to wipe out the wrongs and outrages which disgrace our country? (Cheers.) Can there be one man here whose heart is so dead to all that is great and noble in patriotism that he will not gladly sacrifice all other things for the sake of his country, its liberties, and its greatness? Can we suffer any prejudices, growing out of past differences of opinion, to hinder us from uniting now with all who will act with us to save our country? (Cheers.) We meet to-day to see what measures can be taken to arrest the dangers which threaten our country, and to retrieve it from the evils and burdens resulting from bad government and unwise counsels. I thank God that the strife of arms has ceased, and that once more in the great conventions of our party we can call through the whole roll of States and find men to answer for each. (Tremendous and continued cheering.) Time and events, in their great cycles, have brought us to this spot to renew and invigorate that Constitutional Government which, nearly eighty years ago, was inaugurated in this city. (Loud cheers.) It was here that George Washington, the first President, swore to "preserve, protect, and defend," the Constitution of these United States. (Cheers.) And here, this day, we as solemnly pledge ourselves to uphold the rights and liberties of the American people. Then, as now, a great war which has desolated our land had ceased. Then, as now, there was in every patriotic breast a longing for the blessings of a good government, for the protection of laws, and for sentiments of fraternal regard and affection among the inhabitants of all the States of this Union. When our government, in 1780, was inaugurated in this city, there were glad processions of men and those manifestations of great joy which a people show when they feel that an event has happened which is to give lasting blessing to the land. (Cheers.) To-day, in this same spirit, this vast assemblage meets, and the streets are thronged with men who have come from the utmost borders of our continent. They are filled with the hope that we are about, by our actions, and our policy, to bring back the blessings of good government. It is among the happiest omens which inspirit us now, that those who fought bravely in our late civil war are foremost in their demands that there shall be peace in our land. The passions of hate and malice may linger in meaner breasts, but we find ourselves upheld in our generous purposes by those who showed true courage and manhood on the field of battle. (Cheers.) In the spirit, then, of George Washington, and of the patriots of the Revolution, let us take the steps to reinaugurate our government, to start it once again on its course to greatness and prosperity. (Loud cheers.) May Almighty God give us the wisdom to carry out our purposes, to give to every State of our Union the blessings of peace, good order, and fraternal affection!

Mr. SEYMOUR closed amid long-continued and tremendous cheering.

Mr. GEORGE W. WOODWARD, of Pennsylvania. — I present a written communication from a highly respectable citizen of Pennsylvania, and ask that it may be referred to the Committee on Platform, without reading.

The communication was referred as requested.

At the request of the President the Vice-Presidents elect then took seats on the platform.

Mr. ISAAC E. HIESTER, of Pennsylvania. — I beg to have referred to the Committee on Resolutions the resolutions of the State Conventions of Pennsylvania and Michigan.

Agreed to.

Mr. BROOKS, of New York, offered the following resolutions, —

Resolutions adopted at a Special Council of the National Labor Union, assembled at New York, July 2, 1868.

Whereas, The right to labor and its reward is self-evident; and whereas the excess or want of work is a fruitful source of ignorance, disease, and crime; and whereas the tendency of legislation and monopoly is to restrict the freedom, cripple the energies, and purloin the earnings of industry; therefore,

Resolved, That the producing classes, agricultural, mining, mechanical, intellectual and moral, are the most important portion of all communities; and that distributors, financiers, and statesmen, together with their aids, civil and military, are of secondary consequence, being simply created of the former to disseminate wealth, maintain order, conserve justice, and keep intact the integrity of the nation.

Resolved, That the national honor must be preserved by paying its debts in good faith, and that every debt of the government, not specifically contracted to be paid in gold, should be paid in the lawful currency of the United States; that the bonds, when redeemable, should be paid in legal-tender notes, or exchanged for other bonds at three per cent., convertible into lawful money, at the pleasure of the holder.

Resolved, That the public interest demands the withdrawal of the circulating notes of the national banks, and the substitution of legal-tender Treasury certificates in their stead.

Resolved, That we demand equal taxation on every species of property, according to its real value.

Resolved, That no more of the public domain should be granted to any corporation, under any pretext whatever, and the lands not disposed of should be withdrawn from the market and granted to actual settlers.

Resolved, That we return our thanks to the majorities in Congress and in such State Legislatures as have, in their wisdom, deemed it right and proper to pass the Eight-Hour Law; and we call upon the proper authorities in the United States and the States above mentioned to show their respect for the same by enforcing its demand.

Resolved, That the low wages, long hours, and damaging service to which multitudes of working girls and women are doomed, destroy health, imperil virtue, and are a standing reproach to civilization; that we would urge them to learn trades, engage in business, join our labor unions, or use any other honorable means to persuade or force men to render unto every woman according to her works.

Resolved, That we urge upon the industrial classes in every Congressional and State district, county, city, or town, to press these principles upon the public notice, and to support no man for Congress, or any State Legislature, or any other office of profit or trust, who is not fully pledged to their support.

Resolved, That we recommend to the people, throughout the nation, to hold mass meetings to ratify the principles of the National Labor Union, adopted at Chicago, August, 1867, and herein set forth, and to vote only for those candidates who indorse them; and unless these principles are adopted by one of the two great parties — we care not which — we advise the National Labor Union, at its annual convention, soon to be held in this city, to put in nomination an independent labor candidate for the Presidency, and rally the masses to his support.

The PRESIDENT. — I have here a memorial from the Women's Suffrage Association, with the request that it be handed to the Committee on Resolutions.

Loud cheers, laughter, and cries of "Hear! Hear!" "Read! Read!"

The PRESIDENT. — I may mention that this document is signed by Miss Susan B. Anthony.

Cries, "Read it! read it!"

The Secretary read the communication as follows, —

WOMEN'S SUFFRAGE ASSOCIATION OF AMERICA,
37 PARK ROW, Room 20,
New York, July 4, 1868.

ELIZABETH CADY STANTON,
MRS. HORACE GREELEY,
SUSAN B. ANTHONY,
ABBY HOPPER GIBBONS,
} Central Committee.

To the President and Members of the National Democratic Convention:

GENTLEMEN, — I address you by letter to ask the privilege of appearing before you, during the sittings of this Convention, to demand the enfranchisement of the women of America; the only class of citizens wholly unrepresented in the government; the only class (not guilty of crime) taxed without representation, tried without a jury of their peers, governed without their consent. And yet in this class are found many of your most noble, virtuous, law-abiding citizens, who possess all the requisite qualifications of voters. Women have property and education. We are not "idiots, lunatics, paupers, criminals, rebels," nor do we "bet on elections." We lack, according to your constitutions, but one qualification — that of sex — which is insurmountable (Laughter), and therefore equivalent to a deprivation of suffrage; in other words, the "tyranny of taxation without representation." We desire to lay before you this violation of the great fundamental principles of our government for your serious consideration, knowing that minorities can be moved by principles as majorities are only by votes. Hence we look to you for the initiative step in the redress of our grievances. The party in power have not only failed to heed our innumerable petitions, asking the right of suffrage, poured into Congress and State Legislatures, but they have submitted a proposition to the several States to insert the word "*male*" in the Federal Constitution, where it never has been, and thereby put up a new barrier against the enfranchisement of women. This fresh insult to the women of the republic, who so bravely shared the dangers and sacrifices of the late war, has roused us to more earnest and persistent efforts to secure those rights, privileges, and immunities which belong to every citizen under government. As you hold the Constitution of the Fathers to be a sacred legacy to us and to our children forever, we ask you to save it from this desecration, which deprives one-half our citizens of the right of representation in the government. Over this base proposition the nation has stood silent and indifferent. While the dominant party have, with one hand, lifted up two millions black men and crowned them with the honor and dignity of citizenship, with the other they have dethroned fifteen million white women, — their own mothers and sisters, their own wives and daughters, — and cast them under the heel of the lowest order of manhood. We appeal to you, not only because you, being in a minority, are in a position to consider principles, but because you have been the party heretofore to extend the suffrage. It was the Democratic party that fought most valiantly for the removal of the "property qualification" from all white men, and thereby placed the poorest ditch-digger on a political level with the proudest millionnaire. This one act of justice to working-men has perpetuated your power, with but few interruptions, from that time until the war. And now you have an opportunity to confer a similar boon on the women of the country, and thus possess yourselves of a new talisman that will ensure and perpetuate your political power for decades to come.

While the first and highest motive we would urge on you is the recognition in all your action of the great principles of justice and equality that are the foundation of a Republican government, it is not unworthy to remind you that the party that takes this onward step will reap its just reward. It needs but little observation to see that the tide of progress in all countries is setting toward the enfranchisement of women, and that this advance step in civilization is destined to be taken in our day. We conjure you, then, to turn from the dead questions of the past to the vital issues of the hour. The *brute form* of slavery ended with the war. The black man is a soldier and a citizen. He holds the bullet and the ballot in his own right hand. Consider his case settled. Those weapons of defence and self-protection can never be wrenched from him. Yours the responsibility now to see that no new chains be forged by bondholders and monopolists for enslaving the labor of the country. The late war, seemingly in the interest of slavery, was fought by unseen hands for the larger liberties of the *whole* people. It was not a war between North and South, for the principle of class and caste knows neither latitude or longitude. It was a war of ideas — of Aristocracy and Democracy — of capital and labor — the same that has convulsed the race through the ages, and will continue to convulse future generations until justice and equality shall reign upon the earth. I desire, therefore, an opportunity to urge on this Convention, the wisdom of basing its platform on universal suffrage, as well as universal amnesty, from Maine to California, and thus to take the first step toward a peaceful and permanent reconstruction.

In behalf of the Woman's Suffrage Association of America.

Respectfully yours, SUSAN B. ANTHONY.

Applause greeted various portions of the document.

It was referred to the Committee on Credentials.

Mr. NELSON, of Tennessee, offered the following, —

Resolved, That the Committee appointed by the National Convention of the ninth of June last, to present to this Convention a memorial of the grievances of Tennessee under Radical rule, be admitted to seats in this Convention, and permitted to present said report.

Which was adopted.

Report of the Committee on Credentials.

Mr. WAYNE GRISWOLD, Chairman of the Committee on Credentials, presented the following, which was read, —

To the Chairman of the National Democratic Convention:

Your Committee on Credentials beg leave to report, — that we have examined the credentials of every State in the Union, and we find that each has the full number of delegates to which it is entitled under the call of the National Democratic Executive Committee. While we report the following as the names of the delegates from the respective States, your Committee rejoice that this Convention presents to the nation and to the world a full and complete representation from every State in the American Union. (Loud cheering.)

They also report the following resolution, —

Resolved, That the Committee on Credentials recommend that three delegates from each Territory, and four from the District of Columbia, be admitted to seats on the floor of this Convention, without the privilege of voting in its proceedings.

List of Delegates.
ALABAMA
DELEGATES AT LARGE.
Reuben Chapman, Lewis E. Parsons,
John A. Winston, James H. Clauton.

DISTRICT DELEGATES.
1. C. C. Langdon,
   R. G. Scott, Jr.
2. J. T. Holtzclaw,
   W. C. Oates.
3. W. H. Barnes,
   M. J. Bulger.
4. Samuel Ruffin,
   John J. Jolly.
5. Wm. M. Lowe,
   James L. Sheffield.
6. R. O. Pickett,
   Thomas J. McCellan.

ARKANSAS.
DELEGATES AT LARGE.
P. O. Thweat, A. H. Garland,
B. D. Turner, E. C. Boudinot.

DISTRICT DELEGATES.
1. Robert Smith,
   Jacob Frolich.
2. John W. Wright,
   John M. Harrell.
3. J. S. Dunham
   R. C. Davis.

CALIFORNIA.
DELEGATE AT LARGE.
Thomas Hays (deceased). M. G. Gillette.

DISTRICT DELEGATES.
1. R. C. Page,
   A. Jacoby,
   Joseph Roberts.
2. John Bigler,
   Richard Heath,
   A. H. Rose.
3. E. Steele,
   Charles S. Fairfax,
   W. Woodward.

CONNECTICUT.
DELEGATES AT LARGE.
Wm. W. Eaton, Benjamin Stark,
Tilton E. Doolittle, James H. Hoyt.

DISTRICT DELEGATES.
1. Henry A. Mitchell,
   Geo. D. Hastings.
2. John Kendrick,
   Isaac Arnold.
3. James A. Hovey,
   Marvin H. Sanger.
4. Matthew Bulkley,
   Donald D. Warner.

COLORADO.
DELEGATES AT LARGE.
Hugh Butler, Capt. Craig,
H. B. Morse, T. J. Campbell,
M. Anker, G. Blayton.

DELAWARE.
James A. Bayard, Thos. B. Bradford,
Charles Beasten, James Ponder,
George W. Cummins, Curtis W. Wright.

DISTRICT OF COLUMBIA.

J. D. Hoover,	Wm. Flinn,
Charles Allen,	R. S. Davis,
Jas. G. Berret,	C. Wendell,
T. A. Tolson,	Louis Schade,
Esau Pickrell, B. T. Swart,	Jno. B. Blake.

FLORIDA.

F. R. Cotton,	Thos. Randall,
Wilkinson Call,	S. Fairbanks,
J. P. Sanderson,	Chas. Davis,
C. E. Dyke,	S. H. Owens,
W. D. Barnes,	A. F. Smith,
C. H. Smith,	A. Hewling,
J. C. McLean,	J. B. Brown,
H. Wright,	E. C. Love,
Jas. McKay,	R. L. Campbell,
W. H. Robinson,	W. W. Van Ness,
E. M. L'Engie, A. J. Peeber,	J. J. Williams.

GEORGIA.

DELEGATES AT LARGE.

A. H. Colquitt,	H. S. Fitch,
Geo. Barnes,	J. B. Gordon.

DISTRICT DELEGATES.

1. W. T. Thompson,
   P. C. Pendleton.
2. A. H. Hood,
   C. W. Styles.
3. H. Buchanan,
   J. L. Mustin.
4. W. A. Reid,
   C. Peeples.
5. A. R. Wright,
   E. H. Pottle.
6. Phil. R. Simmons,
   E. Steadman.
7. D. P. Hill, L. Tumlin.

ILLINOIS.

DELEGATES AT LARGE.

W. J. Allen,	W. R. Morrison,
George W. Shutt,	W. T. Dowdall,
W. F. Story,	W. A. Richardson.

DISTRICT DELEGATES.

1. Thomas A. Hoyne,
   W. C. Goudy.
2. R. S. Malony,
   A. M. Harrington.
3. William P. Malburn,
   Bernard H. Truesdale.
4. Charles Buford,
   George Edmunds.
5. W. H. O'Brien,
   James S. Eckles.
6. Charles E. Boyer,
   J. H. McConnell.
7. John Donlon,
   Thomas Brewer.
8. Dr. R. B. M. Wilson,
   Charles A. Keyes.
9. Henry L. Bryant,
   Lyman Lacy.
10. Edward Y. Rice,
    D. M. Woodson.
11. Samuel K. Casey,
    Joseph Cooper.
12. Timothy Grearye,
    W. A. J. Sparks.
13. William H. Green, George W. Wail.

INDIANA.
DELEGATES AT LARGE.
D. W. Voorhies,
J. E. McDonald,
Graham V. Fitch,
Wm. E. Niblack.

DISTRICT DELEGATES.
1. A. T. Whittlesey,
W. S. Turner.
2. Jas. A. Cravens,
David Huffstetter.
3. H. W. Harrington,
W. T. Pate.
4. Lafe Devlin,
John W. Carleton.
5. W. H. Talbott,
D. G. Vawter.
6. Samuel H. Buskirk,
C. G. Patterson.
7. W. D. Manson,
Harris Reynolds.
8. R. P. Effinger,
J. M. Dickson.
9. E. Sturgis,
Adam Wolf.
10. Jas. R. Slack,
S. W. Sprott.
11. T. J. Merrifield,
C. H. Reeve.

IOWA.
DELEGATES AT LARGE.
A. C. Dodge,
John H. O'Neil,
D. O. Finch,
George H. Parker.

DISTRICT DELEGATES.
1. John Rhinehart,
Patrick Gibbon.
2. T. S. Bardwell,
W. E. Brennan.
3. William McClintock,
Ray B. Griffin.
4. Samuel H. Fairall,
P. H. Bousquett.
5. J. D. Test,
J. N. Udell.
6. H. E. J. Boardman,
E. B. Holbrook.

KANSAS.
George W. Glick,
Andrew J. Mead,
Wilson Shannon, Jr.,
Charles W. Blair,
Isaac Sharp,
Thomas P. Fenlon.

KENTUCKY.
DELEGATES AT LARGE.
R. H. Stanton,
J. A. Spalding,
William Preston,
J. G. Carlyle.

DISTRICT DELEGATES.
1. W. B. Machen,
J. A. Flournoy.
2. Gano Henry,
C. B. Vance.
3. H. L. Dulam,
A. J. Rhea.
4. E. A. Graves,
C. B. Mattingly.
5. T. L. Jefferson,
Littleton Cooke.
6. Lucius Desha,
F. A. Boyd.
7. B. F. Buckner,
J. Hart Gibson.
8. Edward Turner,
James B. McCreary,
9. Thomas Turner,
A. L. Martin.

LOUISIANA.
DELEGATES AT LARGE.
1. J. B. Steadman,
   B. F. Jonas.
2. Jas McClosky,
   T. A. Carke.

DISTRICT DELEGATES.
1. Durant Laponte,
   Louis St. Martin.
2. R. L. Gibson,
   James B. Eustis.
3. J. A. Kennard.
4. J. H. Hardy,
   J. McEnry.
5. N. D. Coleman,
   George W. McCramie,
   W. W. Smallwood.

MAINE.
DELEGATES AT LARGE.
Richard D. Rice,
Samuel J. Anderson,
David R. Hastings,
James C. Madigan.

DISTRICT DELEGATES.
1. Ira T. Drew,
   Sylvanus C. Blanchard.
2. J. A. Linscott,
   Moses Riggs.
3. James A. Creighton,
   Isaac Reed.
4. Henry Hudson,
   Marcellus Emory.
5. P. J. Carleton,
   J. C. Talbot.

MARYLAND.
DELEGATES AT LARGE.
Richard B. Carmichael,
George R. Dennis,
Montgomery Blair,
Charles J. McGwinn.

DISTRICT DELEGATES.
1. Hiram McCullough,
   Edward Floyd.
2. Stephenson Archer,
   Wm. Byrnes.
3. Wm. Pynkney White,
   Geo. W. Benson.
4. Andrew R. Syester,
   Outerbridge Horsey.
5. John D. Bowling,
   Geo. Fred. Maddox.

MASSACHUSETTS.
DELEGATES AT LARGE.
Josiah G. Abbott,
Josiah Bardwell,
Reuben Noble,
G. W. Gill.

DISTRICT DELEGATES.
1. Edward Merrill,
   Nicholas Hathaway.
2. S. B. Thaxter,
   Edward Avery,
3. James M. Keith,
   Michael Doherty.
4. Peter Harvey,
   Thomas Whittemore.
5. Charles G. Clark,
   C. O. Morse.
6. D. W. Lawrence,
   George Johnson.
7. W. W. Warren,
   Gardner Prouty.
8. George L. Chesbro,
   James E. Estabrook.
9. Frank Pratt,
   L. B. Jaquith.
10. Abijah W. Chapin,
    John R. Briggs.

MICHIGAN.
DELEGATES AT LARGE.
John Moore,
Byron G. Stout,
Robert McClelland,
Charles E. Stuart.

DISTRICT DELEGATES.
1. Wm. A. Moore,
   Mich. A. Patterson.
2. Fred. V. Smith,
   Walter G. Beckwith.
3. John L. Butterfield,
   A. M. Hart.
4. John F. Godfrey,
   John C. Blanchard.
5. E. B. Winans,
   Seymour Brownell.
6. S. M. Axford,
   Clarence E. Eddie.

MINNESOTA.
DELEGATES AT LARGE.
A. G. Chatfield,
James J. Green,
W. A. Gorman,
Winthrop Young.

DISTRICT DELEGATES.
1. E. A. McMahon,
   George D. Snow.
2. Isaac Staples,
   Thos. N. Sheehey.

MISSISSIPPI.
DELEGATES AT LARGE.
W. S. Featherston,
E. C. Walthall,
W. T. Martin,
E. M. Yerger.

DISTRICT DELEGATES.
1. Orlando Davis,
   F. B. Irby.
2. R. M. Brown,
   S. A. Jonas.
3. G. P. M. Turner,
   H. L. Jarnagin.
4. T. A. Marshall,
   E. Barksdale.
5. J. S. Holt,
   T. R. Stockdale.

MISSOURI.
DELEGATES AT LARGE.
Jas. O. Brodhead,
A. J. P. Garesche,
Thomas L. Price,
Bernard Schwartz.

DISTRICT DELEGATES.
1. Erastus Wells,
   Stilson Hutchins.
2. Carl Daenzer,
   David Murphy.
3. Thomas H. Bird,
   J. W. Everson.
4. O. S. Fahnestock,
   Nathan Bray.
5. Jno. F. Phillips,
   N. M. Givan.
6. Sam'l L. Sawyer,
   John B. Hale.
7. Wm. A. Ridenbaugh,
   Charles A. Mansur.
8. John M. Glover,
   Thos. B. Reed.

9. W. D. Hunter,   A. J. Reed.

NEBRASKA.
G. L. Miller,
G. N. Crawford,
Chas. F. Porter,
J. Sterling Morton,
John Black,
Peter Smith.

NEW HAMPSHIRE.

DISTRICT DELEGATES.

1. Anson S. Marshall,
   Albert R. Hatch.
2. George H. Pierce,
   Isaac Adams.
3. James M. Campbell,
   John Proctor.
4. Horatio Colony,
   H. W. Parker.
5. John G. Sinclair,   E. D. Rand.

NEW JERSEY.

DELEGATES AT LARGE.

Jacob K. Wortendyke,   Richard F. Stevens,
Thomas McKeen,   F. D. Latroop.

DISTRICT DELEGATES.

1. Samuel Still,
   Isaac M. Smalley.
2. Henry S. Little,
   Chas. D. Hendrickson.
3. Ryneas H. Vechtes,
   Miles Ross.
4. David Dodd,
   Thomas Kays.
5. John R. Mullaney,   George Peters.

NEW YORK.

DELEGATES AT LARGE.

Horatio Seymour,   Samuel J. Tilden,
Sanford E. Church,   Henry C. Murphy.

DISTRICT DELEGATES.

1. Erastus Brooks,
   John Armstrong.
2. Jas. B. Craig,
   Wm. Marshall.
3. Alex. McCue,
   Jas. Murphy.
4. Joseph Dowling,
   S. S. Cox.
5. Wm. M. Tweed,
   John Morrissey.
6. Emanuel B. Hart,
   Oswald Ottendorfer.
7. Chas. G. Cornell,
   August Belmont.
8. Augustus Schell,
   A. Oakey Hall.
9. P. B. Sweeney,
   Edw. Jones.
10. Collin Talmie,
    Robert Cochran.
11. Jas. B. Decker,
    C. H. Winfield.
12. Henry A. Tilden,
    Chas. Wheaton.
13. Jacob Hardenburgh,
    Geo. Beach.
14. Wm. Cassidy,
    A. A. Hunt.
15. Moses Warren,
    Emerson E. Davis.
16. Timothy Hoyle,
    Halsey R. Wing.
17. Sam'l B. Gordon,
    Darius W. Lawrence.
18. Cornelius A. Russell,
    Col. Simeon Sammons.
19. Luther J. Burdett,
    John F. Hubbard, Jr.
20. Allen C. Beach,
    Lorenzo Caryl.
21. Francis Kernan,
    Geo. H. Sanford.
22. Wm. F. Allen,
    Chas. Stebbins, Jr.
23. Jas. P. Haskins,
    John A. Green, Jr.
24. Elmore P. Ross,
    Chas. L. Lyon.
25. Joseph L. Lewis,
    Lester B. Faulkner.
26. Hiram A. Beebe,
    Jeremiah McGuire.
27. Marshall B. Champlain,
    Dan'l C. Howell.
28. Geo. W. Miller,
    Henry J. Sickles.
29. Sherburn B. Piper,
    Henry A. Richmond.
30. Joseph Warren,
    Wm. Williams.
31. Chas. H. Lee,   Jonas K. Button.

NEVADA.

W. G. Monroe,
George G. Berry,
D. E. Buel,
L. P. Drexler,
John E. Doyle,
W. M. Seawell.

NORTH CAROLINA.

DELEGATES AT LARGE.

W. N. H. Smith,
W. L. Cox,
Wm. A. Wright,
Jno. F. Hoke.

DISTRICT DELEGATES.

1. M. W. Ransom,
   D. M. Carter,
   P. H. Winston.
   R. H. Smith.
2. M. E. Manly,
   Geo. Howard.
3. Robert Strange,
   N. A. McLean.
4. W. J. Green,
   R. B. Haywood.
5. Bed. Brown,
   J. M. Leach.
6. Z. B. Vance,
   J. M. Long.
7. Thos. L. Clingman,
   L. McD. Tate.

OHIO.

DELEGATES AT LARGE.

Geo. W. McCook,
C. L. Vallandigham,
John G. Thompson,
W. W. Armstrong.

DISTRICT DELEGATES.

1. Jos. C. Butler,
   J. C. Collins.
2. Theodore Cook,
   H. C. Lord.
3. Geo. E. Pugh,
   Wm. G. Gilmore.
4. John E. Cummins,
   John E. Matchett.
5. R. R. McKee,
   F. C. LeBlond.
6. David Tarbill,
   J. M. Trimble.
7. Jacob Reinhard,
   Geo. W. Morgan.
8. H. T. Van Fleet,
   W. M. Randall.
9. Thos. Beer,
   John A. Williams.
10. John Maidlow,
    J. G. Healey.
11. John Hamilton,
    J. W. Collings.
12. E. B. Olds,
    Wayne Griswold.
13. Frank H. Hurd,
    Wm. Veach.
14. T. J. Kenney,
    Neal Power.
15. Hugh J. Jewett,
    Wylie S. Oldham.
16. William Lawrence,
    Henry Boyles.
17. Jas. B. Estep,
    Jas. H. Quinn.
18. Morrison Foster,
    H. H. Dodge.
19. R. O. Bate,
    D. C. Coleman.

OREGON.

E. L. Bristow,
N. M. Bell,
O. Joynt,
W. W. Page,
Judge P. Bruin,
J. C. Avery.

PENNSYLVANIA.
DELEGATES AT LARGE.

George W. Woodward,
William Bigler,
James Campbell,
Isaac E. Heister.

DISTRICT DELEGATES.

1. Wm. McMullin,
   D. M. Naglee.
2. Wm. M. Reilly,
   Wm. C. Patterson.
3. Henry R. Linderman,
   John E. Faunce.
4. Jeremiah McKibbin,
   P. McEntee.
5. Charles M. Hurley,
   H. P. Ross.
6. B. M. Boyer,
   John D. Stiles.
7. John H. Brinton,
   Jackson Lyons.
8. Hiester Clymer,
   Jeremiah Hagenman.
9. Wm. Patton,
   A. J. Steinman.
10. Francis W. Hughes,
    David S. Hammond.
11. E. W. Hamlin,
    Henry S. Mott.
12. Jasper B. Stark,
    Ralph B. Little.
13. Michael Meyler,
    David Lowenberg.
14. David M. Crawford,
    Wm. H. Miller.
15. John A. Magee,
    John Gibson.
16. George W. Brewer,
    John R. Donahue.
17. James Burns,
    Owen Clark.
18. George A. Auchenbach,
    Wm. Brindle.
19. Byron D. Hamlin,
    Wm. L. Scott.
20. Wm. L. Corbett,
    Gaylord Church.
21. John L. Dawson,
    James B. Sansom.
22. John A. Strain,
    John B. Guthrie.
23. R. H. Kerr,
    John T. Bard.
24. A. A. Purman,
    David S. Morris.

RHODE ISLAND.

Chas. S. Bradley,
Alfred Anthony,
Lyman Pierce,
Edward Newton,
Thos. Steere,
Ed. W. Brunsen,
William H. Allen
Amasa Sprague.

SOUTH CAROLINA.

(*Appointed by the April Convention.*) DELEGATES AT LARGE.

B. F. Perry,
James Chesnut,
J. A. Inglis,
A. P. Aldrich.

DISTRICT DELEGATES.

1. W. S. Mullins,
   J. B. Kershaw.
2. C. Tracey,
   W. L. Bonham.
3. J. S. Preston,
   W. B. Stanley.
4. A. Burt,
   W. D. Simpson.

(*Appointed by the June Convention.*) DELEGATES AT LARGE.

Wade Hampton,
J. B. Campbell,
C. M. Furman,
J. P. Carroll.

DISTRICT DELEGATES.

1. A. L. Manning,
   R. Dozier.
2. C. H. Simonton,
   John Hunckel.
3. M. W. Gary,
   A. D. Frederick.
4. T. S. Farrow.

TENNESSEE.

DELEGATES AT LARGE.
T. A. R. Nelson, A. G. P. Nicholson,
N. B. Forrest, Edmund Cooper.

DISTRICT DELEGATES.
1. James White, 5. W. B. Bate,
   W. C. Kyle. I. D. Walker.
2. John Williams, 6. John F. House,
   R. M. Edwards. Dorsay B. Thomas.
3. P. H. Marbry, 7. Wm. Connor,
   W. J. Ramage. W. T. Caldwell.
4. H. C. McLaughlin, 8. A. W. Campbell,
   Joseph H. Thompson. J. W. Leftwich.

TEXAS.

DELEGATES AT LARGE.
Horace Boughton, Ashbel Smith,
Stephen Powers, Gustavus Schleicher.

DISTRICT DELEGATES.
1. James M. Burroughs, 3. J. D. Giddings,
   Daniel A. Veitch. E. J. Gurley.
2. H. R. Runnels, 4. G. W. Smith,
   George W. Wright. George Ball.

VERMONT.

DELEGATES AT LARGE.
H. B. Smith, Henry Keys,
Isaac McDaniels, P. S. Benjamin.

DISTRICT DELEGATES.
1. E. R. Wright, 3. Waldo Brigham,
   George H. Simmons. J. J. Deavitt.
2. George H. Weeks,
   C. N. Davenport.

VIRGINIA.

DELEGATES AT LARGE.
T. A. Bocock, J. B. Baldwin,
F. McMullen, F. L. Kemper,
George Blow, Jr., T. S. Flourney.

DISTRICT DELEGATES.
1. B. B. Douglas, 5. R. H. Glass,
   H. S. Neal. William Martin.
2. John Goode, 6. J. C. Southall,
   John R. Kilby. Samuel W. Coffman.
3. James A. Barbour, 7. John R. Tucker,
   Robert Ould. Ro. Y. Conrad.
4. Robert Ridgway, 8. Joseph Kent,
   Thomas F. Goode. William B. Aston.

WEST VIRGINIA.
DELEGATES AT LARGE.
John Hall, Henry S. Walker,
John W. Kennedy, John J. Davis.

DISTRICT DELEGATES.
1. J. W. Gallaher, 2. H. G. Davis,
   J. N. Camden. J. A. F. Martin.
3. C. A. Sperry, B. H. Smith.

WISCONSIN.
DELEGATES AT LARGE.
H. L. Palmer, Nelson Dewey,
S. Clark, Gabriel Bouck.

DISTRICT DELEGATES.
1. James A. Mallory, 4. F. O. Thorp,
   John Mather. F. W. Horn.
2. E. B. Dean, Jr., 5. George Reid,
   S. T. Thorn. S. A. Pease.
3. Jas. G. Knight, 6. Thomas B. Tyler,
   Charles G. Rodolf. Allen Dawson.

Mr. Cox, of New York. — I move that the report be so amended that all the delegates in attendance from the District of Columbia be admitted to seats in this Convention on the terms mentioned in the report.

Mr. REEVES, of Indiana, moved to lay the amendment on the table. Not agreed to.

A delegate from Arkansas offered the following amendment, —

Resolved, That the delegates from New Mexico and the other Territories of the United States be entitled to all the privileges of delegates from the several States, and that on all questions before the Convention each Territory, through its delegation, shall be entitled to one vote.

The question was taken on the amendment, and it was not agreed to.

The report of the Committee on Credentials was then adopted.

Mr. KERR, of Pennsylvania, offered the following resolution, —

Resolved, That it is the duty of every friend of constitutional liberty to sustain the President in his efforts to preserve the dignity of the nation, and the sacred rights of all the people against Radical usurpation and revolution. (Cheers.) He has survived the partisan malignity of impeachment by the integrity of men sworn to do their duty, and he now stands confidently, proudly, and above them, the most exalted man in the nation, repelling the assaults of the enemies of his country. (Cheers.)

The PRESIDENT. — The resolution will be referred to the Committee on Resolutions.

Mr. NELSON, of Tennessee, offered the following resolution, —

Resolved, That the credentials of Mr. J. Waldron, who claims to be an alternate delegate from the Seventh Congressional District of Tennessee, be referred to the Committee on Credentials.

The credentials were so referred.

Mr. NELSON. — I would state to the Convention that Mr. Waldron appeared at a meeting of the Tennessee delegation this morning and claimed to be the alternate of the delegate from the Seventh District, presenting a certificate signed by the Secretary of the District Convention. I wish that the certificate also be referred to the Committee on Credentials.

The certificate was referred.

Mr. FENELON, of Kansas, offered the following resolution, —

Resolved, That the honor, dignity, and solemn obligations of the government to its foreign-born citizens demand that the flag of the nation shall protect them everywhere, precisely the same as native-born citizens. (Great applause.)

The resolution was referred to the Committee on Resolutions.

Mr. WRIGHT, of Delaware, offered the following resolution, —

Resolved, That a committee of one from each State, to be selected by the delegations thereof, be appointed to form a National Executive Committee.

The resolution was adopted.

Mr. HALL, of New York, offered the following resolution, —

Resolved, That the nation's thanks are due to Chief Justice Chase for his distinguished ability, impartiality, and fidelity to constitutional duty in presiding over the Court of Impeachment. (Cheers.)

The resolution was referred to the Committee on Resolutions.

Mr. RICHARDSON, of Illinois. — Mr. Chairman, the resolution just adopted by the Convention, in relation to the appointment of a National Executive Committee, has not been executed; and I ask that the roll of the States may be called in order that we may appoint a National Executive Committee.

The President requested the gentleman to reduce his motion to writing.

Mr. W. M. RANDALL, of Ohio, offered the following resolution, —

Resolved, That we are in favor of increasing the pensions of soldiers' widows and orphans of the late Federal Army by giving them the equivalent of gold.

The resolution was referred to the Committee on Resolutions.

Mr. REEVE, of Indiana, offered the following resolution, —

Resolved, That while we recognize no man's right to thanks for doing his duty, we congratulate the President of the United States upon his successful preservation from the assaults of his enemies. (Applause.)

The resolution was referred to the Committee on Resolutions.

Mr. RICHARDSON, of Illinois. — Mr. Chairman, I understand from a number of gentlemen that they are not prepared now to name their member of the Executive Committee, and I modify my motion that each delegation report the name of its member to the Clerk to-morrow morning.

The motion prevailed.

Mr. HURLEY, of Pennsylvania, offered the following resolution, —

Resolved, That the amnesty proclamation of Andrew Johnson, President of the United States, be read by the Secretary.

Mr. E. BROOKS, of New York. — I move to amend the resolution so as to make it read, "That the amnesty proclamation of the President of the United States be approved by this Convention."

The question was put on the amendment offered by Mr. Brooks, which prevailed.

Mr. S. S. Cox, of New York, offered the following resolution, which was received with applause and referred to the Committee on Resolutions, —

Resolved, That this Convention approve of the doctrine applied by Secretary Marcy in the Kozta case, so that not merely full naturalization, but a declaration of intention in good faith, shall be the shield of American citizenship abroad.

Mr. Clark, of Wisconsin. — I would like to inquire what has been done with the original resolution in regard to the amnesty proclamation. The amendment offered by the gentleman from New York (Mr. Brooks) was adopted, but nothing has been done since in regard to the original resolution.

The President. — The Chair understood that the amendment of the gentleman from New York (Mr. Brooks) was more in the nature of a substitute than amendment, and that it was adopted; but if it is the will of the Convention that the original resolution be voted upon, the Chair will put the question.

Cries of "No, no!"

Mr. Brewer, of Pennsylvania, offered the following resolution, which was adopted unanimously, —

Resolved, That the thanks of this Convention be tendered to Hon. Henry L. Palmer for the able, impartial, and satisfactory manner in which he discharged the duties of temporary chairman.

The President. — What is the further pleasure of the Convention?

Mr. Bigler, of Pennsylvania. — As there seems to be no business before the Chair, and as the Convention is in a very comfortable and fit condition to proceed with important business, I move that the Convention do now proceed to nominate a candidate for President of the United States. (Cheering.)

Mr. Phillips, of Missouri. — I ask the gentleman to allow me first to offer this resolution, —

Resolved, That the Delegates in this Convention pledge themselves, in advance of any nomination, to support the nominees of this Convention.

Unanimously adopted.

Mr. Hutchins, of Missouri, offered the following amendment to the resolution of Mr. Bigler, —

Resolved, That no steps be taken towards the nomination of a candidate for the Presidency until after the platform shall have been presented.

Mr. Hutchins. — I ask for a vote by States on that amendment.

The Secretary commenced calling the roll, and several States responded.

Mr. Bigler. — I am under the impression that there is a misapprehension as to the importance of the resolution I have offered. It is not intended that we shall proceed to ballot for the candidates immediately. The motion was intended to present the names, to nominate them; then proceed to fix an hour at which we will ballot for candidates. The amendment, as it stands now, involves the question of nominating the candidates in advance of a platform. For myself, I am in favor of that policy. The gentleman will see, therefore, that this is not the place for his amendment.

A Delegate, from Michigan. — I rise to a point of order; that it is not in order to make remarks after the Clerk has commenced to call the roll.

Mr. Bigler. — I have proceeded simply in explanation, for there is some misunderstanding of my motion. I wish simply to say to the gentleman from Missouri (Mr. Hutchins), that the place for his amendment will be when the motion is substituted to proceed to ballot.

Several DELEGATES. — "Order!" "order!"

The PRESIDENT. — The gentleman from Pennsylvania (Mr. Bigler) is requested to suspend one moment. The gentleman from Michigan raises the point of order that he is not in order, the calling of the roll having commenced. Unless there are objections, however, the gentleman from Pennsylvania will be allowed to state the effect of his resolution, as it seems that it is not understood by the Convention, and therefore the amendment of the gentleman from Missouri is not exactly germane to the subject. The resolution does not require that the committee shall proceed to select its candidate, but merely shall now present names of candidates for consideration. Am I correct?

Mr. BIGLER. — Yes, sir, and fix the hour for the ballot.

The PRESIDENT. — The Clerk will read the resolution.

The Clerk read the resolution, and also the amendment.

The PRESIDENT. — Does the gentleman from Missouri insist upon his amendment?

Mr. HUTCHINS. — I do. If it is not in order as an amendment, I will offer it as a substitute.

The PRESIDENT. — The amendment is in order. The Clerk will proceed to call the list of States, upon the amendment offered by the gentleman from Missouri (Mr. Hutchins).

The Clerk proceeded to call the roll.

The vote from Kentucky having been announced in the negative, a delegate from Kentucky, who did not announce his name, stated that six of the delegates voted for the amendment, and desired their votes to be so recorded.

The delegation from New York asked leave to retire for consideration. There being no objection, leave was granted.

The vote was as follows, —

	Yeas.	Nays.		Yeas.	Nays.
Alabama	8	—	Missouri	10	1
Arkansas	5	—	Nebraska	—	3
California	5	—	Nevada	3	—
Connecticut	6	—	New Hampshire	—	5
Delaware	3	—	New Jersey	7	—
Florida	3	—	N. Carolina	4½	4½
Georgia	9	—	New York	—	—
Illinois	—	16	Ohio	21	—
Indiana	13	—	Oregon	3	—
Iowa	8	—	Pennsylvania	—	26
Kansas	3	—	Rhode Island	4	—
Kentucky	—	11	South Carolina	6	—
Louisiana	7	—	Tennessee	10	—
Maine	—	—	Texas	—	6
Maryland	—	7	Vermont	4	1
Massachusetts	12	—	Virginia	—	10
Michigan	8	—	West Virginia	5	—
Minnesota	4	—	Wisconsin	8	—
Mississippi	4	—			

Decided as carried by 189½ to 90½, New York and Maine not voting.

A delegate from California moved that the Convention do now adjourn until to-morrow morning at ten o'clock. Lost.

Mr. BELMONT, of New York, offered the following, —

Resolved, That the thanks of the Convention be given to the Sachems and members of the Tammany Society for having provided and surrendered their magnificent edifice for the accommodation of the Convention, and for their courteous and efficient assistance given to the National Committee in their preparations for the Convention. (Applause.)

The resolution was unanimously adopted.

A delegate from Pennsylvania offered the following, —

Resolved, That it is the sense of this Convention, that in all future Democratic Conventions the candidate who shall receive a majority of all the votes of the Electoral College shall be declared the nominee of the Convention.

Cries of " No! no! "

The delegate asked that it be referred to the Committee on Resolutions.

The PRESIDENT. — The resolution will be so referred if there be no objection.

Mr. J. A. SPAULDING, of Kentucky, offered the following, —

Resolved, That the persons whose names may be presented to this Convention as candidates for the nomination for President and Vice-President be pledged to support the nominees. (Applause.)

The resolution was adopted.

A number of delegates here tried to obtain the floor.

The PRESIDENT. — The Convention will be in order. If delegates will allow us to dispose of the resolutions already sent up, we shall get along with our business much more rapidly. The Chair will try and recognize members in their order. But these resolutions are entitled to precedence. In no other way can the records of this Convention be preserved in order.

Mr. MATTINGLY, of Kentucky, offered the following, —

Resolved by this Convention, That the President of the United States be requested to issue a proclamation of universal amnesty. (Applause.)

Mr. DAWSON, of Pennsylvania. — Mr. Chairman, I hope that that resolution will be put to a direct vote. I regard it as the most important resolution yet presented to this Convention, and I trust it will meet with unanimous support.

The resolution was then again read and adopted.

Mr. BERNARD SCHWARTZ, of Missouri, offered the following, —

Resolved, That the Radical party in establishing two different currencies — one a depreciated paper currency for the masses of the people, the other a gold currency to pay the bondholders' interest — acted in direct violation of the best interests of the people; that honesty requires the speedy payment of the public debt, which can only be done by an economical administration of the government, and a judicious system of equalized taxation, so as to bring the country gradually back to specie payments, and that all efforts to try to force the payment of the five-twenty funded debt in coin before that time, are in direct violation of law and justice.

The PRESIDENT. — This resolution will be referred to the Committee on Resolutions, unless the Convention shall otherwise direct.

Mr. REED, of Missouri, offered the following, —

Resolved, That in all cases where a call of States is demanded, in taking a vote, the business of the Convention be suspended for five minutes to enable delegations to consult.

The resolution was adopted.

Mr. CHARLES E. STUART, of Michigan. — I desire, sir, to have the resolution read, which this Convention has adopted, referring resolutions to the Committee on Resolutions, without debate. It seems, sir, that we are acting upon resolutions that, under the order of this body, are to go to the Committee on Resolutions.

Mr. MURPHY, of New York, stated that the resolution which he had offered yesterday, was as follows, —

Resolved, That a committee of two from each State be selected by the delegates thereof to be appointed a Committee on Resolutions; and that resolutions relating to the platform of the Democratic party be referred to that committee without debate.

Mr. CRAWFORD, of Nevada, offered the following, —

Resolved, That the action of the government in prescribing the conditions of admission of States into the Federal Union, is a violation of the reserved rights of the States, and an infamous usurpation of power. (Cheers.)

Referred to the Committee on Resolutions.

Mr. EMERSON, of Missouri, offered the following, —

Resolved, That the Committee on Platform be informed of the action of this Convention, and requested to report the platform at the earliest possible moment. (Applause.)

Mr. STUART, of Michigan. — The Committee on Resolutions are laboring as rapidly as possible in that work. We organized on Saturday evening, and continued our labors till ten minutes past twelve o'clock. Of course we did nothing yesterday. The resolutions are in the hands of sub-committees, and we hope they will report to-day. I trust, therefore, this explanation will be satisfactory to the gentleman.

Mr. PRESTON, of Kentucky. — The sub-committee are engaged on these resolutions, and the chairman will soon be ready to report.

Mr. VALLANDIGHAM, of Ohio, moved that when this Convention adjourn, it adjourn until three o'clock this afternoon.

Mr. STANTON, of Kentucky, moved to amend by making the hour four o'clock instead of three.

Mr. VALLANDIGHAM accepted the amendment.

The motion, as amended, was carried.

Mr. B. M. BOYER, of Pennsylvania. — I offer the following, —

Resolved, That Andrew Johnson, President of the United States, by his able, zealous, and patriotic defence of the Constitution of this country, has entitled himself to the gratitude of this nation, and to the praise and blessings of the friends of constitutional liberty throughout the world. (Applause.)

Mr. BOYER. — This being a resolution not referring to the platform of principles, but simply an acknowledgment, on the part of this Convention, of the national gratitude to a fearless and patriotic defender of the Constitution, I ask that it may be at once submitted, without debate, to the vote of this Convention.

Objection being offered, the President ruled that the resolution could not be acted upon as requested.

Mr. RICHARDSON, of Illinois. — I move to refer to the Committee on Resolutions, all resolutions that are upon the President's table, without reading.

The PRESIDENT. — The resolution is not in accordance with the rules, inasmuch as it would carry all resolutions to the Committee on Resolutions.

Mr. RICHARDSON. — Of course I do not mean to refer to that committee those resolutions that have already been acted upon. My resolution is intended to include only such resolutions as are now upon the President's table unacted upon.

The resolution was reduced to writing, as follows, —

Resolved, That all resolutions upon all subjects now upon the President's table be referred to the Committee on Resolutions, without being read.

The resolution was adopted.

On motion of Mr. WHITE, of Maryland, the Convention then adjourned.

Afternoon Session.

The Convention assembled pursuant to adjournment. The President, on taking the Chair, was greeted with three cheers.

The PRESIDENT. — The Secretary will read to the Convention a letter that has just been received by the Chair.

The Secretary read the following, —

NEW YORK, July 6, 1868.

MY DEAR SIR, — A Committee of Conservative Soldiers and Sailors, from the Convention now in session in this place, desires to present itself to the Convention of which you are President, with an address in answer to the invitation to the privileges of the floor, and it will be glad to know at what time you will receive it.

We will be glad to be received as soon as it is convenient to the Convention.

Very respectfully yours,

W. B. FRANKLIN, *President*.

Hon. HORATIO SEYMOUR, President National Democratic Convention.

Mr. WOODWARD, of Pennsylvania. — I move that a committee of five be appointed by the Convention to wait upon the Committee of the Soldiers and Sailors' Convention, and invite them to come upon the floor.

The motion prevailed.

The President appointed the following gentlemen to constitute said Committee: Mr. Woodward, of Pennsylvania; General McCook, of Ohio; Mr. Miller, of Nebraska; General Richardson, of Illinois, and Mr. Steele, of California.

General McCook asked to be excused from serving on the committee, as he was about to leave the hall, and suggested that General George W. Morgan be appointed in his place; which suggestion was adopted.

The Soldiers and Sailors' Committee, headed by the flag borne by Sergeant Bates, was received with loud cheers, the delegates rising.

Mr. BREWER, of Pennsylvania, offered the following resolution, —

Resolved, That no gentleman shall be declared the nominee of this Convention for President of the United States, unless he shall receive two-thirds of all the votes cast.

Mr. VALLANDIGHAM, of Ohio. — I rise to the point of order that already this Convention has adopted the two-thirds rule, and that this motion is only superfluous.

The resolution passed by this Convention adopts the rules of the Convention of 1860.

Mr. BREWER, of Pennsylvania. — I do not desire to debate, but simply to say —

Mr. VALLANDIGHAM. — I rise to another point of order, that a point of order is not debatable.

At the suggestion of the President, the resolution was withdrawn to allow the Chair to inform himself upon the point.

Mr. WOODWARD, of Pennsylvania, presented the Committee from the Convention of the Soldiers and Sailors.

The Committee, on appearing in the hall, were received with the greatest enthusiasm, and, as they passed to the front of the room, they were greeted with cheer upon cheer. Cheers were also given for General Franklin, General Slocum, and others.

The Committee were requested to take positions upon the platform.

The PRESIDENT. — The Chair has the honor to present to the Convention General Franklin, as one who represents here the Conservative Soldiers and Sailors of our country, who desire peace, union, and fraternal regard. (Tremendous cheering.)

General FRANKLIN. — I have been deputed by the Conservative Soldiers and Sailors' Convention sitting in this place, to present to you the Committee. This Committee has for its Chairman, General H. W. Slocum, of this State, and it has prepared an address which it desires now to make known to the members of this Convention. (Cheers.)

General SLOCUM appeared, and was greeted with great applause. He stated that the address referred to would be read by Colonel O'Beirne, the Secretary of the committee.

Colonel O'BEIRNE read as follows, —

Address of the Soldiers and Sailors.

MR. PRESIDENT AND GENTLEMEN OF THE CONVENTION, — We are instructed by the unanimous vote of the Convention of the Union Soldiers and Sailors to return to you our thanks for extending to us the privileges of the floor of your Convention. (Cheers.) The objects for which we assembled are clearly set forth in the address of our presiding officers. Our Convention is composed of two thousand delegates, elected to represent every State and Territory in the Union, who have all served in the Union army or navy, every one of whom firmly believes that in co-operating at this time with the conservative party of the country, he is still engaged in the same cause for which he risked his life during the war, viz., to preserve the Union and maintain the supremacy of the Constitution. (Loud applause.) We believe that the objects now being perpetrated in the name of Republicanism and loyalty are not less alarming than were those committed by the armed foes of the government during the war. (Applause.) The party now in power has destroyed the equality of the States, has forced the Southern States to submit to have their constitutions and laws framed by ignorant negroes just released from a condition of servitude, while at the North it has denied the negro (although comparatively well educated) the right of suffrage. (Cheers.) It has attempted to influence the decision of the highest judicial tribunal of the land, by calling public meetings of excited partisans to condemn, in advance, all members of the court who might refuse to act in accordance with their dictation, while the leading journalists of the party, since the close of the impeachment trial, have denounced and vilified in the most unmeasured terms the once chosen leaders of their own party, going so far in some instances as to threaten them with personal violence, and for no other reason than that they were unwilling to perjure themselves at the behest of party. (Cheers.) It has freely removed political disabilities from men at the North, who, before and during the war, were the most violent and malignant rebels, but who have since become the sycophants of the party in power, while it continues to persecute those in the same localities who have always been true to the Union, but are now unwilling to be ruled by their recently emancipated slaves at the South. (Applause.) It has denied official positions to hundreds of the veterans of the war, most of whom are disabled by wounds received in battle, while it has foisted into place partisans of its own, having no claims upon the government, several of whom, fortunately for the country, have, during the past few months, become inmates of penitentiaries. It has placed the general of our armies beyond the control of the President of the United States (to whom the Federal Constitution makes him subordinate), has nominated him for the Presidency, and the events of the last few months indicate that, by the use of the army thus under his supreme control, there is a determination to cause the electoral votes of the Southern States to be cast for himself through force and fraud. (Cheers.) We solemnly declare our convictions that the free institutions of the country have never been in greater jeopardy than at this time, and we look to the deliberations of the Democratic party now assembled in Convention with the deepest anxiety, feeling that upon its action depends the future prosperity of our nation. We earnestly trust and believe that no devotion to men or adherence to past issues will be permitted to endanger the success of the great party to which the country now looks with anxious eye for permanent peace and the prosperity of our free institutions. (Loud applause.) We believe that there are living half a million men who have served in the Union army and navy, who are in sympathy and in judgment opposed to the acts of the party in power, and at least another half a million of men who have heretofore acted with the Republican party, but who, reviewing with alarm the recent acts of that party, are now anxious for a change of administration, with a platform of principles reviving no dead issues, and looking only to the arrest of existing evils, and with candidates whose fidelity to the Constitution and devotion to the country cannot be questioned. We shall co-operate with you in this campaign with a degree of enthusiasm and confidence that will bring victory to our standard and salvation to the country. (Loud cheering.)

  W. B. FRANKLIN,   DUNCAN S. WALKER,
  H. W. SLOCUM,   THOMAS KIBBY SMITH,
  J. W. DENVER,   A. W. BRADBURY,
  JOHN A. MCCLERNAND, JAS. K. O'BEIRNE,
  WM. W. AVERELL,   JAMES PARKER,
  WM. F. SMITH,   ELI C. KINSLER,
  JAMES MCQUADE,   GORDON GRANGER,
  JOHN LOVE,   THOMAS EWING, JR.,
  C. E. PRATT,   R. B. MITCHELL,
  JOHN J. PECK,   E. B. BROWN.

At the conclusion of the reading of the address, three cheers were given for the soldiers and sailors, and calls were made for Gen. Thomas Ewing, Jr., of Ohio, who was introduced to the Convention, and was greeted by a round of applause.

Speech of General Ewing.

GENTLEMEN OF THE CONVENTION, — If it were appropriate for me, it would be impossible, for lack of voice, to express to this Convention the thankfulness which I and the members of the Convention and of the Committee feel for the cordial and enthusiastic manner of this reception. We feel that the members of the two Conventions, however widely separated their paths may have been in the past, will march, henceforth, in one line. (Applause.) We earnestly wish to accomplish the purposes of the war as we understand them — (Applause) — the truly cordial, unconditional restoration of this Union. (Applause.) We have no sympathy for those purposes that have been falsely and dishonestly substituted by the Republican party for the avowed objects of the war. (Applause.) We care not for their dogmas of negro suffrage; we abhor their measures of white disfranchisement. (Applause.) We look upon them as enemies of the Republic, when we see them endeavoring, by means of that power, which a great, confiding people entrusted to them, to undermine and overthrow the settled foundations of our government. (Applause.) We cannot, we shall not, associate with them longer. (Applause.) We earnestly wish to associate with the great body of the Democracy, North and South (Applause); with thousands against whom we fought during the war (Applause); with thousands who felt perhaps coldly in the North towards the Union cause while the war went on, with all of those who now cordially accept as the established theory of the Constitution that the Union is unseverable, and who will stand by and defend the Constitution as interpreted by the government and the Supreme Court. (Applause.) Since our meeting here we have had the pleasure of friendly intercourse with many of the most prominent of the Generals of the Confederate army. (Applause.) Knowing them to be men of honor, comparing views with them, and feeling that their views and our views as to the present and future policy of this government coincide, we will take them by the hand as brothers. (Applause.) Forgetting past issues and passions, we will recognize political enemies only in those who are plotting to overthrow the Union of the States and our constitutional form of government, and we will recognize political friends in all of those who will sustain us in endeavoring to overthrow that party. (Applause.) I thank you, gentlemen of the Convention, for the very unexpected honor of being called upon to address you, and beg you will excuse me for this extempore effort.

Cries of " Go on."

Three cheers were given for General Ewing.

Mr. W. D. TURNER, of Illinois, proposed three cheers for the soldiers and sailors of the army and navy represented by the Convention at Cooper Institute. The cheers were given.

Mr. DOWDELL, of California, offered the following resolution, which was adopted,—

Resolved, That the address of the Soldiers and Sailors' Convention, just read by their Secretary, be received and entered upon the minutes of our proceedings, and become a part and parcel of the proceedings of this Convention.

Mr. MILLER, of Pennsylvania. — Will it be in order for me, sir, to ask for information of the Chair, whether individual delegates of this Convention may not be at liberty from this time until the adjournment of this Convention, to file resolutions with the Secretary of the Convention, making them a part of the proceedings? I move that the further introduction of resolutions be suspended from this time. If I have any purpose in making that motion, it is to endeavor to see some end of the introduction of resolutions by the members of this Convention. Every delegate seems to feel that he will not have fulfilled his mission as a delegate, unless he has spread upon the record a resolution, and, to such an extent, as, in my judgment, not to add very much to the strength of our proceedings when published to the world.

The PRESIDENT. — The gentleman from Pennsylvania should reduce his resolution to writing.

Mr. MILLER, of Pennsylvania. — I withdraw it. (Laughter.)

Mr. EATON, of Connecticut. — There was a resolution passed this morning that the platform should first be determined upon before any ballot should be taken for President. I understand, however, that the Committee on the Platform will not be able to report until to-morrow morning, and therefore I move to reconsider the vote upon the resolution.

Mr. BUEL, of Nevada. — I move to lay the motion of the gentleman from Connecticut (Mr. Eaton) on the table.

Several delegates called for a vote by yeas and nays upon the motion to lay on the table.

Mr. VALLANDIGHAM. — Will not the effect of the motion to lay on the table, supposing it carried, be to continue the resolution in force?

The PRESIDENT. — The Chair understands that such will be the effect.

Mr. VALLANDIGHAM. — Then I hope it will not prevail.

Mr. SCOTT, of Pennsylvania. — Do I understand that, if the motion to lay on the table is carried, it carries the original resolution with it?

The PRESIDENT. — No. The gentleman from Connecticut (Mr. Eaton) moves to reconsider the vote upon the resolution this morning. The gentleman from Nevada (Mr. Buel) moves to lay that motion on the table. The Chair understands that the effect will simply be to carry with it the motion of the gentleman from Connecticut (Mr. Eaton), leaving the rule to stand, that no nominations shall be made until after the adoption of the platform.

Mr. STANTON, of Kentucky. — I understand the rule adopted this morning to be, that when a vote by States was to be taken, delegates should first have five minutes for consultation and deliberation.

The PRESIDENT. — Yes. A vote by States is now called for, and in five minutes from this time it will be taken.

After five minutes' consultation the vote was taken by States upon laying upon the table the motion to reconsider, and the motion was rejected by the following vote, —

	Yeas.	Nays.		Yeas.	Nays.
Alabama	8	—	Nebraska	—	33
Arkansas	5	—	Nevada	3	—
California	5	—	New Hampshire	—	5
Connecticut	—	6	New Jersey	5½	5½
Delaware	3	—	New York	—	33
Florida	3	—	North Carolina	3	6
Georgia	9	—	Ohio	—	21
Illinois	—	16	Oregon	2	1
Indiana	13	—	Pennsylvania	—	26
Iowa	—	8	Rhode Island	4	—
Kansas	1½	1½	South Carolina	6	—
Kentucky	—	11	Tennessee	10	—
Louisiana	—	7	Texas	6	—
Maine	3	3½	Vermont	5	—
Maryland	½	6½	Virginia	—	10
Massachusetts	12	—	West Virginia	2½	2½
Michigan	8	—	Wisconsin	8	—
Minnesota	4	—			
Missouri	7½	3½	Total	142	172
Mississippi	7	—			

The PRESIDENT. — The question is now upon the adoption of the resolution of the gentleman from Connecticut (Mr. Eaton), that the Convention now reconsider the resolution adopted this morning.

Cries of "Question!" "Question!"

A vote by States was called for, and the Chair announced a recess of five minutes, to enable the different delegates to consult.

Mr. SLACK, of Maryland. — I move to adjourn until ten o'clock to-morrow morning.

The motion was lost.

Mr. BREWER, of Pennsylvania. — I move that when this Convention adjourn it adjourn to meet to-morrow morning at ten o'clock, and that hereafter the Convention upon adjournment will fix that hour for its meeting.

Carried.

The PRESIDENT. — The Clerk will now call the States in their order, for the purpose of taking the vote upon the resolution before the Convention.

Mr. FINCH, of Iowa. — I move that this Convention now adjourn.

The motion to adjourn was lost.

The Secretary again read the resolution to reconsider the vote on the resolution that there be no balloting for candidates for President and Vice-President until after the report of the Committee on Resolutions be received and adopted.

The vote by States was then taken with the following result, —

	Yeas.	Nays.		Yeas.	Nays.
Alabama	—	8	Nebraska	—	—
Arkansas	—	5	Nevada	—	3
California	—	5	New Hampshire	5	—
Connecticut	6	—	New Jersey	2½	4½
Delaware	1	—	New York	33	—
Florida	—	3	North Carolina	6	3
Georgia	1	—	Ohio	21	—
Illinois	16	—	Oregon	1	—
Indiana	13	—	Pennsylvania	26	—
Iowa	3½	—	Rhode Island	—	4
Kansas	1½	—	South Carolina	—	6
Kentucky	11	—	Tennessee	—	10
Louisiana	—	7	Texas	—	6
Maine	3	—	Vermont	—	5
Maryland	6½	—	Virginia	—	10
Massachusetts	—	12	West Virginia	2½	2½
Michigan	—	8	Wisconsin	—	8
Minnesota	1½	2			
Mississippi	—	7	Total	179½	137
Missouri	5½	5½			

The PRESIDENT. — The question before the Convention is the resolution of the gentleman from Pennsylvania. A delegate from California has moved an amendment to that resolution, which is first in order. It will be read by the Clerk. It was in the hands of the Chair before other resolutions.

The Secretary read the resolution of Mr. Hammond, of California, as follows, —

Resolved, That Candidates for President may now be put in nomination, but that no ballot be had until a platform of principles is adopted.

Mr. BIGLER. — I make a point of order on the amendment. It is precisely in substance what this body has voted down repeatedly. Therefore it is not in order.

The PRESIDENT. — The motion of the gentlemen from Pennsylvania was this: Not that the Convention should proceed to ballot, but that the Convention should proceed to nominate candidates. The gentleman from California proposes by his amendment so to modify that resolution that no vote shall be taken to nominate until after the adoption of the resolutions. The Chair thinks that is a resolution different from any that has been offered heretofore, and is a modification of the resolution of the gentleman from Pennsylvania.

Mr. BIGLER. — It would be in order provided it was divided.

The PRESIDENT. — It is in the power of the gentleman to call a division of the question.

Mr. BIGLER. — I call for a division of the question. So far as it regards excluding a ballot until a platform is adopted is one division; all that which precedes it is another.

Mr. VALLANDIGHAM. — What became of the motion of the gentleman from Missouri? If I understand it is still undisposed of. This proposition can only come in as amendment to the amendment, no further amendment being in order.

The PRESIDENT. — The gentleman from Ohio (Mr. Vallandigham) is right. The question before the Convention is the adoption of the resolution of the gentleman from Missouri, which had escaped the attention of the Chair.

The Secretary read as follows, —

Resolved, That no balloting for candidates for President or Vice-President be had until after the report of the Committee on Resolutions shall have been received and adopted.

The resolution having been read, —

Mr. HUTCHINS, of Missouri. — That resolution, with the permission of the gentleman who seconded it, I beg leave now to withdraw.

Mr. BIGLER. — Then I desire to modify that resolution, and to move that the States be called in their regular order, and that the candidates be presented, and that there be conceded to each State five minutes to present the claims and character of the candidate whose name it desires to submit to the Convention.

The PRESIDENT. — The gentleman from Pennsylvania now modifies his resolution so that it shall read as follows, —

Resolved, That the call of States be called in their regular order, and that each State be allowed to present the name of any candidate for the Presidency, and that the delegates have five minutes allowed them to present their views upon their candidate. (Applause.)

Mr. BREWER. — I second the resolution of the gentleman from Pennsylvania (Mr. Bigler). It occurred to me this morning when the motion was made by the gentleman from Pennsylvania to put in nomination candidates to be voted for, for the offices of President and Vice-President, that it was out of order and out of the usual custom of the Democratic party. Heretofore, in all national Conventions, every State has had the right and been permitted to vote for any gentleman in this country, — whomsoever they might feel disposed to vote for. If we place in nomination some candidates, and they should then conclude that the nominations should close, there would be no power by which the Convention could afterwards go for a man whose name had not been already presented to the Convention. I second this resolution, because I consider it correct, and the other resolution incorrect and contrary to the usages and practices of the Democratic party. We desire that every State shall present and vote for the candidate of her choice.

Mr. HAMMOND, of California. — Now I apprehend that it will be in order for me to offer my resolution, as there is no original resolution pending. I offer the following resolution as a substitute for the whole matter, —

Resolved, That candidates for the Presidency may now be placed in nomination, but that no balloting be had until the platform of principles is adopted. (Applause.)

Mr. GRAVES, of Kentucky, moved the previous question.

The motion not being seconded, the vote was taken on the amendment of Mr. Hammond, and the question decided in the negative.

The question recurred on the resolution of the delegate from Missouri.

Mr. BIGLER. — I shall be obliged to call for a division of that resolution, as the latter clause of the resolution has already been decided three times in succession.

The PRESIDENT. — The gentleman from Pennsylvania calls for a division of the question upon the ground that the resolution contains two distinct propositions The first part of the resolution is : "*Resolved*, That candidates for the Presidency be now placed in nomination;" and the second point: "That no balloting be had until the platform of principles is adopted." Mr. Bigler proposes now to vote upon the first branch, after which a vote will be taken upon the latter proposition.

Mr. BIGLER. — Mr. President, I withdraw my call for a division.

The amendment was lost.

The question recurred on the resolution of Mr. Bigler. It was adopted.

Mr. JAMES PONDER, of Delaware, moved that the Convention do now adjourn.

The vote on adjournment was taken by States, with the following result, —

	Yeas.		Nays.
Alabama	8	Connecticut	6
Arkansas	5	Georgia	1
California	5	Indiana	13
Delaware	3	Iowa	1½
Florida	3	Kentucky	11
Georgia	8	Maine	2½
Illinois	16	Maryland	7
Iowa	6½	Missouri	3
Kansas	3	Nebraska	3
Louisiana	7	New Hampshire	3
Maine	4	New Jersey	2½
Massachusetts	12	North Carolina	3
Michigan	8	Ohio	21
Minnesota	4	Pennsylvania	26
Mississippi	7	West Virginia	2½
Missouri	6½		
Nevada	3	Total	106
New Hampshire	2		
New Jersey	4½		
New York	33		
North Carolina	6		
Oregon	3		
Rhode Island	4		
South Carolina	6		
Tennessee	10		
Texas	6		
Vermont	5		
Virginia	10		
West Virginia	2½		
Wisconsin	8		
Total	209		

The Convention then adjourned until Tuesday at ten o'clock.

The delegates from the Territories admitted to seats on the floor in pursuance of the resolution adopted, were: Thomas W. Betts, of Idaho Territory; Thomas E. Evershed, of Arizona Territory.

THIRD DAY.

July 7, 1868.

The President being slightly indisposed, although present on the platform, the Convention was called to order by General THOMAS L. PRICE, of Missouri.

The President *pro tem.* introduced Rev. Dr. PLUMMER, who opened the proceedings by the following prayer, the whole convention rising.

Prayer.

Almighty and Glorious Jehovah, Father of men and of nations, we approach Thy eternal and propitious throne, confessing that we are sinful and deserve not the least of all Thy manifold mercies. Though we, as a people, have seen afflictions by the rod of Thy wrath, yet Thou hast punished us less than our iniquities deserve. We have insulted and provoked Thee to anger by our ingratitude, unbelief, and love of the world; by our pride, profaneness, and forgetfulness of Thee. Oh! forgive us our sins. In days gone past Thou hast greatly blessed us; our history is full of striking instances of Thy goodness; our brothers have told us true and wonderful stories of Thy love and mercy; even now we enjoy many favors wholly gracious. We thank Thee for the precious things of Heaven, for the dew, and for the deep that worketh beneath, and for the precious fruits brought forth by the sun, and for the precious things put forth by the moon, and for the chief things of the ancient mountains, and for the precious things of the lasting hills, and for the precious things of the earth, and above all for the good will of Him who dwelt in the bush. We bless Thee for Thy countless benefits, temporal and spiritual. Continue to do us good. Chasten us, yet in measure, for our good; but smite us not in Thy hot displeasure. Let the solemn event by which Thou hast suddenly removed a member of this body from the fleeting scenes of time to the awful realities of eternity be sanctified to us all. In mercy, pity and sustain the family thus cast into deep sorrow.* Pour not upon us the vials of Thy wrath. Spare us according to the greatness of Thy mercy. In Thy tender compassion compose our public agitations; protect the injured; relieve the distressed; judge the widow; be the orphans' God; cause all human sufferings to lead men to repentance and to Thee; make all our people devout worshippers of the God of Heaven; let violence no more be heard in our land, wasting nor destruction in our borders; give our senators wisdom; make our officers peaceful and our exactors righteous; so bless us that our men shall call our walls salvation and our gates praise. Oh! send us, when, how, and by whom Thou wilt, but send us enlargement and deliverance; allay the vindictive passions of men; teach them to forgive and to forget, to pity and to bless. Let the mountains bring forth grace, and the little hills righteousness. O Lord our God, be thou our shield, our glory, and the lifter up of our heads. Guide the deliberations of this Convention to such conclusions as shall promote Thy glory and the public welfare. Deliver not this nation over to misrule, to despotism, to anarchy, to sectional animosity, nor to internecine strifes. Preserve to us and our posterity unimpaired the liberties, civil and religious, received from our fathers, and bought with their toils and tears and blood. So will we, Thy people and the sheep of thy pasture, show forth Thy praise forever and ever, through Jesus Christ, our strength and Redeemer. Amen.

Mr. BIGLER, of Pennsylvania.—I move to dispense with the reading of the journal of yesterday's proceedings. (The motion prevailed.)

* Referring to the death of Peter Cagger, of New York.

Resolutions from Alex. H. Stephens.

Mr. WRIGHT, of Delaware. — I hold in my hand a series of resolutions, which I have received from Hon. Alexander H. Stephens, of Georgia — (Applause) — which I ask to have read and referred to the Committee on Resolutions.

The resolutions were read as follows, and were received with repeated applause.

Resolved, That in the future, as in the past, we will adhere with unswerving fidelity to the Union under the Constitution as the only solid foundation of our strength, security, and happiness as a people, and as a framework of government equally conducive to the welfare and prosperity of all the States — both Northern and Southern.

Resolved, That the Union established by the Constitution is a Union of States Federal in its character, composed of States thereby united, and is incapable of existence without the States as its continuing integral parts; and, therefore, the perpetuation of the Union in its integrity depends upon the preservation of the States in their political integrity,—the government of the United States being a Federal Republic, and not a consolidation of the whole people into a nation.

Resolved, That the perpetuation of the Union, and the maintenance of the government as both were established by the Constitution, and as both under the Constitution have been expounded in the foregoing resolutions, in conformity with the venerable teachings of Jefferson, Madison, and Jackson, have ever been held as cardinal doctrines of the Democratic party; and they are now reiterated with increased earnestness under the solemn conviction that only by bringing back the administration of the government to the time-honored principles (on which for sixty years there was such unparalleled happiness and prosperity); and in rescuing it from those who have ever held the Constitution itself to be no better than a "covenant with death and an agreement with Hell;" whose revolutionary policy and measures have brought such general discord, strife and war with its attendant ills upon a large portion of the country, and such wide-spread demoralization throughout the whole of it.

Resolved, That the Democratic party, in sustaining the Federal administration in the late unhappy conflict of arms, did so in good faith, with the hope and earnest wish to maintain the principles above set forth, and with no view of "waging war" on the part of the Northern States "in any spirit of oppression" against their brethren of the South, nor for any purpose of conquest or subjugation, nor purpose of overthrowing or interfering with the rights or established institutions of the States; but to defend and maintain the supremacy of the Constitution, and to preserve the Union with all the dignity, equality, and rights of the several States unimpaired. The subjugation of these States, or the holding of them as conquerred territory, would be, in the judgment of the Convention, the destruction of the Union itself.

Resolved, That the highest meed of patriotism is due, and should ever be rendered to all those who, in the recent war, perilled life or fortune for the maintenance of the Union, and the beneficent system of American Government thereby established upon the fundamental principles set forth in the foregoing resolution; but we have neither thanks nor sympathy for those who entered or carried on the contest for the subjugation of States, or for the subjugation by Federal authority of the white race in any of the States to the dominion of the black. The right of suffrage, of who shall exercise political power, is a matter that rests, under the Constitution, exclusively with the several States. There it properly belongs, and there it should continue ever to remain.

The resolutions were referred to the Committee on Resolutions.

Mr. RICHARDSON, of Illinois. — I move that all resolutions hereafter introduced to the Convention be referred to the Committee on Resolutions without reading. We shall commit some mistake, or indorse some doctrine that we can not defend upon the stump, and ought not to defend, if we pass all resolutions that are presented here.

Mr. BRADFORD, of Delaware. — I am opposed to that motion, because I think it is due to those that offer them that they shall be read before the Convention.

Mr. TARBILL, of Ohio. — I move to amend the motion of the gentleman from Illinois, so that it shall apply only to resolutions touching the principles of the platform.

Mr. RICHARDSON. — I accept that. I do not know exactly how we are to determine what does refer to the platform, but I will accept the proposition.

Mr. BIGLER, of California. — I have in my possession resolutions adopted by the California Democratic State Convention, which I simply wish to present to go with the others, and ask that they be read.

Mr. COX, of New York. — I wish to say to the Convention that there is no necessity for the motion of the gentleman from Illinois (Mr. Richardson), and I think he will withdraw it when he understands that the Committee on Resolutions are now ready to report, and there will be no occasion for further resolutions of this kind.

Mr. BIGLER, of Pennsylvania. — I move to lay the motion of the gentleman from Illinois upon the table.

Resolutions of the California Convention.

The Secretary read the following resolutions presented by ex-Gov. Bigler of California, adopted by the California Labor Convention, —

Resolved, That it is not only the patriotic duty, but the deliberate purpose of the Democratic party never to submit to be governed by the negro, nor by those claiming to be elected by negro suffrage; and we do earnestly recommend the adoption of this resolution by the National Convention of the Democracy, which shall assemble in July next.

Resolved, That the eight-hour law system of labor is a Democratic measure, and ought of right to become a national principle, making eight hours a legal day's work on all public works in the United States; that our delegation to the National Convention are requested to use their endeavors to incorporate this declaration in the National Platform.

Mr. RICHARDSON, of Illinois. — I move to refer these resolutions and any that may be offered hereafter, to the Committee on the Platform, and I insist upon that question.

Mr. BIGLER. — I move to lay that motion on the table.

The question was put on the motion to lay on the table, and it was rejected.

The question recurred upon the motion of Mr. Richardson.

Mr. VALLANDIGHAM. — I submit that if the resolution is adopted in that form it carries to the table even a motion to proceed to vote for President, as well as any other form of proceeding.

Committee on Resolutions.

Mr. Cox, of New York. — I rise to a point of order that the Committee on Resolutions have the right to report at any time, and are now seeking the recognition of the Chair for that purpose, and that other business should not interfere with the report of the Committee.

Mr. MURPHY, of New York, Chairman of the Committee on Resolutions. — I am directed by the Committee on Resolutions to report the Platform, which I hold in my hand, and which I ask permission to read to the Convention. (Applause.)

Mr. MONROE, of Nevada. — I am directed by gentlemen around me to call the attention of the Chair to the fact that it will be interesting and important to us all to hear each word of the resolutions. While the venerable gentleman was praying for us this morning I noticed that his voice, weak as it was, could be heard all over the hall. I heard every word distinctly, and if it takes from now until next winter to restore order so that we can hear the resolutions, I think it ought to be done, so that we may be able to act intelligently upon the platform.

The PRESIDENT *pro tem*. — Gentlemen, you will please take your seats and keep profound silence. We hope that there will be not a whisper in the hall while the resolutions are being read. Mr. Murphy, of New York, will proceed to read the resolutions.

Mr. Murphy then advanced to the stage, amid much cheering, and read the Platform as follows, —

The Platform.

The Democratic party in National Convention assembled, reposing its trust in the intelligence, patriotism, and discriminating justice of the people; standing upon the Constitution as the foundation and limitation of the powers of the government, and the guaranty of the liberties of the citizen; and recognizing the questions of slavery and secession as having been settled for all time to come by the war, or the voluntary action of the Southern States in Constitutional Conventions assembled, and never to be renewed or reagitated; does, with the return of peace, demand,

First. Immediate restoration of all the States to their rights in the Union, under the Constitution, and of civil government to the American people.

Second. Amnesty for all past political offences, and the regulation of the elective franchise in the States, by their citizens.

Third. Payment of the public debt of the United States as rapidly as practicable. All moneys drawn from the people by taxation, except so much as is requisite for the necessities of the government, economically administered, being honestly applied to such payment, and where the obligations of the government do not expressly state upon their face, or the law under which they were issued does not provide, that they shall be paid in coin, they ought, in right and in justice, be paid in the lawful money of the United States.

Fourth. Equal taxation of every species of property, according to its real value, including government bonds and other public securities.

Fifth. One currency for the government and the people, the laborer and the office-holder, the pensioner and the soldier, the producer and the bond-holder.

Sixth. Economy in the administration of the government, the reduction of the standing army and navy; the abolition of the Freedmen's Bureau; and all political instrumentalities designed to secure negro supremacy; simplification of the system and discontinuance of inquisitorial modes of assessing and collecting internal revenue, so that the burden of taxation may be equalized and lessened, the credit of the government increased and the currency made good; the repeal of all enactments for enrolling the State militia into national forces in time of peace; and a tariff for revenue upon foreign imports, such as will afford incidental protection to domestic manufactures, and as will, without impairing revenue, impose the least burden upon, and best promote and encourage the great industrial interests of the country.

Seventh. Reform of abuses in administration; the expulsion of corrupt men from office; the abrogation of useless offices; the restoration of rightful authority to, and the independence of the executive and judicial departments of the government; the subordination of the military to the civil power, to the end that the usurpations of Congress and the despotism of the sword may cease.

Eighth. Equal rights and protection for naturalized and native-born citizens at home and abroad; the assertion of American nationality, which shall command the respect of foreign powers, and furnish an example and encouragement to people struggling for national integrity, constitutional liberty, and individual rights, and the maintenance of the rights of naturalized citizens against the absolute doctrine of immutable allegiance and the claims of foreign powers to punish them for alleged crimes committed beyond their jurisdiction.

In demanding these measures and reforms we arraign the Radical party for its disregard of right, and the unparalleled oppression and tyranny which have marked its career.

After the most solemn and unanimous pledge of both Houses of Congress to prosecute the war exclusively for the maintenance of the government and the preservation of the Union under the Constitution, it has repeatedly violated that most sacred pledge, under which alone was rallied that noble volunteer army which carried our flag to victory.

Instead of restoring the Union, it has, so far as in its power, dissolved it, and subjected ten States, in time of profound peace, to military despotism and negro supremacy.

It has nullified there the right of trial by jury; it has abolished the habeas corpus, that most sacred writ of liberty; it has overthrown the freedom of speech and of the press; it has substituted arbitrary seizures and arrests, and military trials and secret star-chamber inquisitions, for the constitutional tribunals; it has disregarded in time of peace the right of the people to be free from searches and seizures; it has entered the post and telegraph offices, and even the private rooms of individuals, and seized their private papers and letters without any specific charge or notice of affidavit, as required by the organic law; it has converted the American capitol into a Bastile; it has established a system of spies and official espionage to which no constitutional monarchy of Europe would now dare to resort; it has abolished the right of appeal, on important constitutional questions, to the Supreme Judicial tribunal, and threatens to curtail, or destroy, its original jurisdiction, which is irrevocably vested by the Constitution; while the learned Chief Justice has been subjected to the most atrocious calumnies, merely because he would not prostitute his high office to the support of the false and partisan charges preferred against the President. Its corruption and extravagance have exceeded anything known in history, and by its frauds and monopolies it has nearly doubled the burden of the debt created by the war; it has stripped the President of his constitutional power of appointment even of his own Cabinet. Under its repeated assaults the pillars of the government are rocking on their base, and should it succeed in November next and inaugurate its president, we will meet as a subject and conquered people amid the ruins of liberty and the scattered fragments of the Constitution.

And we do declare and resolve, That ever since the people of the United States threw off all subjection to the British crown, the privilege and trust of suffrage have belonged to the several States, and have been granted, regulated, and controlled exclusively by the political power of each State respectively, and that any attempt by Congress, on any pretext whatever, to deprive any State of this right, or interfere with its exercise, is a flagrant usurpation of power, which can find no warrant in the Constitution; and if sanctioned by the people will subvert our form of government, and can only end in a single centralized and consolidated government, in which the separate existence of the States will be entirely absorbed, and an unqualified despotism be established in place of a federal union of co-equal States; and that we regard the reconstruction acts, so called, of Congress, as such an usurpation, and unconstitutional, revolutionary, and void.

That our soldiers and sailors, who carried the flag of our country to victory against a most gallant and determined foe, must ever be gratefully remembered, and all the guaranties given in their favor must be faithfully carried into execution.

That the public lands should be distributed as wisely as possible among the people, and should be disposed of either under the pre-emption or homestead laws, or sold in reasonable quantities, and to none but actual occupants, at the minimum price established by the government. When grants of the public lands may be deemed necessary for the encouragement of important public improvements, the proceeds of the sale of such lands, and not the lands themselves, should be so applied.

That the President of the United States, Andrew Johnson, in exercising the powers of his high office, in resisting the aggressions of Congress upon the Constitutional rights of the States and the people, is entitled to the gratitude of the whole American people; and, in behalf of the Democratic party, we tender him our thanks for his patriotic efforts in that regard.

Upon this platform the Democratic party appeals to every patriot, including all the Conservative element, and all who desire to support the Constitution and restore the Union, forgetting all past differences of opinion, to unite with us in the present great struggle for the liberties of the people; and that to all such, to whatever party they may have heretofore belonged, we extend the right hand of fellowship, and hail all such co-operating with us as friends and brethren.

At the conclusion of the reading of the platform, Mr. Murphy said, —

As might have been expected in the preparation of this platform there were differences of opinion, which, however, upon consultation, have vanished. I say to this Convention that this platform has received the unanimous approval of the Committee. (Great applause.) And, sir, in view of this fact, I move the previous question upon its adoption. (Applause.)

The SECRETARY. — Mr. Murphy, of New York, Chairman of the Committee on Resolutions, moves the previous question on the Platform. The question now before the Convention is, Shall the previous question be ordered?

Cries of "Question!" "question!"

The previous question was seconded, and the main question ordered, by an overwhelming and unanimous vote.

A DELEGATE. — I should like to hear those resolutions read again.

Cries of "No, no!" and "Question!"

The President *pro tem.* put the question upon the adoption of the Platform, and an unanimous and tremendous vote was given in the affirmative. Not a single dissenting voice answered in response to the call of those opposed.

A scene of the wildest enthusiasm succeeded; the Convention and the spectators rose *en masse;* cheer upon cheer resounded through the building, and the waving of hats and handkerchiefs, and various demonstrations of applause continued for several minutes.

When quiet was restored the business of the Convention proceeded.

Motion to Proceed to Nominations.

Mr. BIGLER, of Pennsylvania. — I offer the following resolution, —

Resolved, That the Convention do now proceed to nominate a candidate for President of the United States.

Great applause, and cries of "Question!"

The question was put and carried unanimously, amid cheering.

Mr. VALLANDIGHAM. — I move to reconsider the vote by which the resolution of the gentleman from Pennsylvania (Mr. Bigler) was adopted, and to lay that motion on the table.

The motion was agreed to.

Construction of the Two-Thirds Rule.

The PRESIDENT, Hon. HORATIO SEYMOUR (who here resumed the Chair). — Before the Committee proceeds to ballot, to avoid all possible misunderstanding, it is proper that this Convention should understand and clearly define what the two-thirds rule is. The Chair is exceedingly anxious that no question shall be decided by it after a ballot that can, by any possibility, lead to any misunderstanding or any disappointment. The Chair holds itself ready in the construction of the two-thirds rule to be governed by the directions of this Convention. We have adopted the rules which governed the Convention in 1864. The Convention of 1864 adopted the rules that governed the Convention of 1860. I see before me a number of eminent gentlemen — one from Illinois, another from Michigan, and others from other States — who were conspicuous members of that Convention. I was not a member of that body, but I have read through its proceedings with a view of understanding what that rule is. I will direct the Clerk to read the decision of the Convention in Charleston in 1860, and the decision of the Convention when it met again at Baltimore under another chairman, after the unfortunate disruption of that body. When those resolutions have been read, if there is any one who wishes to have any further interpretation of these resolutions, I beg the Convention will act upon this matter now. It is exceedingly important after a vote has been taken, where it is possible that the decisions of the Chair might be held to help or hurt a candidate, — it is exceedingly important that he should make no decisions which are not in accordance with the clear sense of this Convention. The Chair should not have thrown upon it the responsibility of any duty so delicate. If all the delegates to this Convention shall vote when we nominate a candidate, no difficulties can arise. But if all should not vote, the question would come up, should two-thirds of all the members of this Convention, or should two-thirds of those who voted, make the nomination? I, therefore, ask upon this subject that the Convention shall instruct the Chair as to the right interpretation of that resolution.

Mr. RICHARDSON, of Illinois. — Mr. President, I desire to submit a resolution, that two-thirds of all the votes cast shall decide the question. I want to say another thing. I shall not now move to repeal this two-thirds rule, but, after we have nominated a candidate, I shall move its repeal for all future Conventions. It is the most mischievous rule ever adopted by the Democratic party. As soon as we nominate a candidate I shall deem it my duty to bring forward the resolution, so as to prevent its obtaining in all future Conventions. A majority of the party should control the party. I want to get out of the wilderness. (Laughter.) I want to safely land. I want to stand upon the Constitution of our country, and the supreme law of the land.

The Secretary read the resolution, for information, as follows, —

That two-thirds of all the votes cast shall be required to nominate a candidate for President, and Vice-President of the United States.

Mr. KERNAN, of New York. — I believe, Mr. President, and I hope that no real issue will arise in this Convention in reference to the subject-matter of this resolution. Not only do we want to get out of the wilderness, but, for the sake of the country, we want to win in the coming contest. (Great cheering.) Our Convention being, as I rejoice to know, composed of representatives from the Democratic Conservative men of every State in the Union (Applause), I desire that we may act in unison, and that we shall nominate no man in this important contest who does not command the best judgment of two-thirds of the representatives here. (Cheers.) It is, therefore, sir, in no other sense that I rise to ask this Convention not to change the rule which has hitherto prevailed, and not to adopt the resolution of my respected friend from Illinois. I believe, sir, that we should not place ourselves in such a position that the representatives of any one State should affect the result of our deliberations by refusing to act for their constituents in this important contest. Let the delegates from every State give up, not their feelings nor their prejudices, but their judgment in reference to the man who is to be our standard-bearer. (Cheers.) I do not want my judgment to prevail if I find that two-thirds of the gentlemen of the Convention are opposed to my judgment, nor do I want the judgment of others to prevail except they shall succeed in satisfying two-thirds of all the delegates from all the States that the man they select is the one best calculated to lead us on to victory, and rescue us from the misrule of Radical faction. (Great applause.) Therefore I submit that we should adhere to the rule that has hitherto prevailed, vote down the resolution, and go into the ballot like brothers, saying that the man who shall command the votes of two-thirds of the delegates from the States shall be our standard-bearer, and that nobody else shall. (Loud applause.)

Mr. RICHARDSON, of Illinois. — I have said that I was in favor of the two-thirds rule if we make our nominations to-day.

Mr. CLYMER, of Pennsylvania. — Mr. President, I chanced by the kindness of the Committee on Organization to be its chairman. When it reported the rule with reference to what regulations should govern the proceedings of this body, it was deemed important that a very clear understanding should be had upon this important subject, and it may be interesting to you, sir, and this Convention, to know what was the construction placed upon this rule by that committee. I will state that I believe it was the unanimous judgment of that committee, when it reported the rule, that it required, not two-thirds of the vote cast, but two-thirds of the vote of the entire Electoral College to nominate. (Cries of "Good," and applause.) Therefore, I move, sir, to substitute for the resolution of the honorable gentleman from Illinois (Mr. Richardson), the following, which I send to the desk.

A DELEGATE from Louisiana. — Mr. President, I desire to ask what has become of the resolution which was offered by the gentleman from Maryland. I want it read.

Mr. RICHARDSON, of Illinois. — Mr. President, I will withdraw my whole proposition; but I give notice, that when I advance with a candidate to a majority vote, I will camp with the majority, and stay there to the end. (Laughter.)

The PRESIDENT. — If the resolution is withdrawn, the Chair advises this Convention that it should adopt the construction which was put upon this resolution in 1860, by the President of the Convention, at Charleston, and by the President of the Convention, at Baltimore. The Chair understands that the decision at Charleston (which decision was assented to afterwards at Baltimore) was that it required two-thirds of the electoral votes to nominate. (Applause.) In order that the Convention may understand this, I will ask the Secretary to read the decision there made. The only wish of the Chair in this matter is to prevent any possible misunderstanding from arising as to the rule under which we act. With this understanding, if the Convention assents to it, the subject will be dropped.

Mr. WHITE, of Maryland. — Inasmuch as the decision of the Chair is exactly in accordance with my resolution, I will withdraw it.

The Secretary, by direction of the President, then read from the report, the decision of the Chair made at the Democratic Convention of 1860, as follows, —

The resolution passed at Charleston, as understood by the President of this Convention, as understood by the present occupant of the Chair, was not a change in the rule requiring a two-thirds' vote to be given to nominate, but merely a direction given to the Chair, by the Convention, not to declare any one nominated until he had received two-thirds of the votes of the Electoral College; and the present occupant of the Chair will not feel at liberty, under that direction, to declare any one nominated until he gets 202 votes, unless the committee shall otherwise instruct him.

Mr. Bigler, of Pennsylvania, moved that the roll of States be called, and that the delegates of the several States proceed to the nomination of candidates for the Presidency.

A DELEGATE from Delaware. — Several gentleman here desire to know the exact electoral vote.

The PRESIDENT. — The entire electoral vote is 317.

Mr. A. OAKEY HALL, of New York. — I offer the following resolution, —

Resolved, That whereas the following States are represented in this Convention, with the following electoral vote (here follows the official tally, State by State, as part of the resolution), the whole number of delegates in the Convention being 317, two-thirds of which are $211\frac{1}{2}$, that no person shall be nominated unless he shall receive 212 votes.

A delegate moved to lay the resolution on the table.

The PRESIDENT. — The Chair is of the opinion that the Convention has already settled this question, and that the resolution is not in order, because it is simply carrying out what has already been decided.

The PRESIDENT. — Before the States are called, I wish to say one word to the audience. It has been a subject of complaint, and the Chair perhaps has been much at fault, that we have allowed so much latitude to those who have come up to witness our proceedings. There has been so much that went straight to the Democratic heart, that we could not repress such manifestations (Cheers); but while this is true, our audience must remember that so far as the business of this Convention is concerned, it is unfit and improper for them in any degree to attempt to influence its action by their manifestations. And let me say another thing. While the tickets to this Convention have been given out in their proportion to every delegate, in the very nature of things a large share of this audience is drawn from the great city in which we meet. And let me reinforce my appeal to them by another consideration, which I know will sink deep into the heart of every man from New York. It is an act of inhospitality. (Cheers.) I trust, therefore, that, when this Convention shall proceed to ballot, there will at least be no manifestation which shall not show that this Convention, and all who are about us, recognize in every man whose name shall be offered here a true, earnest, and honest man, whom we would all be glad to honor, though we are compelled to make a choice of but one. (Loud applause.)

Mr. BIGLER, of Pennsylvania. — The first proceeding under the order of the Convention, already adopted, will be the nominating of the candidates of the Convention.

VOICES. — "No, no! let us waive that."

Mr. CAVANAUGH, of Montana. — I send to the Chair, and desire to have read, certain resolutions adopted last evening by all the delegates from all the Territories of the United States.

Mr. VALLANDIGHAM. — I am obliged, reluctantly, to raise the point of order that the House is engaged in the performance of another duty, and the resolutions of the gentlemen are clearly not in order.

The PRESIDENT. — The Chair is of opinion that the resolutions are not in order now, as the Convention is in the performance of another order.

Mr. CAVANAUGH. — May I ask a question? At what time may these resolutions be offered, if at all?

After consultation with several delegates, Mr. Cavanaugh withdrew the resolutions.

Mr. TILDEN. — I am desired to suggest to the Chair that it instruct the Secretary of the Convention, when any State shall give in its vote, to call back that vote, in order that there may be no misunderstanding or confusion.

The PRESIDENT. — The Secretary will be so instructed. The Convention will now proceed to name candidates.

Mr. THURMAN, of Ohio. — I wish to say a word. The resolution of the gentleman from Pennsylvania was that this Convention do now proceed to nominate a President. That resolution was agreed to, a motion to reconsider was made, and that resolution was laid on the table; so there is nothing to do but to execute that order. One thing further: a resolution was passed yesterday that the friends of every candidate that should be presented to this Convention should pledge him and themselves to support the nomination that should be made. That would seem to require that the names of the candidates should be presented, and the pledge should be given.

The PRESIDENT. — The Chair understands that the resolution of the gentleman from Pennsylvania contemplated, and that it was the sense of the Convention, that we should now proceed to have the names of the candidates announced.

Mr. BIGLER, of Pennsylvania. — The resolution offered this morning had better be read.

The resolution read as follows, —

Resolved, That the Convention do now proceed to nominate a candidate for President of the United States.

Mr. BIGLER, of Pennsylvania. — That is a general order; under that order all the other forms that are necessary must be first adopted. We must have tellers, and then proceed to ballot.

The PRESIDENT. — How many tellers shall there be?

Mr. BREWER, of Pennsylvania. — I move that the Secretaries of the Convention act as tellers.

Mr. BIGLER. — How many Secretaries are there at the table?

The SECRETARY. — Four.

Mr. BIGLER. — I move that the Secretaries of the Convention act as tellers, and count all the votes that shall be given.

The motion was agreed to.

A delegate from Georgia complained that, owing to the confusion, delegates sitting near the doors leading into the hall could not hear a word.

The PRESIDENT. — The officers of the house will see that good order and quiet are observed.

Mr. MUNRO, of Nevada. — I have one question to ask, upon the answer to which may depend the course which this delegation will adopt in regard to the nomination of candidates. I ask that the President now state what his ruling will be after the closing of the naming of candidates here, — as to whether we can, at any time hereafter, bring forward any new candidate?

The PRESIDENT. — The Chair understands that this Convention has a right, at any time, to bring forward any new candidate it may see fit.

Mr. DODGE, of Ohio. — As a preliminary proceeding, I move that any delegate be now authorized to present the name of any candidate.

Mr. THURMAN, of Ohio. — I suggest to my colleague that his motion is entirely unnecessary.

The PRESIDENT. — The Chair understands that when the Convention resolved to go into the nomination of a candidate for President, they meant to do it in the usual and customary form. At all times it has been the practice of our Conventions to give delegates a chance to name their candidates, and the Chair will so hold unless objections are made.

Mr. THURMAN, of Ohio. — I ask the attention of the Chair to the resolution adopted yesterday: That when a delegate nominates a candidate, he pledge that candidate, and those who support him, to support the nominee of the Convention. He is required to do that by the resolution adopted yesterday.

The PRESIDENT. — The Chair understands that that resolution was unanimously adopted by the Convention, and that its members are so committed. How far candidates themselves may be regarded as pledged I do not know. But I sincerely hope that no doubt will linger in the mind of any delegate upon that subject, and that no one will suspect that any person who allows his name to be brought here as a candidate will not support the nominees of the Convention. (Cheers.)

The Secretary read the resolution passed yesterday, pledging rejected candidates to support the nominee of the Convention.

Mr. TILDEN of New York. — It is the common law of the Democratic party that every candidate is so pledged; and I suggest that if any gentleman here proposes a candidate whom he does not deem to be so pledged, he should mention the exception. (Laughter.)

The PRESIDENT. — The subject is disposed of. The roll of States will now be called, so that the delegates from each State will have an opportunity, if they see fit, to state what candidates they wish to present to the Convention.

The Secretary called the name of Alabama.

The CHAIRMAN of the Delegation. — Alabama makes no nomination.

The Secretary called the name of Arkansas.

The CHAIRMAN of the Delegation. — Arkansas makes no nomination.

The Secretary called the name of California.

Mr. BIGLER. — California makes no nomination.

The Secretary called the name of Connecticut.

Mr. EATON of Connecticut. — It will be remembered, sir —

The PRESIDENT. — If the gentleman will give way a moment — The Chair understands that five minutes is the time allowed to each delegation to present a candidate. If that is the understanding of the Convention, the rule will be enforced.

Nomination of James E. English of Connecticut.

Mr. EATON of Connecticut. — It will be remembered that after passing through a terrible civil war, which lasted for four long and weary years, the clouds of despotism hung all over this broad land. All was gloom, all was darkness, all was desolation. At last, sir, there arose a star in the East, and my own gallant little commonwealth broke through the gloom and elected a

Democratic Governor. (Cheers.) I know I do not say too much when I say that a thrill of joy ran all through the land at the news of that election. (Applause.) A year rolled around, and again, sir, the sterling and gallant Democracy of my little commonwealth elected the same man Governor. Mr. President, the State of Connecticut, the first State to vote Democratic after the war; the State of Connecticut, whose platform for the past ten years has always been a Democratic platform; the State of Connecticut, well knowing that she has but six votes to give here, that she is a small State, and that in all probability eminent and distinguished men of other States will be named, yet comes here and offers you as the standard-bearer of this great Confederacy of Commonwealths her own, executive officer, — Connecticut names JAMES E. ENGLISH as her candidate. (Loud cheering.)

The Secretary called the name of Delaware.

The CHAIRMAN of the Delegation. — Delaware makes no nomination.

The Secretary called the name of Florida.

The CHAIRMAN of the Delegation. — Florida makes no nomination.

The Secretary called the name of Georgia.

The CHAIRMAN of the Delegation. — Georgia makes no nomination.

The Secretary called the name of Illinois.

Mr. RICHARDSON of Illinois. — The State of Illinois will cast her vote for Mr. PENDLETON (Applause); but we leave it to the Ohio delegation to make the nomination.

The Secretary called the name of Indiana.

The CHAIRMAN of the Delegation. — The gentleman for whom the delegation of Indiana design to cast their vote has been already named to the Convention.

The Secretary called the name of Iowa.

The CHAIRMAN of the Delegation. — Iowa makes no nomination, but expects to sustain the nomination made by the State of Ohio.

The Secretary called the name of Kansas.

The CHAIRMAN of the Delegation. — Kansas makes no nomination.

The Secretary called the name of Kentucky.

The CHAIRMAN of the Delegation. — Kentucky makes no nomination.

The Secretary called the name of Louisiana.

The CHAIRMAN of the Delegation. — Louisiana makes no nomination.

The Secretary called the name of Maine.

Nomination of General Hancock.

General ANDERSON of Maine.—I am directed by the majority of the Delegates from Maine to present to this body as a candidate, a gentleman, who, they believe, unites in himself all the best characteristics of the most available candidates, and who, if elected, would be able to discharge acceptably and as well as any other man in the country the duties of the chief executive office of the United States. I present a gentleman, who by his position during the past year has made a record that stands to-day high in the hearts of the whole American people; a gentleman who, appointed to a Military District of the United States, succeeding one who in that position had subordinated his regard for the laws and the Constitution of the country, and his respect for the Chief Magistrate of the United States to his own ambitious longings for wealth and power, standing there as the representative of his Government, interposed the shield of the laws of the country between the tyranny of hard and petty tyrants, and an oppressed and outraged people (Applause); a man, who by nature, gifted with a broad, comprehensive and discriminating intellect, educated in a school which taught him that the government was instituted to afford to its citizens the great cardinal rights of personal liberty, personal security, and the right to acquire and enjoy property, stood there and interposed, between the operations of the military government and the people who had been outraged and oppressed, the law that should accord to them those rights; a gentleman who on another field was one of the brave men in command of troops in the late contest, and united within himself the attributes of lion-hearted courage, and great magnanimity, who fought well for the nation which placed him in command, but held forth the hand of mercy to the enemy when brought beneath his arms; a man who, ever foremost in the fight, held the plume aloft, which, like the helmet of Navarre, was always the oriflamme under which his troops went on either to honorable death or glorious victory. With these words it would seem almost superfluous to give the name; but I will nominate General WINFIELD SCOTT HANCOCK. (Great cheering.)

Nomination of George H. Pendleton, of Ohio.

Mr. EMORY of Maine. — In behalf of what now constitutes the minority, but what I have reason to believe will constitute a majority of the Maine delegation, and in behalf of the laboring masses of Maine, who look to the action of this Convention to relieve them from the burden of debt and taxation under which they are now groaning, I nominate as their choice the Hon. GEORGE H. PENDLETON, of Ohio. (Prolonged applause.)

The Secretary called the name of Maryland.

The CHAIRMAN of the Delegation. — Maryland makes no nomination.

The Secretary called the name of Massachusetts.

The CHAIRMAN of the Delegation. — The State of Massachusetts presents no name at this time.

The Secretary called the name of Michigan.

The CHAIRMAN of the Delegation. — Michigan makes no nomination at this time.

The Secretary called the name of Minnesota.

The CHAIRMAN of the Delegation. — Minnesota makes no nomination at this time.

The Secretary called the name of Mississippi.

The CHAIRMAN of the Delegation. — Mississippi makes no nomination.

The Secretary called the name of Missouri.

The CHAIRMAN of the Delegation. — Missouri makes no nomination.

The Secretary called the name of Nebraska.

The CHAIRMAN of the Delegation. — Nebraska makes no nomination, but will cast her vote for GEORGE H. PENDLETON.

The Secretary called the name of Nevada.

The CHAIRMAN of the Delegation. — Nevada makes no nomination.

The Secretary called the name of New Jersey.

Nomination of Governor Joel Parker, of New Jersey.

Mr. LITTLE, of New Jersey. — Mr. President, the State of New Jersey nominates ex-Governor JOEL PARKER. (Cheers.) He has a national reputation. During the late war he sustained the general government with all the force at his command, but at no time did he permit the Federal power to make any encroachment upon the rights of the State. He is a man who will receive, as we believe, every Democratic and Conservative vote in the country. He is the soldiers' friend; he is the champion of State rights; he belongs to a State that at one time had the only Democratic Governor in all the North; he belongs to a State that elected a Democratic Governor in the midst of the war. I will not detain the Convention by any further expression as to his merits, claims, or qualifications. His record is his highest praise.

The Secretary called the State of New York.

Nomination of Sanford E. Church.

Mr. SAMUEL J. TILDEN. — The State of New York, by the unanimous vote of her delegation, nominates to this Convention one of her own most distinguished citizens; a gentleman honorably associated with her public offices for many years past; trained and experienced in executive administration, of decisive and energetic will; a gentleman who has been repeatedly submitted to the ordeal of a popular vote in the State of New York, and has always come from the trial with distinguished success, and who, if he should be the nominee of this Convention, would help us to achieve in this State a more brilliant triumph than any we have ever yet accomplished: a gentleman whom the delegation can cordially and sincerely recommend to the Convention and the country as fit in all respects to fulfil the greatest civic trust in the world — the chief magistracy of our great republic (Cheers); and who, as a candidate, would be unassailable and available. The delegation from the State of New York submits to this Convention the name of SANFORD E. CHURCH, of New York. (Great cheering.)

The SECRETARY. — The State of New York nominates SANFORD E. CHURCH. (Applause.)

The Secretary called the State of South Carolina.

The CHAIRMAN of the delegation, Mr. PERRY. — The State of South Carolina makes no nomination.

The Secretary called the State of Ohio.

General McCOOK. — Mr. President, Ohio, by the unanimous vote of her Convention, places in nomination the name of GEORGE H. PENDLETON, of Ohio. (Loud cheering.)

The Secretary called Oregon.

The CHAIRMAN of the Delegation, Mr. BRISTOW. — Oregon will make no nomination, but will cast its vote for George H. Pendleton. (Applause.)

The Secretary called the name of Pennsylvania.

Judge WOODWARD. — Mr. President, by a unanimous vote of the delegation of which I have the honor to be the organ, I am instructed to place before the Convention the name of an honored citizen of the State of Pennsylvania as a candidate for the office of President of the United States. Before I pronounce his name, I beg leave to submit a few observations in reference to our nominee. An impression has gained currency that the delegation intends only a personal compliment to their fellow-citizen, and that they do not name him with an earnest purpose of making him a Presidential candidate. Sir, this is a mistake. The delegation intends no mere personal compliment, but a *bona fide* nomination. Their favorite needs no compliments, and desires none. If his countrymen think he can be useful to them in the highest office in their gift, he will do his best to serve them acceptably; but if they prefer another before him, no man will yield a more hearty and cheerful support to whomsoever you may nominate. In this hour of great national peril, the Pennsylvania delegation feel that it is their duty to bring their best offering and lay it upon the altar of our common country. We make the offering with a profound impression of all the solemn obligations of the occasion. It is the best we have to present, and, if accepted, we believe it will prove a present and lasting blessing to our beloved country. We make the nomination in good earnest, but with great deference to the opinions and preferences of others; and we hereby declare our purpose to stand by and support our nominee until a full opportunity shall have been given to other delegations to rally to his standard. Our candidate, if not well known to the nation at large, is well known to the people of Pennsylvania, and will be supported by them with an enthusiasm which no other name can inspire. Born in Connecticut, and reared in the honorable calling of a carpenter, he came, early in life, to Pennsylvania, where, by patient industry, by judicious adaptation of the best means to the best ends, and by uniform good living, he acquired the confidence of his fellow-citizens, and lifted himself from the poverty in which he was cradled into great prosperity and affluence. He stands to-day among the men who have the deepest stake in the material wealth of the nation. He is one of the largest tax-payers in the country. (Applause.) Our delegation are very far from considering mere wealth a qualification for office, but when great wealth has been acquired, not by inheritance, nor by speculation, and still less by peculation and fraud, but by honest industry, by frugality of living, by following the dictates of a sound judgment and a clear understanding, its possession is proof of an organization and administrative intellect capable of, and fitted for, high duties in any sphere of life. The qualities of manhood are well marked by the uses to which individual wealth is devoted. In the instance which I am about to place before the Convention, wealth has not been hoarded, nor hid under a bushel, nor wasted in riotous living, nor squandered on schemes of folly and extravagance, but it has been employed in clearing out and improving farms, developing and working coal mines, building and conducting railroads, establishing furnaces, foundries, and manufactories, and in founding the Lehigh University, — a grand seat of Christian education, and the only institution of learning in our country that has ever been fully endowed, from its start, by individual munificence. If our candidate has not filled the noisy trump of fame, these are the trophies which he has won in the battle of life. He has not gashed the bosom of the earth to make millions of graves for his fellowmen; but he has given employment to the idle, homes to the houseless, bread to the hungry, and clothing to the naked. He has not filled the land with widows and orphans; but widows and orphans have shared his bounties, and the blessing of the widow's God has descended upon his basket and his store. For many years he has been a foremost man among those enterprising benefactors of our race, who are pushing railroads into every part of our extensive country. Railroads are the grandest achievement of modern civilization. They are the highways of the million. They carry population into our remote lands; they build up towns and cities in what had else been the waste places of the earth; they diffuse intelligence, comfort, and cheerful wealth, broadcast, and they bring back to the seaboard cities the products of the forest, the farm, the mine, and the industries of interior communities. The planning, constructing, and managing of a system of connected railroads in so rugged a country as Pennsylvania, adapting them to the heavy tonnage of coal and iron, and to the quick transportation of passengers, and making them profitable to stockholders, as well as beneficial to the public, are labors that demand high qualities of mind, and bear loud testimony to the fitness of our candidate to grapple with complicated problems and to bring them to sound practical solutions.

VOICES. — "Time."

The PRESIDENT. — The time allotted has already expired, but I trust the gentleman will be allowed to proceed and finish his remarks.

Cries of " Go on, go on."

Judge WOODWARD concluded as follows, —

A good business man is what the nation now needs at its head. Orators and warriors are useful in proper places, but through the incompetency and mismanagement of the men who have ruled the country for seven years, debt, taxes, confusion, frauds, and embarrassments of all sorts, have been brought upon us which threaten our utter ruin, and which only a practical wisdom, that has been trained in the business of life, can avert and alleviate. A man so trained does Pennsylvania this day present. The forces of his character are quiet and noiseless, like those better forces of nature which ripen the grain fields and the orchards, and which bear fruits that are "pleasant to the eye and good for food." If there is no brilliance to attract the public gaze to him, there is a pure, solid character, upon which we may build as upon a sure foundation. A Democrat all his life, a Representative in two successive Congresses, an Associate Judge for five years, a communicant of the Protestant Episcopal Church, a man whose integrity has never been questioned, whose big heart embraces all his countrymen, and whose liberal hand is ever open to suffering humanity; such is the man Pennsylvania is proud to present for the consideration of his countrymen. It is a rule of Divine equity that he who has been faithful over a few things, shall be made a ruler over many things. 'Accept our candidate, sir, and you may count his majority in the old Keystone State by tens of thousands. Elect him President, and the thieves and gamblers will no longer seek office, but only hiding-places from the vigilance of a virtuous Executive, and the Republic will feel the instinct of a new life. Pennsylvania nominates for the next President of the United States, the Hon. ASA PACKER. (Applause.)

The Secretary called the State of Rhode Island.

The CHAIRMAN of the Delegation. — The State of Rhode Island makes no nomination.

The Secretary called the State of South Carolina.

The CHAIRMAN of the Delegation. — The State of South Carolina makes no nomination.

The Secretary called the State of Tennessee.

Nomination of President Johnson.

Mr. THOMAS A. R. NELSON, on behalf of the Tennessee delegation, responded as follows, —

I am instructed by the Tennessee delegation to present to this Convention a gentleman whose name is well known to the members of the Convention, to the people of the United States, and to the civilized world. I am directed to present the name of one who for thirty-three years was associated with the Democratic party, and is devoted to the maintenance and support of Democratic principles, — one whose life and position is an exemplification of the true equality of American institutions; one who, springing from poverty and obscurity, has obtained the highest office within the gift of the people; one who has engaged in the mightiest political contest that our nation ever saw (Cheers); one who was in favor of the Union in times that tried men's souls, and who was devoted to its support when the Union needed strength; one who, after his elevation to the Presidency, has been maligned, calumniated, traduced, vilified, and persecuted by the Radical party; one who has stood up nobly to the principles of the Constitution, and who has exemplified the principles that are announced in our declaration of principles to-day: one who has battled for the Constitution against the efforts of those who have attempted to destroy it; who has stood up for the rights of the Executive and Judicial departments against the tyrannical usurpations of Congress; one who has nobly borne himself in this contest while he has filled the place which was assigned him by the American people; one who has ever been faithful among the faithless; who, chosen by the people, has ever had their dearest interests at heart (Cheers); one who deserves the confidence of the whole American people, and will faithfully discharge, in time to come, as he has done in times past, the duties which they have imposed upon him. I am directed to present to the members of this Convention the name of ANDREW JOHNSON, of Tennessee. (Enthusiastic cheering.)

The Secretary called the State of Texas.

The CHAIRMAN of the delegation. — The State of Texas makes no nomination.

The Secretary called the State of Vermont.

Mr. H. B. SMITH, on behalf of the delegation, said, —

Vermont presents no new candidates, but her representatives here will cast their votes as a unit for the only Democratic Governor in New England. Vermont will vote for James E. English. (Applause.)

The Secretary called the State of Virginia.

Mr. JOHN B. BALDWIN, on behalf of the delegation, responded as follows, —

The State of Virginia presents no nomination; but, true to her ancient history, she accepts and will cordially support, as her first choice, the nominee of this Convention. (Applause.)

The Secretary called the State of West Virginia.

Mr. BENJAMIN H. SMITH, chairman of the delegation, responded as follows, —

West Virginia makes no nomination, but pledges herself to the support of George H. Pendleton. (Cheers.)

The Secretary called the State of Wisconsin.

Nomination of James R. Doolittle.

Mr. S. CLARK, on behalf of the delegation, said, —

The delegates from the State of Wisconsin were instructed by the State Convention that sent them here to vote as a unit. A majority of that delegation, controlling the vote of that State, will present to this Convention the name of one of her most distinguished citizens, — a gentleman whose reputation is so world-wide that no eulogy from myself or any other delegate can add a particle to his laurels, — a gentleman who separated himself from the Republican party when it was in the zenith of its glory and power throughout the country and throughout his own State, sacrificing thereby his own personal and political ambition for the good of his country and for the preservation of the Constitution and the liberties of the people. I am directed to present the name of Hon. JAMES R. DOOLITTLE. (Loud cheers.)

Mr. HENRY L. PALMER. — The delegation from Wisconsin has good-naturedly differed in regard to the candidate for the Presidency. The majority has very properly presented the name of the distinguished citizen from our own State. I am, however, instructed by the minority of that delegation to second the nomination of a gentleman who has never been out of the Democratic party — the Hon. George H. Pendleton. (Applause.)

Nominations.

The Secretary announced the following candidates as having been put in nomination, —

James E. English, of Connecticut; George H. Pendleton, of Ohio; Joel Parker, of New Jersey; Sanford E. Church, of New York; Asa Packer, of Pennsylvania; Andrew Johnson, of Tennessee; James R. Doolittle, of Wisconsin.

The following is a table of candidates nominated, —

Alabama, 8 — No nomination.
Arkansas, 5 — No nomination.
California, 5 — No nomination.

Connecticut, 6 — James E. English.
Delaware, 3 — No nomination.
Florida, 3 — No nomination.
Georgia, 9 — No nomination.
Illinois, 16 — No nomination.
Iowa, 8 — No nomination.
Kansas, 3 — No nomination.
Kentucky, 11 — No nomination.
Louisiana, 7 — No nomination.
Maine, 7 — Winfield Scott Hancock; **minority** nominated George H. Pendleton.
Maryland, 7 — No nomination.
Massachusetts, 12 — No nomination.
Michigan, 8 — No nomination.
Minnesota, 4 — No nomination.
Mississippi, 7 — No nomination.
Missouri, 11 — No nomination.
Nebraska, 3 — No nomination.
Nevada, 3 — No nomination.
New Hampshire, 5 — No nomination.
New Jersey, 7 — Ex-Governor Joel **Parker.**
New York, 33 — Sanford E. Church.
North Carolina, 9 — No nomination.
Ohio, 21 — George H. Pendleton.
Oregon, 3 — George H. Pendleton.
Pennsylvania, 26 — Asa Packer.
Rhode Island, 4 — No nomination.
South Carolina, 6 — No nomination.
Tennessee, 10 — Andrew Johnson.
Texas, 6 — No nomination.
Vermont, 5 — James E. English.
Virginia, 10 — No nomination.
West Virginia, 5 — No nomination.
Wisconsin, 8 — James R. Doolittle; minority, George H. Pendleton.

Mr. MILLER, of Pennsylvania. — I move that the Convention now proceed to ballot.

The PRESIDENT. — The Chair understands that the custom has been for the Secretary to call the roll. The several delegations then give in their votes to the Chair through their chairman. If any time is required, five or ten minutes for this purpose will be allowed, if there is no objection.

Mr. CAVANAUGH, of Montana. — Will it now be in order to offer a resolution?

The PRESIDENT. — The Chair understands that the Convention has already decided that it will not give votes to delegates from the Territories.

Mr. CAVANAUGH. — The delegates from these Territories respectfully present a resolution that ought to go upon the record. Do not let this Convention act like the Radical Congress.

Cries of "Order."

The PRESIDENT. — The gentleman is not in order. The Secretary will call the roll.

NATIONAL DEMOCRATIC CONVENTION.   75

Mr. CAVANAUGH. — I appeal from the decision of the Chair.

Mr. VALLANDIGHAM. — An appeal is not in order.

The PRESIDENT. — The clerk will proceed with the call. The chairmen of the respective delegations from each of the States, as they are called, will rise in their places and name the man and the number of votes of the delegation.

The Secretary called the roll as follows, —

First Ballot.

Alabama. — The Chairman of the Delegation: The State of Alabama casts her eight votes for Andrew Johnson, of Tennessee.

Arkansas. — The Chairman of the Delegation: The State of Arkansas casts her five votes for James E. English, of Connecticut.

California. — The Chairman of the Delegation: California asks to pass her vote.

Connecticut. — The Chairman of the Delegation: Connecticut casts her six votes for James E. English.

Delaware. — The Chairman of the Delegation: Delaware has the honor to cast her three votes for that illustrious Buckeye statesman, George H. Pendleton.

Florida. — The Chairman of the Delegation: Florida casts her three electoral votes for Andrew Johnson, of Tennessee.

Georgia. — The Chairman of the Delegation: Georgia casts her nine votes for Andrew Johnson, of Tennessee.

Illinois. — The Chairman of the Delegation: Illinois casts her vote for George H. Pendleton.

Iowa. — The Chairman of the Delegation: The State of Iowa casts her eight votes for George H. Pendleton, of Ohio.

Kansas. — The Chairman of the Delegation: The State of Kansas casts two votes for George H. Pendleton; one-half vote for Thomas Hendricks, and one-half vote for Frank P. Blair.

Kentucky. — The Chairman of the Delegation: The State of Kentucky casts her eleven votes for George H. Pendleton.

Louisiana. — The Chairman of the Delegation: The State of Louisiana casts her votes for Gen. W. S. Hancock.

Maine. — The Chairman of the Delegation: The State of Maine casts four and a half votes for W. S. Hancock, one and a half for George H. Pendleton, one for Andrew Johnson.

Maryland. — The Chairman of the delegation: The State of Maryland casts four and a half votes for George H. Pendleton, two and a half for Andrew Johnson.

Massachusetts. — The Chairman of the Delegation: The State of Massachusetts casts eleven votes for Gen. Hancock, and one vote for George H. Pendleton, of Ohio.

Michigan. — The Chairman of the Delegation: The State of Michigan casts her eight electoral votes for Reverdy Johnson, of Maryland.

Minnesota. — The Chairman of the Delegation: Four votes for George H. Pendleton.

Mississippi. — The Chairman of the Delegation: Mr. President, I am instructed by the Mississippi Delegation to cast her nine votes for W. S. Hancock.

Missouri. — The Chairman of the Delegation: The State of Missouri casts five votes for George H. Pendleton; one vote for S. E. Church, of New York; two and a half votes for Thomas Hendricks; two and a half votes for Gen. Hancock; and a half vote for Andrew Johnson, of Tennessee.

A delegate from California here asked leave to cast the vote of that State, stating that some of the delegates were absent from the room when her name was called.

The PRESIDENT. — The State of California will be again called when the roll of States has been gone through with. It greatly embarrasses the officers of the Convention and the reporters of the press to make announcements out of order.

Nebraska. — The Chairman of the Delegation: The State of Nebraska casts her three votes for George H. Pendleton, of Ohio. (Applause.)

Nevada. — The Chairman of the Delegation: The State of Nevada casts her three votes for ex-Governor Joel Parker, of New Jersey.

New Hampshire. — The Chairman of the Delegation: The State of New Hampshire casts one vote for James R. Doolittle, two votes for Gen. Hancock, and two votes for George H. Pendleton.

New Jersey. — The Chairman of the Delegation: New Jersey casts her seven electoral votes for Joel Parker. (Cheers.)

New York. — The Chairman of the Delegation: New York casts her thirty-three votes for Sanford E. Church. (Cheers.)

North Carolina. — The Chairman of the Delegation: North Carolina casts nine votes for Andrew Johnson. (Cheers.)

Ohio. — The Chairman of the Delegation: Ohio casts twenty-one votes for George H. Pendleton. (Cheers.)

Oregon. — The Chairman of the Delegation: Oregon casts her three votes for George H. Pendleton.

Pennsylvania. — The Chairman of the Delegation: Pennsylvania casts her twenty-six votes for Asa Packer.

Rhode Island. — The Chairman of the Delegation: Rhode Island casts her four votes for James R. Doolittle.

South Carolina. — The Chairman of the Delegation: The State of South Carolina casts her six votes for Andrew Johnson, of Tennessee.

Tennessee. — The Chairman of the Delegation: The State of Tennessee casts her ten votes for Andrew Johnson. (Cheers.)

Texas. — The Chairman of the Delegation: The State of Texas casts her six votes for Andrew Johnson, of Tennessee.

Virginia. — The Chairman of the Delegation: Virginia casts her ten votes for Andrew Johnson, of Tennessee. (Cheers.)

West Virginia. — The Chairman of the Delegation: The State of West Virginia casts her five electoral votes for George H. Pendleton.

Wisconsin. — The Chairman of the Delegation: The Delegates of the State of Wisconsin, under the instructions of our Convention, casts her eight votes for James R. Doolittle.

California. — A DELEGATE: By direction of the Chairman of our Delegation, who is in ill health, I am instructed to cast, as the vote of California, three for Parker, of New Jersey, and two for Pendleton, of Ohio.

NATIONAL DEMOCRATIC CONVENTION.

The Secretary announced the vote as follows, —

Whole number of votes cast	317
James E. English	16
Winfield S. Hancock	33½
George H. Pendleton	105
Joel Parker	13
Sanford E. Church	34
Asa Packer	26
Andrew Johnson	65
James R. Doolittle	13
Frank P. Blair, Jr.	½
Thomas A. Hendricks	2½
Reverdy Johnson	8½

FIRST BALLOT — RECAPITULATION.

STATES.	WHOLE NO.	PENDLETON.	HANCOCK.	CHURCH.	ENGLISH.	PARKER.	PACKER.	A. JOHNSON.	DOOLITTLE.	HENDRICKS.	BLAIR.	R. JOHNSON.
Alabama	8	..	..	..	..	..	..	8	..	..	..	..
Arkansas	5	..	..	..	5	..	..	..	..	..	..	..
California	5	2	..	..	..	3	..	..	..	..	..	..
Connecticut	6	..	..	..	6	..	..	..	..	..	..	..
Delaware	3	3	..	..	..	..	..	..	..	..	..	..
Florida	3	..	..	..	..	..	..	3	..	..	..	..
Georgia	9	..	..	..	..	..	..	9	..	..	..	..
Illinois	16	16	..	..	..	..	..	..	..	..	..	..
Indiana	13	13	..	..	..	..	..	..	..	..	..	..
Iowa	8	8	..	..	..	..	..	..	..	..	..	..
Kansas	3	2	..	..	..	..	..	..	..	½	½	..
Kentucky	11	11	..	..	..	..	..	..	..	..	..	..
Louisiana	7	..	7	..	..	..	..	..	..	..	..	..
Maine	7	1½	4½	..	..	..	..	1	..	..	..	..
Maryland	7	4½	..	..	..	..	..	2½	..	..	..	..
Massachusetts	12	1	11	..	..	..	..	..	..	..	..	..
Michigan	8	..	..	..	..	..	..	..	..	..	..	8
Minnesota	4	4	..	..	..	..	..	..	..	..	..	..
Mississippi	7	..	7	..	..	..	..	..	..	..	..	..
Missouri	11	5	2	1	..	..	..	½	..	2	..	½
Nebraska	3	3	..	..	..	..	..	..	..	..	..	..
Nevada	3	..	..	..	..	..	3	..	..	..	..	..
New Hampshire	5	2	2	..	..	..	..	..	..	1	..	..
New Jersey	7	..	..	..	..	7	..	..	..	..	..	..
New York	33	..	..	33	..	..	..	..	..	..	..	..
North Carolina	9	..	..	..	..	..	..	9	..	..	..	..
Ohio	21	21	..	..	..	..	..	..	..	..	..	..
Oregon	3	3	..	..	..	..	..	..	..	..	..	..
Pennsylvania	26	..	..	..	..	..	26	..	..	..	..	..
Rhode Island	4	..	..	..	..	..	..	..	4	..	..	..
South Carolina	6	..	..	..	..	..	..	6	..	..	..	..
Tennessee	10	..	..	..	..	..	..	10	..	..	..	..
Texas	6	..	..	..	..	..	..	6	..	..	..	..
Vermont	5	..	..	..	5	..	..	..	..	..	..	..
Virginia	10	..	..	..	..	..	..	10	..	..	..	..
West Virginia	5	5	..	..	..	..	..	..	..	..	..	..
Wisconsin	8	..	..	..	..	..	..	..	8	..	..	..
Total	317	105	23½	34	16	13	26	65	13	2½	½	8½

The Secretary called the roll for the second ballot, as follows, —

Second Ballot.

Alabama. — Eight votes for A. Johnson.
Arkansas. — One-half vote for J. E. English; for Joel Parker, two and a half; for A. Johnson, two.
California. — Three votes for Joel Parker; two for A. Johnson.
Connecticut. — Six votes for J. E. English.
Delaware. — Three votes for G. H. Pendleton.
Florida. — Three votes for A. Johnson.
Georgia. — Eight and a half votes for A. Johnson; for Thomas Ewing, Jr., one-half.
Illinois. — Sixteen votes for G. H. Pendleton.
Indiana. — Thirteen votes for G. H. Pendleton.
Iowa. — Eight votes for G. H. Pendleton.
Kansas. — Two votes for G. H. Pendleton; T. A. Hendricks, one-half; Frank Blair, one-half.
Kentucky. — Eleven votes for G. H. Pendleton.
Louisiana. — Seven votes for W. S. Hancock.
Maine. — One and a half votes for G. H. Pendleton; for W. P. Hancock, four and a half; for J. E. English, one.
Maryland. — Four and a half votes for G. H. Pendleton; for A. Johnson, two and a half.
Massachusetts. — One vote for G. H. Pendleton; for W. S. Hancock, eleven.
Michigan. — Eight votes for Reverdy Johnson.
Minnesota. — Four votes for G. H. Pendleton.
Mississippi. — Seven votes for W. S. Hancock.
Missouri. — Five and a half votes for George H. Pendleton; for Gen. Hancock, two votes; for Hendricks, one and a half; for Andrew Johnson, one and a half; and for James R. Doolittle, one-half.
Nebraska. — Three votes for George H. Pendleton.
Nevada. — Three votes for Joel Parker, of New Jersey.
New Hampshire. — Two votes for George H. Pendleton, and three votes for Gen. Hancock.
New Jersey. — Seven votes for Joel Parker.
New York. — Thirty-three votes for Sandford E. Church.
North Carolina. — Eight and a half votes for Andrew Johnson, and one-half vote for Pendleton.
Ohio. — Twenty-one votes for George H. Pendleton.
Oregon. — Three votes for Pendleton.
Pennsylvania. — Twenty-six votes for Asa Packer.
Rhode Island. — Four votes for James R. Doolittle.
South Carolina. — Six votes for Andrew Johnson.
Tennessee. — Ten votes for Andrew Johnson.
Texas. — Six votes for Gen. Hancock.
Vermont. — Five votes for James E. English.
Virginia. — Ten votes for Frank P. Blair, of Missouri. (Applause.)
West Virginia. — Five votes for George H. Pendleton.
Wisconsin. — As before: eight votes for James R. Doolittle.

The Secretary announced the second ballot, —

The whole number of votes cast	317
James E. English	12½
W. S. Hancock	40½
George H. Pendleton	104
Joel Parker	15½
Sanford E. Church	33
Asa Packer	26
Andrew Johnson	52
James R. Doolittle	12½
Thomas A. Hendricks	2
Frank P. Blair, Jr.	10½
Reverdy Johnson	8
Thomas Ewing	½

SECOND BALLOT—RECAPITULATION.

STATES.	WHOLE NO.	*PENDLETON.*	*HANCOCK.*	*CHURCH.*	*ENGLISH.*	*PARKER.*	*PACKER.*	*A. JOHNSON.*	*DOOLITTLE.*	*HENDRICKS.*	*BLAIR.*	*R. JOHNSON.*	*T. EWING, Jr.*
Alabama	8	..	..	..	..	..	..	8	..	..	..	..	..
Arkansas	5	..	..	..	½	2½	..	2	..	..	..	..	..
California	5	..	..	..	..	3	..	2	..	..	..	..	..
Connecticut	6	..	..	..	6	..	..	..	..	..	..	..	..
Delaware	3	3	..	..	..	..	..	..	..	..	..	..	..
Florida	3	..	..	..	..	..	..	3	..	..	..	..	..
Georgia	9	..	..	..	..	..	..	8½	..	..	..	..	½
Illinois	16	16	..	..	..	..	..	..	..	..	..	..	..
Indiana	13	13	..	..	..	..	..	..	..	..	..	..	..
Iowa	8	8	..	..	..	..	..	..	..	..	..	..	..
Kansas	3	2	..	..	..	..	..	..	..	½	½	..	..
Kentucky	11	11	..	..	..	..	..	..	..	..	..	..	..
Louisiana	7	..	7	..	..	..	..	..	..	..	..	..	..
Maine	7	1½	4½	..	1	..	..	..	..	..	..	..	..
Maryland	7	4½	..	..	..	..	..	2½	..	..	..	..	..
Massachusetts	12	1	11	..	..	..	..	..	..	..	..	..	..
Michigan	8	..	..	..	..	..	..	..	..	..	..	8	..
Minnesota	4	4	..	..	..	..	..	..	..	..	..	..	..
Mississippi	7	..	7	..	..	..	..	..	..	..	..	..	..
Missouri	11	5½	2	..	..	..	..	1½	½	1½	..	..	..
Nebraska	3	3	..	..	..	..	..	..	..	..	..	..	..
Nevada	3	..	..	..	..	3	..	..	..	..	..	..	..
New Hampshire	5	2	3	..	..	..	..	..	..	..	..	..	..
New Jersey	7	..	..	..	..	7	..	..	..	..	..	..	..
New York	33	..	..	33	..	..	..	..	..	..	..	..	..
North Carolina	9	½	..	..	..	..	..	8½	..	..	..	..	..
Ohio	21	21	..	..	..	..	..	..	..	..	..	..	..
Oregon	3	3	..	..	..	..	..	..	..	..	..	..	..
Pennsylvania	26	..	..	..	..	..	26	..	..	..	..	..	..
Rhode Island	4	..	..	..	..	..	..	..	4	..	..	..	..
South Carolina	6	..	..	..	..	..	..	6	..	..	..	..	..
Tennessee	10	..	..	..	..	..	..	10	..	..	..	..	.
Texas	6	..	6	..	..	..	..	..	..	..	..	..	..
Vermont	5	..	..	..	5	..	..	..	..	..	..	..	..
Virginia	10	..	..	..	..	..	..	..	..	..	10	..	..
West Virginia	5	5	..	..	..	..	..	..	..	..	..	..	..
Wisconsin	8	..	..	..	..	..	..	..	8	..	..	..	..
Total	317	104	40½	33	12½	15½	26	52	12½	2	10½	8	½

Mr. SCOTT, of Pennsylvania. -- I move that we now adjourn until four o'clock this afternoon.

Mr. VALLANDIGHAM, of Ohio. — That motion is not in order. A motion to adjourn carries the Convention over until ten o'clock to-morrow morning.

The PRESIDENT. — The motion is not in order; for, by the rule adopted by the Convention, a motion to adjourn carried the Convention over until ten o'clock the next day.

Mr. SCOTT. — I withdraw the motion.

Mr. BOYER, of Ohio. — I move that the Convention take a recess until four o'clock.

The President put the motion to take a recess, and declared it lost.

The States were then called in their order. Pending the vote, Judge Woodward, of Pennsylvania, said,—

On behalf of Pennsylvania, I ask leave of the Convention for the delegation to retire for consultation.

The PRESIDENT. — It will be granted unless objection be made.

A DELEGATE. — I object.

The PRESIDENT. — Objection being made, the question will be upon allowing the Pennsylvania delegation to retire for consultation.

The question was put and leave was granted, a recess being taken to allow time for the delegation to retire.

Third Ballot.

The vote was then proceeded with, after recess, as follows, —

Arkansas. — Four votes for F. P. Blair, one-half vote for Andrew Johnson, and one-half vote for James E. English.

California. — Three votes for Parker, one for Pendleton, and one for Andrew Johnson.

Connecticut. — Six votes for English.

Delaware. — Three votes for G. H. Pendleton.

Florida. — Three votes for Reverdy Johnson.

Georgia. — Eight votes for Andrew Johnson, and one vote for Thomas Ewing, Jr., of Ohio.

Illinois. — Thirteen votes for Pendleton.

Iowa. — Eight votes for George H. Pendleton.

Kansas. — Two votes for Pendleton, one-half vote for Thomas E. Hendricks, and one-half vote for Blair.

Kentucky. — Eleven votes for George H. Pendleton.

Louisiana. — Seven votes for Gen. Hancock.

Maine. — Four and a half votes for Gen. Hancock, one and a half for Pendleton, and one for English.

Maryland. — Five votes for Pendleton, and two for Andrew Johnson.

Massachusetts. — Eleven votes for Gen. Hancock, and one for Pendleton.

Michigan. — Eight votes for Reverdy Johnson.

Minnesota. — Four votes for Pendleton.

Mississippi. — Seven votes for Gen. Hancock.

Missouri. — Missouri casts five and a half votes for Pendleton, three and a half for Hendricks, one for Andrew Johnson, and one for Gen. Hancock.

Nebraska. — Three votes for George H. Pendleton.

Nevada. — Two votes for Joel Parker, and one for George H. Pendleton.

New Jersey. — Seven votes for Joel Parker.

New York. — Thirty-three votes for Sanford E. Church.

New Hampshire. — One-half vote for Hendricks, one and a half for George H. Pendleton, and three for Hancock.

South Carolina. — Six votes for Hancock, two for Pendleton, and one for Andrew Johnson.

Ohio. — Twenty-one votes for George H. Pendleton.

Oregon. — The Chairman of the Delegation: Oregon still casts her three votes for the Statesman of the West, the Herald of Victory — George H. Pendleton. (Applause and laughter.)

Pennsylvania. — The Secretary called the State of Pennsylvania; but there was no response.

Rhode Island. — Four votes for James R. Doolittle.

North Carolina. — Three votes for Andrew Johnson, two for Pendleton, and one for Parker.

Tennessee. — Ten votes for Andrew Johnson.

Texas. — Six votes for Hancock.

Vermont. — Five votes for Thomas A. Hendricks.

Virginia. — Ten votes for George H. Pendleton.

West Virginia. — Five votes for George H. Pendleton.

Wisconsin. — Eight votes for James R. Doolittle.

Pennsylvania. — The Delegation from Pennsylvania at this point returned to the hall, and their chairman announced that Pennsylvania cast twenty-six votes for Asa Packer.

The Secretary announced the result of the vote, as follows, —

The whole number of votes cast	317
James E. English	7½
W. S. Hancock	45½
George H. Pendleton	119½
Joel Parker	13
Sanford E. Church	33
Asa Packer	26
Andrew Johnson	34½
James R. Doolittle	12
Thomas A. Hendricks	9½
Frank P. Blair	4½
Reverdy Johnson	11
Thomas Ewing	1

THIRD BALLOT — RECAPITULATION.

STATES.	WHOLE NO.	ENGLISH.	HANCOCK.	PENDLETON.	PARKER.	CHURCH.	PACKER.	A. JOHNSON.	DOOLITTLE.	HENDRICKS.	BLAIR.	R. JOHNSON.	T. EWING, Jr.
Alabama	8							8					
Arkansas	5	½						½			4		
California	5			1	3			1					
Connecticut	6	6											
Delaware	3			3									
Florida	3											3	
Georgia	9							8					1
Illinois	16			16									
Indiana	13			13									
Iowa	8			8									
Kansas	3			2						½	½		
Kentucky	11			11									
Louisiana	7		7										
Maine	7	1	4½	1½									
Maryland	7			5				2					
Massachusetts	12		11	1									
Michigan	8											8	
Minnesota	4			4									
Mississippi	7		7										
Missouri	11		1	5½				1		3½			
Nebraska	3			3									
Nevada	3			1	2								
New Hampshire	5		3	1½						½			
New Jersey	7				7								
New York	33					33							
North Carolina	9		6	2				1					
Ohio	21			21									
Oregon	3			3									
Pennsylvania	26						26						
Rhode Island	4								4				
South Carolina	6			2	1			3					
Tennessee	10							10					
Texas	6		6										
Vermont	5										5		
Virginia	10			10									
West Virginia	5			5									
Wisconsin	8								8				
Total	317	7½	45½	119½	13	33	26	34½	12	9½	4½	11	1

Fourth Ballot.

The Secretary again called the roll, as follows,—

Alabama. — Eight votes for Andrew Johnson.

Arkansas. — Two and a half votes for Pendleton, one and a half for Frank P. Blair, one and a half for Andrew Johnson, and one-half vote for English.

California. — Three votes for Parker, one for Johnson, and one for Pendleton.

Delaware. — Three votes for George H. Pendleton.

Florida. — Three votes for Hancock.

Georgia. — Eight votes for Andrew Johnson, one for Ewing.

Illinois. — Sixteen votes for Pendleton.

Indiana. — Thirteen votes for George H. Pendleton.

Iowa. — Eight votes for Pendleton.

Kansas. — Two votes for Pendleton, one-half for Hendricks, and one-half for Blair.

Kentucky. — Eleven votes for Pendleton.

Louisiana. — Seven votes for Hancock.

Maine. — Four and a half votes for Hancock, one and a half for Pendleton, and one for Hendricks.

Maryland. — Five votes for Pendleton, one and a half for Andrew Johnson, and one-half for Hendricks.

Massachusetts. — Eleven votes for Hancock, one for Pendleton.

Michigan. — Eight votes for Reverdy Johnson.

Minnesota. — Four votes for Pendleton.

Mississippi. — Seven votes for Hancock.

Missouri. — Five votes for Pendleton, two for Hancock, and four for Hendricks.

Nebraska. — Three votes for Pendleton.

Nevada. — Three votes for Joel Parker.

New Hampshire. — Half a vote for Hendricks, one and a half for Pendleton, and three for Hancock.

New Jersey. — Seven votes for Parker.

New York. — Thirty-five votes for Sanford E. Church.

North Carolina. — The Chairman of the Delegation: Nine votes for Horatio Seymour. (Loud and enthusiastic cheering, participated in by the galleries.)

Mr. TILDEN. — Mr. President, I shall give notice if there is any cheering in the galleries in respect to the candidates whose names are mentioned here, that I shall move to clear the galleries.

Mr. RICHARDSON, of Illinois. — I move to clear them now.

A DELEGATE from Michigan. — I suggest to the gentleman from Illinois (Mr. Richardson) that the intimation is sufficient, if he will withdraw his motion.

Mr. RICHARDSON. — Certainly I will withdraw my motion.

The PRESIDENT (Mr. Seymour). — I trust I may be permitted now to make a single remark. Very much to my surprise, my name has been mentioned. I must not be nominated by this Convention. I could not accept its nomination if tendered, which I do not expect. My own inclinations prompted me to decline at the outset; my honor compels me to do so now. I am grateful for any expression of kindness. But I trust it will be distinctly understood that it is impossible, consistent with my position, to allow my name to be mentioned in this Convention against my protest. The Clerk will proceed with the call.

The Secretary then resumed the call, as follows, —

Ohio. — Twenty-one votes for George H. Pendleton.
Oregon. — Three votes for Pendleton.
Pennsylvania. — Twenty-six votes for Packer.
Rhode Island. — Four votes for Doolittle.
South Carolina. — Three votes for Andrew Johnson, two for Pendleton, and one for English.
Tennessee. — Ten votes for Andrew Johnson.
Texas. — Six votes for Hancock.
Vermont. — Five votes for Thomas A. Hendricks.
Virginia. — Ten votes for George H. Pendleton.
West Virginia. — Five votes for Pendleton.
Wisconsin. — Eight votes for James R. Doolittle.

The Secretary announced the result, as follows, —

Whole number of votes cast	317
English	7½
Hancock	43½
Pendleton	118½
Parker	13
Church	33
Packer	26
A. Johnson	32
Doolittle	12
Hendricks	11½
Blair	2
Reverdy Johnson	8
Ewing	1
Seymour	9

FOURTH BALLOT — RECAPITULATION.

STATES.	WHOLE NO.	ENGLISH.	HANCOCK.	PENDLETON.	PARKER.	CHURCH.	PACKER.	A. JOHNSON.	DOOLITTLE.	HENDRICKS.	BLAIR.	R. JOHNSON.	T. EWING, Jr.	SEYMOUR.
Alabama	8							8						
Arkansas	5	½		2½				½		1½				
California	5			1	3			1						
Connecticut	6	6												
Delaware	3			3										
Florida	3		3											
Georgia	9							8					1	
Illinois	16			16										
Indiana	13			13										
Iowa	8			8										
Kansas	3			2						½	½			
Kentucky	11			11										
Louisiana	7		7											
Maine	7		4½	1½							1			
Maryland	7			5					1½	½				
Massachusetts	12		11	1										
Michigan	8											8		
Minnesota	4			4										
Mississippi	7		7											
Missouri	11		2	5						4				
Nebraska	3			3										
Nevada	3				3									
New Hampshire	5		3	1½						½				
New Jersey	7				7									
New York	33					33								
North Carolina	9													9
Ohio	21			21										
Oregon	3			3										
Pennsylvania	26						26							
Rhode Island	4								4					
South Carolina	6	1		2				3						
Tennessee	10							10						
Texas	6		6											
Vermont	5										5			
Virginia	10			10										
West Virginia	5			5										
Wisconsin	8							8						
Total	317	7½	43½	118½	13	33	26	32	12	11½	2	8	1	9

A DELEGATE from Indiana. — Mr. President, the name of one of the most talented and respected citizens of Indiana has been presented here, outside of the delegation from that State, and with respectable strength. It presents a subject, therefore, of grave deliberation upon the part of the delegation from that State, and I am requested by many of the delegates to ask the Convention for permission to retire for the purpose of deliberation.

Permission being granted, the delegation withdrew from the hall.

Mr. FAULKNER, of New York, moved that the Convention adjourn until six o'clock this afternoon.

The PRESIDENT. — The Chair understands from the Secretary that the resolution respecting adjournments, already adopted by the Convention, provides that when the Convention adjourns, it shall adjourn until ten o'clock to-morrow morning. The only way, therefore, to act upon the wish of the delegate from New York, is to take a recess.

A DELEGATE from New York. — I move, then, that the Convention take a recess until four o'clock this afternoon.

A DELEGATE from Nebraska. — I move to amend by taking a recess until seven o'clock this evening.

Neither amendment nor resolution was agreed to.

A DELEGATE from Kansas. — I move the Convention do now adjourn.

The motion was lost.

Fifth Ballot.

The Secretary again called the roll, with the following result, —

Alabama. — Eight votes for Andrew Johnson.

California. — Three votes for Asa Packer, one for Andrew Johnson, and one for George H. Pendleton.

Connecticut. — Six votes for James E. English.

Delaware. — Three votes for George H. Pendleton.

Florida. — Three votes for James R. Doolittle.

Illinois. — Sixteen votes for George H. Pendleton.

Iowa. — Eight votes for George H. Pendleton.

Kansas. — Two votes for George H. Pendleton, one-half for Thomas H. Hendricks, and one-half for F. P. Blair, Jr.

Kentucky. — Eleven votes for George H. Pendleton.

Louisiana. — Seven votes for Winfield S. Hancock.

Maine. — Four and a half votes for Hancock, one and a half for Pendleton, and one for Hendricks.

Maryland. — Five votes for George H. Pendleton, one for Hendricks, and one for Andrew Johnson.

Massachusetts. — Eleven votes for W. S. Hancock, and one for George H. Pendleton.

Michigan. — Eight votes for Mr. Hendricks, of Indiana.

Minnesota. — Four votes for George H. Pendleton.

Mississippi. — Seven votes for Winfield S. Hancock.

Missouri. — Five and a half votes for George H. Pendleton, two for W. S. Hancock, and three and a half for Hendricks.

Nebraska. — Three votes for George H. Pendleton.

Nevada. — Three votes for Parker.

New Hampshire— One-half vote for Thomas A. Hendricks, one and a half for Pendleton, and three votes for W. S. Hancock.
New Jersey.— Seven votes for Joel Parker.
New York.— Thirty-three votes for Sanford E. Church.
North Carolina.— Five and a half votes for Hancock, two and a half for Pendleton, and one for Packer.
Ohio.— Twenty-one votes for Pendleton.
Oregon.— Three votes for Pendleton.
Pennsylvania.— Twenty-six votes for Packer.
Rhode Island.— Four votes for Doolittle.
South Carolina.— Three votes for Andrew Johnson, two for Pendleton, and one for John Quincy Adams, of Massachusetts.
Tennessee.— Ten votes for Andrew Johnson.
Texas.— Six votes for Hancock.
Vermont.— Five votes for Thomas A. Hendricks.
Virginia.— Ten votes for Pendleton.
West Virginia.— Five votes for Pendleton.
Wisconsin.— Eight votes for Doolittle.
Georgia.— Nine votes for Frank P. Blair.
Arkansas.— Three votes for Pendleton, one for Andrew Johnson, and one for English.

Executive Committee.

During the recess the Secretary said,—

I have to request that the delegations that have appointed members of the Executive Committee will please pass them up to the President's table, on slips of paper, with the post-office address, giving their States.

Mr. BRADFORD, of Delaware.— I think the resolution was that a Committee should be appointed, one from each State, to name them.

The PRESIDENT.— The delegates from each State select their own representatives.

Mr. WRIGHT, of Delaware.— I offered that resolution. It was to select one from each State to form a National Executive Committee.

Mr. RICHARDSON, of Illinois.— If the Convention will give me their attention for half a moment, I will say a word in regard to the Territories. Probably in four years from now most of them will be States in the Union. I am for giving them some encouragement, and I desire to make this proposition to the Committee: that they be permitted to appoint upon the National Executive Committee a member from each of the Territories of the United States.

Mr. HART, of New York.— I move to lay that resolution on the table.

The motion was lost.

Mr. TARBILL, of Ohio.— I move to amend the resolution so as to make it include the District of Columbia.

Gen. McCOOK, of Ohio.— The District of Columbia is not a State yet, and it is not represented on this floor.

Mr. D. O. FINCH, of Iowa.— I am in favor of the original proposition, for the reason that the Territories in four years, in all probability, will be States, while the District of Columbia never can be; therefore the amendment should be voted down.

A vote being taken on the amendment, it was declared lost.

The question was then stated to be on the resolution of the gentleman from Illinois, to add to the National Executive Committee one member from each of the Territories.

Mr. BUEL, of Nevada. — I would desire briefly to call attention to the fact that there is territory enough on the other side of the mountains, out of which, we hope, within the next year, at least, to carve ten States. The population of all those Territories are thoroughly Democratic, even including my own friend Brigham Young and his people of Utah. (Laughter.) Now, sir, I don't see the justice of excluding those gentlemen from representation on this committee. This committee is to remain in power for four years. We will have at least four Democratic States in that portion of the country before the expiration of four years. I hope gentlemen will reflect a moment before that is voted down. These men have risked their lives in the settlement of this country, and they carried the faith of their fathers there.

Mr. TILDEN, of New York. — Nothing could give us of the large States more pleasure than to do anything that is reasonable for our friends of the Territories; but in the Constitution of the Executive Committee and the discharge of its important functions, it is enough that a State of 4,000,000 like New York should be neutralized by the small States of the Union. It is enough that a small State of the Union should neutralize Pennsylvania, Ohio, Indiana, Illinois. Let us not add to that inequality by the introduction of delegates into that committee from the Territories having a very small population, who will have an equal influence upon the action of the Democratic party, voting as they do on that committee with these great and populous States. I do not think the request is reasonable; therefore I move to lay the motion on the table.

The PRESIDENT. — The motion of the gentleman from New York is not in order, as a similar one has just been voted down.

Mr. TILDEN. — I move to postpone it indefinitely.

The PRESIDENT. — The Chair will first present a resolution that has been offered by Mr. Riley, of Pennsylvania, by way of amendment.

The resolutions were read as follows, —

Resolved, That the representation of the next National Convention shall be the same as now.

Resolved, That in the event of any new State being admitted, any person who shall be named by the regular Democratic organization of the State shall be recognized as a member of the National Executive Committee.

Resolved, That the place of holding the next National Convention shall be left at the discretion of the National Executive Committee.

The amendment was accepted by Mr. Richardson.

The Secretary announced that the only resolution to be voted on was as follows, —

Resolved, That in the event of any new State being admitted, any person who shall be named by the regular Democratic organization of the State shall be recognized as a member of the National Executive Committee.

The Chair held the rest of the resolution to be unnecessary and out of order.

The resolution was agreed to.

Mr. WHITE, of Maryland. — I move that a committee of three be appointed by this Convention to wait upon the Indiana delegation and inquire if there is any probability of their immediately returning to the Convention, and, if not, that the Convention take a recess.

The motion was agreed to.

The Chair appointed Messrs. White (Md.), Faulkner (N. Y.), and Kerr (Penn.), as the committee.

Mr. FAYETTE MCMULLEN, of Virginia. — Mr. President, it must be perfectly obvious to this Convention now that we can do little, if anything, until we have retired and taken some refreshment. I have been most patient here; and no gentleman from my State, or scarcely from any other Southern State, has opened his mouth. I only rise now for the purpose of submitting a motion that I hope will meet the unanimous concurrence of this body, to wit, that we take a recess until five o'clock.

Mr. STRAIN, of Pennsylvania, seconded the motion.

The PRESIDENT. — Mr. Nelson, of Tennessee, calls the attention of the Chair to the fact that yesterday this Convention passed a resolution inviting a delegation from the State of Tennessee to submit to this body a memorial of the wrongs suffered by that State. The resolution was adopted, and the gentleman asks that Mr. McMullen will withdraw his resolution for the purpose of permitting that committee to be heard at this time.

Mr. MCMULLEN. — Mr. President, Tennessee is my neighbor; I cannot withhold any courtesy asked for by that State. I therefore withdraw my motion with great pleasure, but with the understanding that it is to be renewed when the memorial shall have been presented.

Mr. F. W. BROWN, of Tennessee, then submitted to the Convention the following

Memorial.

To the National Democratic Convention assembled in New York, July 4th, 1868, for the purpose of restoring the rights of States, and re-establishing the ancient liberties of the Republic.

A convention constituted by the people of Tennessee, and representing the great mass of the legitimate body politic of what should be a free and equal State of the FEDERAL UNION, directed your memorialists to make report to this assemblage of freemen of the oppressions, usurpations, and misrule to which this State has been subjected by the minions and agents of the party now in possession of the government of the United States.

The tyranny, of which we on behalf of a great body of American citizens complain, is not the evil supremacy of a mere domestic faction maintaining itself against odds by its own vigor, talent, and courage. On the contrary, if unsupported by the now misdirected powers of the FEDERAL UNION, the ruling oligarchs of our unfortunate commonwealth would not long abide the indignation of an outraged people. It is only because they represent and are executing the policy of the men now wielding the vast weight of Federal authority, who prostitute the resources of a great nation to uphold and protect these petty oppressors of a noble State. that we appeal through you to the people of States yet free to aid us in the redress of wrongs which are intolerable to American freemen, and the longer continuance of which threatens either renewed convulsions or the entire subversion of liberty throughout the Republic.

It is historically true that the present State organism of Tennessee was created in violation of all American precedent. It was not a government established by a majority of the citizens or of the inhabitants. It rests on a vote of *twenty-two thousand*, out of a voting population of *one hundred and sixty thousand*.

It is likewise true that the Confederate soldier and his sympathizer, on the surrender of the armies of the South, recognized the State Government as an exigency of civil war, and were entirely willing to waive its illegality, believing that it would conform in its legislation to the spirit and meaning of the terms of surrender tendered by the United States, and that its administration would be relieved in the midst of peace of whatever harshness the military necessities, out of which it sprung, may have in the first instance required. It was expected that, instead of being confined to the interests of the few that inaugurated its existence, it would be generously and wisely expanded so as to embrace the whole people. Intending to accept in good faith the result of the war, as restoring the old boundaries of the UNION, and re-establishing the authority of the Federal Government over the seceding States, as also the abolition of slavery, our people did not apprehend that a State Government, the foundling of a military camp, would annul the settlement of the questions at issue in the civil war made by the armies in the field. Nor was it anticipated that harder terms would be exacted of the defeated belligerent when unarmed, than had been demanded of him by his brave adversary in the field, when with arms in his hands despair might have renewed his enterprise, and the horrors of a dishonorable submission, more terrible than those of hopeless war, might have recreated his wasted resources. The parole of the Confederate, as understood among all honorable beligerents, guaranteed to him on the part of the supporters of the UNION his pre-existing rights, civil and political, as a citizen, on the condition of obedience to laws, State and Federal. To place the Southern citizen on a lower plane of civil and political liberty than that whereon the northern freeman stood, was a precedent so repugnant to the spirit and letter of all American Constitutions, and so fraught with danger to the Republic, that it was not believed there could emerge from the turbulence of the times a faction so malignant or insane as to propose, much less execute, so monstrous a project. Thus conceiving the situation, the people yielded a cheerful obedience to the State Government inaugurated during the war, confidently calculating that its administration and conduct would be such as would shortly legitimate it in their respect and affections.

These just expectations of the people have not been realized. It soon became apparent that the faction accidentally in power did not intend to recognize the submission of the people to the arms of the UNION, unless for the future they would mortgage to them their opinions and votes. It was not sufficient that they had in good faith resumed their allegiance to Federal authority, so long as they reserved to themselves the right to think and vote as American freemen. To exclude them from all participation in the affairs of government, and reduce them substantially to a condition of alienage, while exacting of them all the duties, and imposing on them all the burdens of citizenship, was deemed the only expedient by which the men then in office could prolong their power.

The amended Constitution proclaimed by the military governor of the State, — Andrew Johnson, — and accepted by those then having Tennessee in custody under Federal military occupation, granted power to the General Assembly to determine the qualifications of voters and the limitation of the elective franchise. It was in the exercise of this power under a constitution confessedly the work of not even *one-third* of the people, that a system of oppression was consummated, which has converted a once free and sovereign State of this *Union* into an odious despotism. The General Assembly first constituted after the proclamation of the amended constitution, when but a few of the citizens could vote, enacted three successive franchise laws, each surpassing the former in harshness and injustice. The result of the legislation on this matter has been *the disfranchisement of more than two-thirds of the whites, and the surrender of the ballot to the negro.* It would be impossible, within the appropriate compass of this memorial, to present in detail the enormities of these franchise acts. We can only briefly advert to them.

These were passed from time to time as the necessities of the authorities required a restricted suffrage to maintain them in office. The only exceptions to the rigor of these laws were those who had, or were supposed to have, assimilated with them in political sentiment. Thus political opinion was made the condition on which AMERICAN CITIZENS should enjoy that franchise, by which alone their liberties can be preserved, — access to the ballot-box. The principle worked out to its full extent enables a temporary majority to render its rule perpetual, or force the people ultimately to relieve themselves by revolutionary violence. The majority of to-day have only to find their present supremacy threatened by a change of opinion in the masses hostile to their policy and power, really converting them into a minority, to justify the line of action pursued in Tennessee. Then the work of excision from the polls may commence, narrowing in still decreasing circles the voting population, by depriving of the ballot such members of the hostile voters, as to leave under the control and for the support of the party in power a majority of the voters, but really an insignificant minority of the people. Then is established an oligarchy, the deadliest foe of popular liberty.

A still more repulsive and tyrannical feature of these disfranchising acts is found in those provisions, which propound to the citizen, in order to exercise the right of suffrage, harsh and inquisitorial oaths, reaching not only his conduct, but his *opinions* in the *past*, and putting upon him the alternative of committing perjury or of becoming his own accuser for the disabling acts and sympathies, which, by the terms of the law, exclude him from the ballot. Thus has been inaugurated, amid the civilization of the nineteenth century, and in a Republic, that odious inquisition into the secret thoughts and private opinions of men, which has been justly deemed the peculiar disgrace of even a remote and barbarous period, of even the most ignorant and cruel despotism.

That provision of the Federal constitution which forbids a State to pass a bill of attainder or *ex post facto* law, has been either audaciously violated, or it is so easy of evasion as to be utterly worthless for the protection of American citizens against the madness of faction or the licentiousness of power;

and the intentions of the framers of that instrument have been utterly frustrated by the ingenious devices of revenge and hatred. For it cannot be denied that, under the pretence of fixing the qualifications of voters, *two-thirds* of the white men of this State have been *divested* of the elective franchise by legislative enactment, as a punishment for assumed offences for which they have never even been challenged by any process of law.

By virtue of the disfranchisement of the great mass of the white people, TENNESSEE is now practically under the dominion of the negro.

It was not, however, until it became apparent that no franchise law, however restrictive or harsh as to the white population, would retain power in the hands of our domestic faction, that the negro was endowed with the ballot. To serve alone their selfish interest, all the great body of the white people of the State, CITIZENS OF THE REPUBLIC, long accustomed, under ancient usage and the laws of the State, to exercise the right of suffrage, were disfranchised, and the lately emancipated African slave, unfitted, according to the universal experience of mankind, for self-government, entrusted with the gravest duties ever devolved on freemen. If this legislation resulted from any conviction, that universal suffrage, regardless of race as a principle, should be introduced into the American system, however foolish and dangerous we might esteem the measure, its projectors would, at least, be entitled to that respect which ever attaches to sincerity. But we are not permitted by the facts to accord to them this consideration. If it was on principle, and from an honest conviction of duty, that the ballot was granted the rude, illiterate, and still semi-barbarous negro, it would have been done at once, and not postponed until every expedient had been tried by the present official incumbents to get along without his vote. Nor would an honest advocate of negro suffrage deem it consistent with his theory to exclude the great body of white people from the elective franchise, while bestowing it on the African race. We are therefore compelled, in justice to the truth of history, to represent all these outrages on the ancient rights, liberties, and privileges of American citizens as perpetrated solely in the interest of a party, and to maintain in official position a particular class. Because the whites would not sustain this class and their policies, they are stripped of their franchises of American freedom, and the African is arrayed against them, for the present dominating over them, — an elevation of an inferior race, however inconvenient and insulting for the present to the superior, to ultimately result, as all intelligent men must know, in the utmost future calamity to the negro.

In the past career of the Republic, party antagonisms have been productive of many evils and great wrongs, — have often been marked by public indecorum and individual depravity; but never before the present, and now passing period in our history has any political organization dared to trample on the substantial liberties of the American citizen, or sought to wrest the elective franchise from those entitled to it by the ancient usage and laws of the Republic. No faction ever before proposed to secure its success by such a crime!

This offence is the more rank, because the act does not stop with striking down the liberties and franchises of the citizen, but heaps upon the victims of this lawlessness the ignominy of political subordination to an inferior race. Did the founders of the Republic ever intend that any part of the white should be subjected to the black race? It concerns the people of the Northern States, who, thank God! are yet free, scarcely less than those represented by your memorialists, to overthrow the infamous policies of which we complain. If our people within the several Southern States are to be taxed, and our domestic policy shaped, by the lately emancipated slave and the irresponsible adventurer, who uses him as an unreasoning instrument of his purpose, so will the Northern citizen be taxed in the *National Assessment* by the same constituency, and through the national legislature his political and material interests will be affected by the same unintelligent and irresponsible vote. To substitute for the intelligent white voter of the South, the negro elector is to expose the interests of the North to almost the same hazard that threatens those of the South. *In this matter, the welfare of the white man in the South cannot be separated from that of the white man in the North.*

Odious and oppressive as are the franchise laws of Tennessee, they have been greatly aggravated in all their evils by the registration acts and their administration. The first statute committed the work of registration to the Clerks of the County Courts, who are officers elected by the people, and therefore so situated as to understand that it was not prudent for them to play the *role* of petty tyrants, or trifle with the rights and liberties of the citizen. But, by a subsequent act, these delicate and responsible duties have been assigned to Commissioners appointed by the Governor, to whom alone they are substantially responsible for their conduct. It is true that there is a provision subjecting these Commissioners to punishment, as for a misdemeanor for *wilful* and *intentional* violation of the law. But when it is considered that, by the terms of the law, the burden of proof as to wilfulness and intention of the corrupt register is thrown on the accusing party, and that it is so easy for the offending officer to have his dereliction construed into a mere mistake, it will be seen that the people are without protection, in this regard, against the corrupt practices or arbitrary action of the registers. To render this very slight and evasive restraint on the conduct of this official utterly insufficient for the security of the people, the legislature has ordered that the counsel fees and costs of suit incurred by him in defending any prosecution, penal or civil, instituted against him for a violation of the rights of the citizen in the performance of his official duty, be paid out of the public treasury, — thus taxing the people to pay the expenses of their oppressors incurred in the perpetration of the wrong. When it is remembered that the tax-payers of the State are those opposed to the faction in power, and consequently those against whom these Commissioners of Registration would be most likely to perpetrate, and do, in fact, work injustice, the vice and tyranny of this legislation must at once become apparent. In effect, it compels freemen to pay for the chains with which they are to be bound.

Additional impunity is secured to these servants of the executive by a statute, which enables them to exclude from the jury-box, by challenge for cause, *any one who is not a voter*. Thus is rendered certain in every trial an *available partisan* influence on the panel, in behalf of the transgressing register.

On the other hand, the authorities controlling the State have not left their interests to the hazard of even the accidental or occasional honesty of these officers. The power has been reserved to the executive to declare, by simple proclamation, the registration of any county void, and to remove, at his sovereign will, any register that may excite his suspicion or incur his displeasure. Thus has been reposed in the executive department of the government the entire control of the ballot-box, and to that end he exercises judicial and executive functions, — judicial, to divest, and that, too, without trial, freemen of privileges duly acquired, — executive, to inflict his own sentence of divestiture, in violation of all principles of free government, against all precedents known to American law, and in utter disregard of the provisions of the constitution. This arbitrary power has been often exercised by the present executive, and always redounding to the advantage of the faction supporting him and his policy. In this state of the case where is there a foothold for those who would lift from earth the prostrate form of Liberty, and reanimate her fainting spirit? Personal ambition and desire for official *preferment* are by every selfish consideration enlisted on the side of absolutism, because all expectants of place must bow to him who can work through the registers any elective result desired. It is vain to expect in any canvass, through a fair and orderly polling, a successful issue for him who opposes in opinion "the powers that be." With the entire control of the ballot-box thus secured in the hands of one man, the exercise of the elective franchise is but a delusive and idle ceremony. Though the result purports to be accomplished through Democratic forms, it is none the less the mere expression of autocratic will. The candid rescript of the emperor would be better, because none could be deceived as to what was the fact in the present, nor deluded by vain hopes as to the future.

In addition to all this, the conviction is general, among the citizens of the State, that while the act of legislation is made easy and rapid for such whites as are known to affiliate with the authorities of the State, and for negroes who are manipulated in the same interest by secret political societies, and army officers in the Freedman's Bureau, the same process is rendered difficult and slow for the whites, who are known to be opposed in sentiment to the now prevailing policies of the State and of Congress. Thus, in many instances, by these indirect methods, the party in place is relieved against a hostile suffrage, from which even their rigorous franchise laws would not protect them.

We are therefore compelled to announce to this Convention that Republican government, as understood by Americans, no longer exists in the State of Tennessee; that freedom of elections, the chief muniment of English and American liberty has perished; that freemen may there be disseized of priceless privileges without the judgment of their peers even, and otherwise than by the laws of the land; and that the order of Warsaw reigns throughout her borders.

The evil effects of this oppressive policy are already plainly manifest in the material condition of the State, and palpably visible on the surface of society. We will briefly advert to them.

The great body of the whites, feeling that they are victims of oppression; that they are unjustly deprived of any share in the government; that they are in all respects fitted by intelligence to participate in affairs of State; and remembering that the political privileges of which they have been deprived constituted a part of their birthright, — are discontented, and apprehend still greater calamities and outrages. They recognize that at present they are neither secure in their property or liberties. Stripped of suffrage, they cannot defend them at the ballot-box. Their foes among the whites, and the negroes granted by the statute the privilege of being armed, while the same is denied to them, deprives them of that sense of security which ever resides with physical power, and places them under a constant menace from the vicious and depraved elements of society. Hence the division between the people and their rulers is something more than the mere array of conflicting opinions, which, with free suffrage, and free speech, seldom breeds civil commotion, or injuriously affects the State. It is in this instance the threatening antagonism between the *oppressor* on the one hand, and the *oppressed* on the other. The apprehension and natural resentment of the latter, and the official insolence and hate of the former, retorting the detestation of which he is conscious, are constantly recurring provocations to physical violence. Experience and history prove that there can be neither happiness nor prosperity for a State thus circumstanced. So long as republican forms are preferred on this continent, no American State can have any assurance of peace and prosperity unless the ballot is free to the white American citizen. The inherent vigor and imperial qualities of the white race will be content with nothing less until they shall agree to accept other political institutions.

It is of the utmost importance to every free State, that those who are the most intelligent, have the largest stake in social order, and possess property, or are interested in property by the hope of accumulation through steady industry, should participate in the government. But, in our unfortunate Commonwealth, this is the very class which are excluded from the management of its affairs. The people are thus deprived in public business of the efficient capacity of their best citizens. Their affairs are consequently in the hands of incapable men, — too often entirely controlled by those who are mere adventurers camped in their midst, like vagrant Huns for the purposes of present plunder, in whose fidelity to their interests and integrity they have not the slighest confidence, and to whom the language of Col. Barré used in the British Parliament to describe a similar class that infested the American colonies, may not inappropriately be applied, when he spoke of the colonial officers as "men sent to spy out their liberties, *to misrepresent their actions*, and to prey upon them, — men whose behavior on many occasions has caused the blood of those sons of liberty to recoil within them!" Yet it would not be strict justice not to admit some honorable exceptions to this rule. But these exceptions serve to modify only to a very limited extent the vices and disorders naturally inherent in such depraved and tyrannical policies. For instance, though we have on the bench some honest judges of respectable ability, it is manifest that the Courts of the State lose their self-possession and quail when confronted by the political ferocity of the hour. Hard is the lot of that people when law shrinks from the defence of her own altars from profanation, and plays the coward within "the holy of holies." England has always accounted it an excess of misfortune whenever her judiciary for a moment lost its fearless independence. Shall American republicans manifest in this matter less sensibility than British subjects? Will they not demand that courts and judges shall stand unmoved amid the tempest of civil strife to defend the right even against their own mad passions?

Those laboring under disabilities as to suffrage and office embrace the highest intellects of the State. Among the disfranchised will be found the aged pioneer, who, with axe and rifle, redeemed from the rude wilderness, and the still ruder savage, our fruitful soil; secured to civilization and culture her lovely valleys and plains, and maintained with Jackson on the ramparts of New Orleans the flag of the Republic. On the same role of alienized citizens will be found the great mass of the descendants of the founders of the Commonwealth, who, representing in their characters, as well as lineage, the virtues and heroism of a worthy ancestory, have themselves, according to their varied abilities, served the country in war or in peace. There must still be added to this aggregate of attainted merit her adopted sons, attracted from every State of the Union, as well as from foreign lands, to her generous hearthstone. We ask if it is no grievance, no wrong, to TENNESSEE, that, in the administration of her affairs, she should be deprived of the intelligence and virtue, both at the ballot-box, and in office, of her noblest people? Is there no wrong in thus deposing from their chartered rights this great and worthy body of American citizenship?

The property and accumulating industry of the State being excluded from all available influence in the construction of the legislature is, in fact, taxed without representation. The property of the State is without representation, because the great mass of those who hold it are disfranchised, and the few property holders who have been so fortunate as to secure legislation cast fruitless votes against the vagabondage that now controls at the hustings the destinies of the Commonwealth. It is the same case with the large proportion of the laboring white men. The negroes whose votes create the taxing body, have, with scarcely a single exception, no property to be taxed. They do not even pay a poll assessment, and are either in fact, or permitted by the county authorities for political advantage, to be paupers to an excessive extent, and a charge on the taxes wrung from the disfranchised whites. Put in place by such a constituency, and most generally himself unaffected by any tax which he may create, it is not to be expected that the legislator would be at all economical in dealing with the financial affairs of the State, or that he would particularly care if taxation should become so excessive as to amount to practical confiscation.

The result is just what might be expected. The debt of the State is continually increased, her resources diminished, and her taxation fearfully enhanced. By unusual and enormous levies on her merchants, trade is driven from our cities and State to other cities and States. The returns of mechanical industry are consumed in obtaining a meagre support and paying taxes, leaving no accumulations behind. The farmer, who should be independent, can scarcely, with the most favorable seasons, balance his books. Our courts in many parts of the State are besieged by clamorous tax-payers seeking by litigation either to be relieved of unconstitutional assessments, or to delay their collection. In fine, property impoverishes. Thrift but accumulates for the tax-gatherer laws, while the foreigner and citizen of other States are repelled from our borders by the same misrule. Thus our miserable State, with the finest climate that ever blest the most fruitful and varied soil, is wasted in every fibre and muscle.

We have, in the presentation of the political condition of Tennessee, abstained from impeaching individual corruption and private dereliction. We designed to arraign a hideous *system* of oppression, fix attention on the great principles of constitutional liberty violated, and expose hateful, and, therefore, unwise policies. The best ministers of tyrannical laws will become depraved, and vicious administrations will necessarily breed bad men. Nor has our State, in this regard, enjoyed immunity, but, on the contrary, has been duly afflicted by these additional aggravations of her situation. To depict these, however, might plausibly subject us to the imputation of partisan heat. It is the system at which we strike. Destroy that, and the offenders disappear with their offences, soon to be forgotten, like other calamities of life, in restored happiness and a resumed prosperity. The business of our paper is not to accuse this or that man, this or that official, but to present to the members of this Convention, and through them to the people of the North, the grave and solemn question, — whether a sovereign State of the FEDERAL UNION shall be retained in bondage, and thousands of her people made miserable; to remind the Northern States that once consenting to the enslavement of any one of the Federal circle, they but prepare for the divestiture at some future day of their own sovereign rights; to remind the people that for them to instigate, or even permit, the degradation and vassalage of an American citizen is to forge their own manacles for future imposition, and to adjust their own limbs for the gyves of the oppressor.

T. W. BROWN,
J. E. BURLEY,
WM. A. QUARLES, } *Committee.*
J. H. CALLENDER,
WM. CLARE,

After the reading of the memorial, a delegate from Indiana stated that his delegation were still in consultation, and not ready to return to the hall; but that, in the mean time, he was authorized, on behalf of the delegation, to cast the vote of that State as heretofore, — thirteen for Mr. Pendleton.

The Secretary announced the vote on the fifth ballot, as follows,—

The whole number of votes cast	317
James E. English	7
W. S. Hancock	46
George H. Pendleton	122
Joel Parker	13
Sanford E. Church	33
Asa Packer	27
Andrew Johnson	24
James R. Doolittle	15
Thomas A. Hendricks	19½
Frank P. Blair	9½
Reverdy Johnson	—
Thomas Ewing, Jr.	—
J. Q. Adams	1

FIFTH BALLOT—RECAPITULATION.

STATES.	WHOLE NO.	ENGLISH.	HANCOCK.	PENDLETON.	PARKER.	CHURCH.	PACKER.	A. JOHNSON.	DOOLITTLE.	HENDRICKS.	BLAIR.	R. JOHNSON.	T. EWING, Jr.	ADAMS.
Alabama	8							8						
Arkansas	5	1		3				1						
California	5			1	3			1						
Connecticut	6	6												
Delaware	3			3										
Florida	3								3					
Georgia	9										9			
Illinois	16			16										
Indiana	13			13										
Iowa	8			8										
Kansas	3			2						½	½			
Kentucky	11			11										
Louisiana	7		7											
Maine	7		4½	1½						1				
Maryland	7			5				1		1				
Massachusetts	12		11	1										
Michigan	8									8				
Minnesota	4			4										
Mississippi	7		7											
Missouri	11		2	5½						3½				
Nebraska	3			3										
Nevada	3				3									
New Hampshire	5		3	1½						½				
New Jersey	7				7									
New York	33					33								
North Carolina	9		5½	2½			1							
Ohio	21			21										
Oregon	3			3										
Pennsylvania	26						26							
Rhode Island	4								4					
South Carolina	6			2				3						1
Tennessee	10							10						
Texas	6		6											
Vermont	5										5			
Virginia	10			10										
West Virginia	5			5										
Wisconsin	8								8					
Total	317	7	46	122	13	33	27	24	15	19½	9½			1

Mr. TILDEN, of New York. — The New York delegation ask leave to retire for the purpose of designating their member for the National Executive Committee.

Cries of "No! no! no!"

The question was put upon granting the request of the New York delegation, and it was decided lost.

The Secretary then proceeded with the call of the roll, and called again the State of

Alabama. — Eight votes for Andrew Johnson.
Arkansas. — Four for Blair, one for Johnson.
California. — Three for Parker, one for Pendleton, one for Packer.
Connecticut. — Six for English.
Delaware. — Three for Pendleton.
Florida. — Three for Hendricks.
Georgia. — Eight and a half for Pendleton, one-half for Blair.
Illinois. — Sixteen for Pendleton.
Indiana. — No response was made, the delegation being out.
Iowa. — Eight for Pendleton.
Kansas. — Two and a half for Hendricks, one and a half for Blair.
Kentucky. — Eleven for Pendleton.
Louisiana. — Four and a half for Hancock, one and a half for Pendleton, one for Hendricks.
Maryland. — Five and a half for Pendleton, one for Andrew Johnson, a half for Hendricks.
Massachusetts. — Eleven for Hancock, one for Pendleton.
Michigan. — Eight for Hendricks.
Minnesota. — Four for Pendleton.
Mississippi. — Seven for Hancock.
Missouri. — Four for Pendleton, two and a half for Hancock, three for Hendricks; one for Andrew Johnson.
Nebraska. — Three for Pendleton.
Nevada. — Three for Joel Parker.
New Hampshire. — One-half for Hendricks, one and a half for Pendleton, three for Gen. Hancock.
New Jersey. — Seven for Parker.
New York. — Thirty-three for Sanford E. Church, of New York.
North Carolina. — Eight and a half for Hendricks, two and a half for Pendleton.
Ohio. — Twenty-one for Pendleton.
Oregon. — Three for Pendleton.
Pennsylvania. — Mr. CLYMER: The Chairman of the Pennsylvania Delegation being temporarily absent, has asked me to perform the duty for him, to announce that Pennsylvania casts twenty-six votes for Packer.
Rhode Island. — Rhode Island gives four votes for James R. Doolittle.
South Carolina. — Six for Gen. Hancock.
Tennessee. — Ten for Andrew Johnson.
Texas. — Six for Hancock.
Vermont. — Five for Hendricks.

Virginia. — Ten for George H. Pendleton. (Applause.)
West Virginia. — Five for Pendleton.
Wisconsin. — Eight for Doolittle.
Indiana. — The CHAIRMAN of the Delegation: The Indiana Delegation are still in consultation. In the mean time, I shall venture to cast the vote as before, — thirteen for Pendleton.

NATIONAL DEMOCRATIC CONVENTION.

The Secretary announced the result, as follows, —

Total number of votes cast	316½
James E. English	6
W. S. Hancock	47
George H. Pendleton	122½
Joel Parker	13
Sanford E. Church	33
Asa Packer	27
Andrew Johnson	21
James R. Doolittle	12
Thomas A. Hendricks	30
Frank P. Blair	5

SIXTH BALLOT — RECAPITULATION.

STATES.	WHOLE NO.	ENGLISH.	HANCOCK.	PENDLETON.	PARKER.	CHURCH.	PACKER.	A. JOHNSON.	DOOLITTLE.	HENDRICKS.	BLAIR.
Alabama	8							8			
Arkansas	5							1			4
California	5			1	3		1				
Connecticut	6	6									
Delaware	3			3							
Florida	3									3	
Georgia	9			8½							½
Illinois	16			16							
Indiana	13			13							
Iowa	8			8							
Kansas	3			2						½	½
Kentucky	11			11							
Louisiana	7		7								
Maine	7		4½	1½						1	
Maryland	7			5½					1	½	
Massachusetts	12		11	1							
Michigan	8									8	
Minnesota	4			4							
Mississippi	7		7								
Missouri	11		2½	4				1		3	
Nebraska	3			3							
Nevada	3				3						
New Hampshire	5		3	1½						½	
New Jersey	7				7						
New York	33					33					
North Carolina	9			1½						8½	
Ohio	21			21							
Oregon	3			3							
Pennsylvania	26							26			
Rhode Island	4								4		
South Carolina	6		6								
Tennessee	10							10			
Texas	6		6								
Vermont	5									5	
Virginia	10			10							
West Virginia	5			5							
Wisconsin	8								8		
Total	317	6	47	122½	13	33	27	21	12	30	5

Mr. CARTER, of North Carolina. — It is quite obvious, sir, that we are accomplishing nothing. I therefore move that we adjourn until to-morrow morning at ten o'clock.

Many DELEGATES. — "No, no."

Mr. CLYMER. — I move to amend by saying that we take a recess until seven o'clock this evening.

The CHAIRMAN. — The question must first be put on the motion to adjourn.

The motion was rejected.

Mr. CLYMER. — I move to take a recess until seven o'clock this evening.

The motion was rejected.

Mr. CAMPBELL, of Pennsylvania. — The Pennsylvania Delegation ask leave to retire for consultation.

The question was put, and leave was refused.

Mr. STEVENS, of New Jersey. — I move that we take a recess until six o'clock.

The question was put, and the result was doubtful.

The PRESIDENT. — The list of States will be called, for it is impossible for the Chair to decide the question.

A DELEGATE. — I move to adjourn.

The CHAIRMAN. — The motion is not now in order, as the Chair is not now certain what the result of the last vote was. The Clerk will read a communication.

Endorsement of the Platform by the Soldiers and Sailors' Convention.

The Secretary read the following communication to the Convention.

Resolved, That the declaration of principles adopted by the Democratic National Convention be, and the same are hereby approved.

Ordered, That the Secretary communicate to the Democratic Convention a copy of the above resolution forwith.

JAMES O'BIERNE,
Secretary Soldiers and Sailors' Convention.

To the Democratic Convention.

Mr. RICHARDSON, of Illinois. — I move that the document just received from the Soldiers' and Sailors' Convention be put upon the record of the Convention and made part of the proceedings.

The motion prevailed.

Mr. D. M. CARTER, of North Carolina. — I move we take a recess until six o'clock this evening.

NATIONAL DEMOCRATIC CONVENTION.

The vote was taken on the motion, by States, as follows: affirmative, 99; negative, 218.

	Yeas.	Nays.		Yeas.	Nays.
Alabama	—	8	Nebraska	—	3
Arkansas	—	5	Nevada	3	—
California	—	5	New Hampshire	5	—
Connecticut	—	6	New Jersey	7	—
Delaware	1	2	New York	—	33
Florida	—	3	North Carolina	9	—
Georgia	9	—	Ohio	—	21
Illinois	—	16	Oregon	—	3
Indiana	—	13	Pennsylvania	26	—
Iowa	8	—	Rhode Island	4	—
Kansas	—	3	South Carolina	—	6
Kentucky	—	11	Tennessee	—	10
Louisiana	—	7	Texas	—	6
Maine	—	7	Vermont	5	—
Maryland	—	7	Virginia	10	—
Massachusetts	—	12	West Virginia	5	—
Michigan	—	8	Wisconsin	—	8
Minnesota	—	4			
Mississippi	7	—	Total	99	218
Missouri	—	11			

Mr. WHITE, of Maryland. — I move we now adjourn.

The CHAIRMAN. — The motion now is that the Convention do adjourn. It carries us over until the regular meeting to-morrow, at ten o'clock.

The SECRETARY. — I am requested by the National Committee to say that the chairmen of the respective delegations will call at the National Committee rooms, in this building, this evening, at eight o'clock, and receive their tickets of admission. Tickets may be obtained on an order sent by any chairman of a delegation. I have also to announce that the delegation of Pennsylvania are requested to meet this evening at Irving Hall, at eight o'clock.

The Secretary announced that the vote on the motion to adjourn stood 218 for the motion, to 99 against, as follows, —

	Yeas.	Nays.		Yeas.	Nays.
Alabama	8	—	Nebraska	2	—
Arkansas	5	—	Nevada	—	3
California	5	—	New Hampshire	—	5
Connecticut	6	—	New Jersey	—	7
Delaware	2	1	New York	33	—
Florida	3	—	North Carolina	—	9
Georgia	—	9	Ohio	21	—
Illinois	16	—	Oregon	3	—
Indiana	13	—	Pennsylvania	—	26
Iowa	—	8	Rhode Island	—	4
Kansas	3	—	South Carolina	6	—
Kentucky	11	—	Tennessee	10	—
Louisiana	7	—	Texas	6	—
Maine	7	—	Vermont	—	5
Maryland	7	—	Virginia	—	10
Massachusetts	12	—	West Virginia	—	5
Michigan	8	—	Wisconsin	8	—
Minnesota	4	—			
Mississippi	—	7	Total	218	99
Missouri	11	—			

The Convention, at three and a half o'clock, was declared adjourned until Wednesday morning, at ten o'clock.

FOURTH DAY.

July 8, 1868.

The Convention was called to order by the President, Hon. HORATIO SEYMOUR.

On motion of General McCOOK, the reading of the minutes of yesterday's proceedings was dispensed with.

Mr. WELLS, of Missouri, asked that the names of the Executive Committee be read.

The Secretary read the names as follows, —

The National Executive Committee.

Alabama. — John Forsyth, Mobile.
Arkansas. — John M. Harrell, Little Rock.
California. — John Bigler, Sacramento City.
Connecticut. — Wm. M. Converse, Franklin.
Delaware. — Samuel Townsend, Newcastle.
Florida. — Charles E. Dyke, Tallahassee.
Georgia. — A. H. Colquit, Albany.
Illinois. — Wilbur F. Storey, Chicago.
Indiana. — William E. Niblack, Vincennes.
Iowa. — Daniel O. Finch, Des Moines.
Kansas. — Isaac E. Eaton, Leavenworth City.
Kentucky. — Thomas C. McCreery, Owensboro.
Louisiana. — James McCloskey, New Orleans.
Maine. — Sylvanus R. Lyman Portland.
Maryland. — Odin Bowie, Prince George.
Massachusetts. — Frederick O. Prince, Boston.
Michigan. — William A. Moore, Detroit.
Minnesota. — Charles W. Nash, St. Paul.
Mississippi. — Charles E. Hooker, Jackson.
Missouri. — Charles A. Mants, St. Louis.
Nebraska. — G. L. Miller, Omaha.
Nevada. — J. W. McCorkle, Virginia City.
New Hampshire. — Harry Bingham, Littleton.
New Jersey. — John McGregor, Newark.
New York. — August Belmont, New York City.
North Carolina. — Thomas Bragg, Raleigh.
Ohio. — John G. Thompson, Columbus.
Oregon. — J. C. Hawthorn, Portland.
Pennsylvania. — Isaac Eskister, Lancaster.
Rhode Island. — Gideon Bradford, Providence.
South Carolina. — Charles H. Simonton, Charleston.
Tennessee. — John W. Leftwich, Memphis.
Texas. — John Hancock, Austin.
Vermont. — H. B. Smith, Milton.
Virginia. — John Goode, Norfolk.
West Virginia. — John Hall, Point Pleasant.
Wisconsin. — Frederick W. Horn, Cedarburg.

Mr. TARBELL, of Ohio. — I move that without further delay we proceed to the calling of the States.

Mr. GRAHAM V. FITCH, of Indiana. — Before proceeding with the call of the States, Indiana claims the right heretofore conceded to other States, to present the name of one of her most talented citizens as a candidate for nomination by this Convention. The name is known to the Convention, for he has already received a respectable vote here. That vote, however, came from other than his own State, a tribute to the worth of one of the best and purest men in the nation. (Applause.) Circumstances which occurred before the connection of his name with the nomination rendered it, in the estimation of the delegation from his State, highly proper and right that they should give their vote a reasonable length of time for the distinguished candidate from Ohio. In the opinion of a majority of the delegation from Indiana that time has passed, and they are left to vote their own preference, and what they believe to be the preference of their people. From this opinion a minority of the delegation dissent, and deem that their obligation to sustain Mr. Pendleton is not yet discharged. The majority have no desire to control, and make no attempt to control, even if there was the slightest probability of the attempt being successful, the action of that minority. We concede to them the best of motives, a desire merely to conscientiously discharge a delegated trust. The citizen, whose name we are about to present, is a man of unimpeached private character and unimpeached public record. He is a gentleman, sir, in all the relations of life. He is not, he never was, an office-seeker himself, but whatever position has been bestowed upon him by the partiality of the citizens of his own State has been bestowed unsought and by acclamation. He is second to no man within our borders in ability, in devotion to the Union, in attachment to the principles of Democracy, in integrity of purpose, and in firmness in the discharge of duty. That citizen is Thomas A. Hendricks. (Loud applause.)

A DELEGATE from Indiana. — On behalf of the minority of the delegation from the State of Indiana, I claim the privilege here to state in a few words the reasons that governed our action. A majority of the delegation following in the lead of the votes being cast for Mr. Hendricks, a gentleman who commands the highest respect and confidence in the State of Indiana in all the positions that he has held, and the one he now holds, have decided to cast their votes for him. Without impugning the honor of any man from the State of Indiana, I wish to give the reasons why I cannot go with them. On the 5th day of January last the Democracy of Indiana assembled at Indianapolis in such array of numbers and talent as never before assembled in that State, and they adopted a resolution expressing a preference for George H. Pendleton (Cheers) over the most determined and persistent opposition. In respect to that resolution, at the first meeting of the delegation in this city (and no gentleman on the delegation will controvert it), it was agreed that the vote of Indiana should be cast for Mr. Pendleton so long as there was a reasonable hope of his nomination. (Cheers.) A majority of the delegation have rescinded that resolution, as I suppose they have a right to do. I merely claim that by the record, and by my conscientious conviction, my duty as a delegate of the State of Indiana is, so long as there is a reasonable hope of his nomination, to vote for George H. Pendleton, of Ohio. (Cheers.)

The SECRETARY. — A majority of the delegation from Indiana have placed in nomination the name of Thomas A. Hendricks. (Cheers.)

The CHAIRMAN. — If there is no other nomination, the Secretary will now proceed to call the roll of the States.

The Seventh Ballot.

The call of States was then made.

The ballot then proceeded, as follows, —

Alabama. — A unit for Pendleton.

Arkansas. — A unit for Hendricks.

California. — Three votes for George H. Pendleton, one and a half for Hancock, and one-half for Hendricks.

Connecticut. — (Passed for the present.)

Delaware. — Three votes for George H. Pendleton. (Cheers.)

Florida. — Three votes for Hendricks.

Georgia. — Eight votes for George H. Pendleton, and one for Hendricks.

Illinois. — Sixteen votes for Pendleton.

Indiana. — (Passed for the present.)

Iowa. — Eight votes for Pendleton.

Kansas. — Two votes for Pendleton, half a vote for Hendricks, and half a vote for Frank P. Blair.

Kentucky. — Eleven votes for Pendleton.

Louisiana. — Seven votes for Hancock.

Maine. — Hancock four and a half, Pendleton one and a half, and Hendricks one.

Maryland. — Six and a half for Pendleton, and one and a half for Hendricks.

Massachusetts. — Eleven votes for Hancock, and one for Pendleton.

Michigan. — Eight for Hendricks.

Minnesota. — Four for Pendleton.

Mississippi. — Seven for Pendleton.

Missouri. — Four for Pendleton, five for Hendricks, one for Andrew Johnson, and one-half for Hancock.

Nebraska. — Three for Pendleton.

Nevada. — Three for Pendleton.

New Hampshire. — Half for Hendricks, one and a half for Pendleton, and three for Hancock.

New Jersey. — Seven for Joel Parker.

New York. — Thirty-three for Sanford E. Church.

North Carolina. — Nine for General Hancock.

Ohio. — Twenty-one votes for George H. Pendleton.

Oregon. — The Chairman of the Delegation, Mr. Bell. Mr. President, in casting the vote of my State this morning, it is with a feeling that the Democracy has recently achieved an overwhelming victory over the policy of the Chicago Convention.

Cries of "Order, order."

The PRESIDENT. — Is the gentleman going to announce a new candidate?

Mr. BELL. — No, sir.

The PRESIDENT. — Then you are not in order.

Mr. BELL. — I desire simply to give the reason for our vote this morning.

The PRESIDENT. — If you desire to make a new nomination, that is in order.

Mr. BELL. — Well, sir, I will simply say that I wish to nominate George H. Pendleton. (Laughter and cheers.)

Pennsylvania. — Twenty-six votes for Packer.

Rhode Island. — Four votes for Doolittle.

South Carolina. — Six votes for Andrew Johnson.

Tennessee. — Five and a half votes for Andrew Johnson, and four and a half for Pendleton.

Texas. — Six votes for General Hancock.

Vermont. — Five votes for Hendricks.

Virginia. — Ten votes for Pendleton.

West Virginia. — Five votes for Pendleton.

Wisconsin. — Eight votes for Doolittle.

Connecticut. — Six votes for English.

Indiana. — Nine and a half for Hendricks, and three and a half for Pendleton.

The Secretary announced the result, as follows, —

Total number of votes cast	316½
James E. English	6
W. S. Hancock	42½
George H. Pendleton	137½
Joel Parker	7
Sanford E. Church	33
Asa Packer	26
Andrew Johnson	12½
James R. Doolittle	12
Thomas A. Hendricks	39½
Frank P. Blair	½

SEVENTH BALLOT—RECAPITULATION.

STATES.	WHOLE NO.	ENGLISH.	HANCOCK.	PENDLETON.	PARKER.	CHURCH.	PACKER.	A. JOHNSON.	DOOLITTLE.	HENDRICKS.	BLAIR.
Alabama	8	..	..	8	..	..	..	..	..	..	..
Arkansas	5	..	..	..	..	..	..	..	..	5	..
California	5	..	1½	3	..	..	..	..	..	½	..
Connecticut	6	6	..	..	..	..	..	..	..	..	..
Delaware	3	..	..	3	..	..	..	..	..	..	..
Florida	3	..	..	..	..	..	..	..	..	3	..
Georgia	9	..	..	8	..	..	..	..	..	1	..
Illinois	16	..	..	16	..	..	..	..	..	..	..
Indiana	13	..	..	3½	..	..	..	..	..	9½	..
Iowa	8	..	..	8	..	..	..	..	..	..	..
Kansas	3	..	..	2	..	..	..	..	..	½	½
Kentucky	11	..	..	11	..	..	..	..	..	..	..
Louisiana	7	..	7	..	..	..	..	..	..	..	..
Maine	7	..	4½	1½	..	..	..	..	..	1	..
Maryland	7	..	..	6½	..	..	..	..	..	½	..
Massachusetts	12	..	11	1	..	..	..	..	..	..	..
Michigan	8	..	..	..	..	..	..	..	..	8	..
Minnesota	4	..	..	4	..	..	..	..	..	..	..
Mississippi	7	..	..	7	..	..	..	..	..	..	..
Missouri	10½	..	½	4	..	..	..	1	..	5	..
Nebraska	3	..	..	3	..	..	..	..	..	..	..
Nevada	3	..	..	3	..	..	..	..	..	..	..
New Hampshire	5	..	3	1½	..	..	..	..	..	½	..
New Jersey	7	..	..	..	7	..	..	..	..	..	..
New York	33	..	..	..	..	33	..	..	..	..	..
North Carolina	9	..	9	..	..	..	..	..	..	..	..
Ohio	21	..	..	21	..	..	..	..	..	..	..
Oregon	3	..	..	3	..	..	..	..	..	..	..
Pennsylvania	26	..	..	..	..	..	26	..	..	..	..
Rhode Island	4	..	..	..	..	..	..	..	4	..	..
South Carolina	6	..	..	..	..	..	..	6	..	..	..
Tennessee	10	..	..	4½	..	..	..	5½	..	..	..
Texas	6	..	6	..	..	..	..	..	..	..	..
Vermont	5	..	..	..	..	..	..	..	..	5	..
Virginia	10	..	..	10	..	..	..	..	..	..	..
West Virginia	5	..	..	5	..	..	..	..	..	..	..
Wisconsin	8	..	..	..	..	..	..	..	8	..	..
Total	316½	6	42½	137½	7	33	26	12½	12	39½	½

NATIONAL DEMOCRATIC CONVENTION.

Mr. TILDEN, of New York. — Mr. President, by the rule adopted by the New York delegation, the chairman is instructed to convene a meeting upon the requisition of any five members. I have received such a requisition, and I respectfully ask of the Convention leave to retire for the purpose of consultation.

The PRESIDENT *pro tem*, GEN. THOMAS L. PRICE. — If there be no objection, the delegation from New York will have leave to retire.

Mr. FINCH. — I object.

The question was put upon allowing the New York delegation to retire for consultation, and it was agreed to.

The President *pro tem.* put the question upon proceeding immediately to another ballot, and it was agreed to.

Mr. CLYMER moved that the Convention take a recess of fifteen minutes, which was agreed to.

The Convention accordingly took a recess of fifteen minutes.

Eighth Ballot.

The Convention proceeded to the eighth ballot for a candidate for President, and the Secretary called the roll of States, as follows, —

Alabama. — Seven for Pendleton.
Arkansas. — Five for Hendricks.
California. — Three and a half for Pendleton and one and a half for Hancock.
Connecticut. — Six for English.
Delaware. — Three for Pendleton.
Florida. — Three for Hendricks.
Georgia. — Nine for Pendleton.
Illinois. — Sixteen for Pendleton.
Indiana. — Nine and a half for Hendricks, and three and a half for Pendleton.

Mr. REEVES. — Mr. Chairman, as one of the delegation from Indiana, I have twice announced that I will withhold my vote; but it has been announced both times. It should be nine votes for Hendricks and two and a half for Pendleton.

Mr. FITCH, Chairman of the Delegation. — My friend is mistaken. I announced his vote for George H. Pendleton.

Mr. REEVES. — It must not be counted for anybody.

Mr. FITCH. — Leave the record as it is.

Mr. REEVES. — Does the chairman of the delegation insist upon my casting my vote against my will.

The PRESIDENT *pro tem.* — By the order of the Convention, each chairman is allowed to cast the vote of the delegation.

Mr. REEVES. — Well, sir, Mr. Fitch, nor no other man, can cast my vote.

Iowa. — Eight for Pendleton.
Kansas. — Two for Pendleton, one-half for Hendricks, and one-half for Frank P. Blair.
Kentucky. — Eleven for Pendleton.
Louisiana. — Seven for Pendleton.

Maine. — Four and a half for Hancock, one and a half for Pendleton, and one for Hendricks.

Maryland. — Six for Pendleton, and one for Hendricks.

Massachusetts. — Eleven for Hancock, and one for Pendleton.

Michigan. — Eight for Hendricks.

Minnesota. — Four for Pendleton.

Mississippi. — Seven for Pendleton.

Missouri. — Five for Pendleton, five for Hendricks, one-half for Hancock, and one-half for Andrew Johnson.

Nebraska. — Three for Pendleton.

Nevada. — Three for Pendleton. (Cheers.)

New Hampshire. — One-half vote for Hendricks, one and a half for Pendleton, three for Hancock. (Applause.)

New Jersey. — Seven for Parker.

New York — had not returned when her name was reached, and was passed temporarily.

North Carolina. — Four and a half for Pendleton, three and a half for Hendricks, and one for Hancock.

Ohio. — Gen. McCook: Twenty-one for Pendleton. It is hardly worth while to call her. (Laughter and cheers.)

Oregon. — Three for Pendleton. (Applause.)

Pennsylvania. — Pennsylvania, not being ready when her name was called, was temporarily passed.

Rhode Island. — Four for Doolittle.

North Carolina. — Six for Pendleton.

Tennessee. — Five and a half for Johnson, and four and a half for Pendleton. (Applause.)

Texas. — Six for Pendleton. (Applause.)

Vermont. — Five for Hendricks. (Great applause.)

Virginia. — Nine and a half votes for Pendleton, one-half vote for Hancock.

West Virginia. — Five for Pendleton. (Great applause.)

Wisconsin. — Eight for Doolittle.

New York. — Mr. TILDEN: Mr. President, I am instructed by the unanimous vote of the New York delegation, and with the concurrence and approval of Sanford E. Church (whom it is but justice to say the delegation from New York would have preferred if within their power to make the nominee) —

Gen. McCook. — I call the gentleman to order.

Cries of "Order!" "Go on!" and "Vote!"

Mr. TILDEN. — New York casts her thirty-three votes for Thomas A. Hendricks. (Continued cheering and applause.)

NATIONAL DEMOCRATIC CONVENTION.

The Secretary announced the vote on the eighth ballot, as follows, —

The whole number of votes cast	317
James E. English	6
W. S. Hancock	28
George H. Pendleton	156½
Joel Parker	7
Sanford E. Church	—
Asa Packer	26
Andrew Johnson	6
James R. Doolittle	12
Thomas A. Hendricks	75
Frank P. Blair	½

EIGHTH BALLOT — RECAPITULATION.

STATES.	WHOLE NO.	ENGLISH.	HANCOCK.	PENDLETON.	PARKER.	CHURCH.	PACKER.	A. JOHNSON.	DOOLITTLE.	HENDRICKS.	BLAIR.
Alabama	8	..	..	8	..	..	..	..	..	..	..
Arkansas	5	..	..	..	..	..	..	..	..	5	..
California	5	..	1½	3½	..	..	..	..	..	..	..
Connecticut	6	6	..	..	..	..	..	..	..	..	..
Delaware	3	..	..	3	..	..	..	..	..	..	..
Florida	3	..	..	..	..	..	..	..	..	3	..
Georgia	9	..	..	9	..	..	..	..	..	..	..
Illinois	16	..	..	16	..	..	..	..	..	..	..
Indiana	13	..	..	3½	..	..	..	..	..	9½	..
Iowa	8	..	..	8	..	..	..	..	..	..	..
Kansas	3	..	..	2	..	..	..	..	..	½	½
Kentucky	11	..	..	11	..	..	..	..	..	..	..
Louisiana	7	..	..	7	..	..	..	..	..	..	..
Maine	7	..	4½	1½	..	..	..	..	..	1	..
Maryland	7	..	..	6	..	..	..	..	..	1	..
Massachusetts	12	..	11	1	..	..	..	..	..	..	..
Michigan	8	..	..	..	..	..	..	..	..	8	..
Minnesota	4	..	..	4	..	..	..	..	..	..	..
Mississippi	7	..	..	7	..	..	..	..	..	..	..
Missouri	11	..	½	5	..	..	..	½	..	5	..
Nebraska	3	..	..	3	..	..	..	..	..	..	..
Nevada	3	..	..	3	..	..	..	..	..	..	..
New Hampshire	5	..	3	1½	..	..	..	..	..	½	..
New Jersey	7	..	..	..	7	..	..	..	..	..	..
New York	33	..	..	..	..	..	..	..	..	33	..
North Carolina	9	..	1	4½	..	..	..	..	..	3½	..
Ohio	21	..	..	21	..	..	..	..	..	..	..
Oregon	3	..	..	3	..	..	..	..	..	..	..
Pennsylvania	26	..	..	..	..	..	26	..	..	..	..
Rhode Island	4	..	..	..	..	..	..	..	4	..	..
South Carolina	6	..	..	6	..	..	..	..	..	..	..
Tennessee	10	..	..	4½	..	..	..	5½	..	..	..
Texas	6	..	6	..	..	..	..	..	..	..	..
Vermont	5	..	..	..	..	..	..	..	..	5	..
Virginia	10	..	½	9½	..	..	..	..	..	..	..
West Virginia	5	..	..	5	..	..	..	..	..	..	..
Wisconsin	8	..	..	..	..	..	..	..	8	..	..
Total	317	6	28	156½	7	..	26	6	12	75	½

A Delegate from Pennsylvania. — I move that the Convention take a recess for fifteen minutes.

The motion was lost.

Ninth Ballot.

The Secretary called the roll of States on the ninth ballot, with the following result, —

Alabama. — Eight for Pendleton.
Arkansas. — Five for Hendricks.
California. — Three and a half for Pendleton, one and a half for Hancock.
Connecticut. — Six for English.
Delaware. — Three for Pendleton.
Florida. — Three for Hendricks.
Georgia. — Nine for Pendleton.
Illinois. — Sixteen for Pendleton.
Indiana. — Nine and a half for Hendricks, three for Pendleton, and one-half declining,
Iowa. — Eight for Pendleton.
Kansas. — Two for Pendleton, one-half for Hendricks, one-half for Blair.
Kentucky. — Eleven for Pendleton.
Illinois. — Seven for Pendleton.
Maine. — Four and a half for Hancock, one and a half for Pendleton, one for Hendricks.
Maryland. — Four and a half for Pendleton, two and a half for Hendricks.
Massachusetts. — Eleven for Hancock, and one for Pendleton.
Michigan. — Eight for Hendricks. (Applause.)
Minnesota. — Four for Pendleton.
Mississippi. — Seven for Pendleton.
Missouri. — Four for Pendleton, six for Hendricks, and one for Hancock.
Nebraska. — Three for Pendleton.
Nevada. — Three for Pendleton.
New Hampshire. — One-half for Hendricks, one and a half for Pendleton, and three for Hancock.
New Jersey. — Seven for Parker.
New York. — Thirty-three for Hendricks.
North Carolina. — Six and a half for Hendricks, one for Hancock, one for Pendleton, and one-half for Packer.
Ohio. — Twenty-one for Pendleton.
Oregon. — Three for Pendleton.
Pennsylvania. — Twenty-six for Packer.
Rhode Island. — Four for Doolittle.
South Carolina. — Six for Hancock. (Applause.)
Tennessee. — Five and a half for Johnson, and four and a half for Pendleton.
Texas. — Six for Hancock. (Applause.)
Vermont. — Five for Hendricks. (Applause.)
Virginia. — Nine and a half for Pendleton, and one-half vote for Hancock.
West Virginia. — Five for Pendleton.
Wisconsin. — Eight for Doolittle.

NATIONAL DEMOCRATIC CONVENTION.   113

The Secretary announced the vote on the ninth ballot, as follows, —

The whole number of votes cast	316½
James E. English	6
W. S. Hancock	34½
George H. Pendleton	144
Joel Parker	7
Sanford E. Church	—
Asa Packer	26½
Andrew Johnson	5½
James R. Doolittle	12
Thomas A. Hendricks	80½
Frank P. Blair	½

NINTH BALLOT—RECAPITULATION.

STATES.	WHOLE NO.	ENGLISH.	HANCOCK.	PENDLETON.	PARKER.	CHURCH.	PACKER.	A. JOHNSON.	DOOLITTLE.	HENDRICKS.	BLAIR.	R. JOHNSON.	T. EWING, Jr.	ADAMS.
Alabama	8			8										
Arkansas	5									5				
California	5		1½	3½										
Connecticut	6	6												
Delaware	3			3										
Florida	3									3				
Georgia	9			9										
Illinois	16			16										
Indiana*	13			3						9½				
Iowa	8			8										
Kansas	3			2						½	½			
Kentucky	11			11										
Louisiana	7		4½	1½						1				
Maine	7			7										
Maryland	7			4½						2½				
Massachusetts	12		11	1										
Michigan	8									8				
Minnesota	4			4										
Mississippi	7			7										
Missouri	11		1	4						6				
Nebraska	3			3										
Nevada	3			3										
New Hampshire	5		3	1½						½				
New Jersey	7				7									
New York	33									33				
North Carolina	9		1	1			½			6½				
Ohio	21			21										
Oregon	3			3										
Pennsylvania	26						26							
Rhode Island	4								4					
South Carolina	6		6											
Tennessee	10			4½				5½						
Texas	6		6											
Vermont	5									5				
Virginia	10		½	9½										
West Virginia	5			5										
Wisconsin	8								8					
Total	317	6	34½	144	7		26½	5½	12	80½	½			

* ½ not voting.

Tenth Ballot.

The SECRETARY. — The Convention will now proceed with the tenth ballot.

Alabama. — Eight for Pendleton.

Arkansas. — Five for Hendricks.

California. — One and a half for Hancock; three and a half for Pendleton.

Connecticut. — The chairman of the delegation, Mr. Eaton, announced the vote of the State as follows: Mr. Pendleton, three votes; Mr. English, three votes.

Mr. HOVEY, of Connecticut. — I rise to a point of order. Connecticut, if I understand it, casts six votes for James E. English.

Mr. EATON — I have the honor of being chairman of the Connecticut delegation. I did not suppose, sir, that there was a member of that delegation who would question my integrity.

The PRESIDENT. — The gentlemen will come to order. Delegations must settle their own questions outside of this Convention. (Loud cheers.)

Mr. EATON. — Mr. Chairman, when one of the delegates from my State rises here and charges me with a dishonorable act, I propose to vindicate my character.

The PRESIDENT. — The gentleman will come to order. The vote of each State will be received through its chairman.

Mr. KENDRICK, of Connecticut. — I wish to inquire in what way we can have this thing rectified.

The PRESIDENT. — The State of Connecticut will be passed for the moment until the delegation can settle this matter among themselves. The Secretary will call the next State.

Delaware. — Three for Pendleton.

Florida. — Three for Hendricks.

Georgia. — Eight for Pendleton, and one for Hendricks.

Illinois. — Sixteen for Pendleton.

Indiana. — Three for Pendleton, a half for Packer, nine and a half for Hendricks.

Iowa. — Eight for Pendleton. (Applause.)

Kansas. — Two for Pendleton, one-half for Hendricks, one-half for Blair.

Kentucky. — Eleven for Pendleton.

Louisiana. — Seven for Pendleton.

Maine. — Four and a half for Hancock, one and a half for Pendleton, one for Hendricks.

Maryland. — Four and a half for Pendleton, two and a half for Hendricks.

Massachusetts. — Eleven for Hancock, one for Pendleton.

Michigan. — Eight for Hendricks.

Minnesota. — Four for Pendleton.

Mississippi. — Seven for Pendleton.

Missouri. — One and a half for Hancock, four for Pendleton, one-half for Johnson, five for Hendricks.

Nebraska. — Three for Pendleton.

Nevada. — Three for Pendleton.

New Hampshire. — Three for Hancock, one and a half for Pendleton, and a half for Hendricks.

New Jersey. — Seven for Parker.

New York. — Thirty-three for Hendricks. (Applause.)

North Carolina. — Five and a half for Hendricks, two and a half for Pendleton, and one for Packer.

Ohio. — Twenty-one for Pendleton.

Oregon. — Three for Pendleton.

Pennsylvania. — Twenty-six for Packer.

Rhode Island. — Four for Doolittle.

South Carolina. — Six for Hancock.

Tennessee. — Five and a half for Johnson, and four and a half for Pendleton.

Texas. — Six for Hancock.

Vermont. — Five for Hendricks.

Virginia. — Nine and a half for Pendleton, and one-half for Hancock.

West Virginia. — Five for Pendleton.

Wisconsin. — Eight for Doolittle.

Connecticut. — Three for Pendleton, and three for Hendricks.

Mr. REEVES, of Indiana. — My vote by register of the Clerk was put down to Mr. Packer. The chairman of the delegation announced one-half not voting.

Mr. FITCH, Chairman of the Indiana Delegation. — The gentleman is correct. I announced one-half not voting.

The Secretary announced the result, as follows, —

Total number of votes cast	317
W. S. Hancock	34
George H. Pendleton	147½
Joel Parker	7
Asa Packer	27½
Andrew Johnson	6
James R. Doolittle	12
Thomas A. Hendricks	82½
Frank P. Blair	½

TENTH BALLOT—RECAPITULATION.

STATES.	WHOLE NO.	HANCOCK.	PENDLETON.	PARKER.	PACKER.	A. JOHNSON.	DOOLITTLE.	HENDRICKS.	BLAIR.
Alabama	8	..	8	..	..	..	..	..	..
Arkansas	5	..	..	..	..	..	..	5	..
California	5	1½	3½	..	..	..	..	..	..
Connecticut	6	..	3	..	..	..	..	3	..
Delaware	3	..	3	..	..	..	..	..	..
Florida	3	..	..	..	..	..	..	3	..
Georgia	9	..	8	..	..	..	..	1	..
Illinois	16	..	16	..	..	..	..	..	..
Indiana	13	..	3	..	..	½	..	9½	..
Iowa	8	..	8	..	..	..	..	..	..
Kansas	3	..	2	..	..	..	..	½	½
Kentucky	11	..	11	..	..	..	..	..	..
Louisiana	7	..	7	..	..	..	..	..	..
Maine	7	4½	1½	..	..	..	..	1	..
Maryland	7	..	4½	..	..	..	..	2½	..
Massachusetts	12	11	1	..	..	..	..	..	..
Michigan	8	..	..	..	..	..	..	8	..
Minnesota	4	..	4	..	..	..	..	..	..
Mississippi	7	..	7	..	..	..	..	..	..
Missouri	11	1½	4	..	..	½	..	5	..
Nebraska	3	..	3	..	..	..	..	..	..
Nevada	3	..	3	..	..	..	..	..	..
New Hampshire	5	3	1½	..	..	..	..	½	..
New Jersey	7	..	..	7	..	..	..	..	..
New York	33	..	..	..	..	..	..	33	..
North Carolina	9	..	2½	..	..	1	..	5½	..
Ohio	21	..	21	..	..	..	..	..	..
Oregon	3	..	3	..	..	..	..	..	..
Pennsylvania	26	..	..	..	26	..	..	..	..
Rhode Island	4	..	..	..	..	..	4	..	..
South Carolina	6	6	..	..	..	..	..	..	..
Tennessee	10	..	4½	..	..	5½	..	..	..
Texas	6	6	..	..	..	..	..	..	..
Vermont	5	..	..	..	..	..	..	5	..
Virginia	10	½	9½	..	..	..	..	..	..
West Virginia	5	..	5	..	..	..	..	..	..
Wisconsin	8	..	..	..	..	..	8	..	..
Total	317	34	147½	7	27½	6	12	82½	½

NATIONAL DEMOCRATIC CONVENTION. 117

Eleventh Ballot.

The Secretary called the roll of the States as follows, —

Alabama. — Eight for Pendleton.
Arkansas. — Five for Hendricks.
California. — Three for Pendleton, one for Hendricks, eleven for Hancock.
Connecticut. — Three for Pendleton, three for Hendricks.
Delaware. — Three for Pendleton.
Florida. — Three for Hendricks.
Georgia. — Eight for Pendleton, one for Hendricks.
Illinois. — Sixteen for Pendleton.
Indiana. — Nine and a half for Hendricks, three for Pendleton.
Iowa. — Eight for Pendleton.
Kansas. — Two for Pendleton, two and a half for Hendricks, and one-half for Blair.
Kentucky. — Eleven for Pendleton.
Louisiana. — Seven for Pendleton.
Maine. — Four and a half for Hancock, one and a half for Pendleton, one for Hendricks.
Maryland. — Four and a half for Pendleton, two and a half for Hendricks.
Massachusetts. — Eleven for Hancock, one for Pendleton.
Michigan. — Eight for Hendricks.
Minnesota. — Four for Pendleton.
Mississippi. — Seven for Pendleton.
Missouri. — Four for Pendleton, six for Hendricks, and one for Hancock.
Nebraska. — Three for Pendleton.
Nevada. — Three for Pendleton.
New Hampshire. — One-half for Hendricks, one-half for Doolittle, one and a half for Pendleton, and two and a half for Hancock.
New Jersey. — Seven for Parker.
New York. — Mr. MULLIN: thirty-three for Thomas A. Hendricks. (Great applause.)
North Carolina. — Nine for Hendricks. (Great applause.)
Ohio. — Twenty-one for Pendleton.
Oregon. — Three for the "Young Greenback of the West," Geo. H. Pendleton. (Cheers and laughter.)
Pennsylvania. — Twenty-six for Packer.
Rhode Island. — Four for Doolittle. (Applause.)
South Carolina. — Six for Hancock.
Tennessee. — Five and a half for Johnson, four and a half for Pendleton.
Texas. — Six for Hendricks.
Vermont. — Five for Hendricks. (Applause.)
Virginia. — Nine and a half for Pendleton, one and a half for Hancock.
West Virginia. — Five for Pendleton.
Wisconsin. — Eight for Doolittle.

The Secretary announced the result, as follows, —

Total number of votes cast	316½
W. S. Hancock	32½
George H. Pendleton	144½
Joel Parker	7
Asa Packer	26
Andrew Johnson	5½
James R. Doolittle	12½
Thomas A. Hendricks	88
Frank P. Blair	½

ELEVENTH BALLOT — RECAPITULATION.

STATES.	WHOLE NO.	HANCOCK.	PENDLETON.	PARKER.	PACKER.	A. JOHNSON.	DOOLITTLE.	HENDRICKS.	BLAIR.
Alabama	8	..	8	..	..	..	..	..	..
Arkansas	5	..	..	..	..	..	..	5	..
California	5	1	3	..	..	..	..	1	..
Connecticut	6	..	3	..	..	..	..	3	..
Delaware	3	..	3	..	..	..	..	..	..
Florida	3	..	..	..	..	..	..	3	..
Georgia	9	..	8	..	..	..	..	1	..
Illinois	16	..	16	..	..	..	..	..	..
Indiana*	13	..	3	..	..	..	..	9½	..
Iowa	8	..	8	..	..	..	..	..	..
Kansas	3	..	2	..	..	..	..	½	½
Kentucky	11	..	11	..	..	..	..	..	..
Louisiana	7	..	7	..	..	..	..	..	..
Maine	7	4½	1½	..	..	..	..	1	..
Maryland	7	..	4½	..	..	..	..	2½	..
Massachusetts	12	11	1	..	..	..	..	..	..
Michigan	8	..	..	..	..	..	..	8	..
Minnesota	4	..	4	..	..	..	..	..	..
Mississippi	7	..	7	..	..	..	..	..	..
Missouri	11	1	4	..	..	..	..	6	..
Nebraska	3	..	3	..	..	..	..	..	..
Nevada	3	..	3	..	..	..	..	..	..
New Hampshire	5	2½	1½	..	..	..	½	½	..
New Jersey	7	..	..	7	..	..	..	..	..
New York	33	..	..	..	..	..	..	33	..
North Carolina	9	..	..	..	..	..	..	9	..
Ohio	21	..	21	..	..	..	..	..	..
Oregon	3	..	3	..	..	..	..	..	..
Pennsylvania	26	..	..	..	26	..	..	..	..
Rhode Island	4	..	..	..	..	..	4	..	..
South Carolina	6	6	..	..	..	..	..	..	..
Tennessee	10	..	4½	..	..	5½	..	..	..
Texas	6	6	..	..	..	..	..	..	..
Vermont	5	..	..	..	..	..	..	5	..
Virginia	10	½	9½	..	..	..	..	..	..
West Virginia	5	..	5	..	..	..	..	..	..
Wisconsin	8	..	..	..	..	..	8	..	..
Total	317	32½	144½	7	26	5½	12½	88	½

* ½ not voting.

Twelfth Ballot.

The Secretary then called the roll of States on the twelfth ballot, as follows, —

Alabama. — Eight for Pendleton.
Arkansas. — Five for Hendricks.
California. — One and a half for Hendricks, and one-half for Chase.

At the announcement of the half vote for Salmon P. Chase, prolonged cheering rose from the galleries and hall. As it began to subside, several hisses were heard, which immediately caused a more enthusiastic renewal of the applause, which continued for several minutes.

Mr. LITTLETON COOKE, of Kentucky, moved that the galleries be cleared.

A DELEGATE, from Wisconsin. — Mr. President, the galleries are filled with people, some of whom have come two thousand miles to witness the proceedings of the Convention. They are good Democrats, and they have a right to applaud when they please. (Great cheering in the galleries, and to some extent on the floor.) We depend on these people to elect our ticket, and they have a right to cheer for any one. (Cheers.)

Mr. CLARK, of Massachusetts. — Mr. President, as a member of the Massachusetts delegation, I must coincide with the gentleman who has just spoken. Those men in the galleries have come, some of them, a great distance to witness our deliberations.

The PRESIDENT *pro. tem.* — The Chair will state that every effort will be made by the ushers and the marshals to preserve order. The Chair has no power to suppress cheers, only hissing and bad conduct. The Chair would suggest to the lobby both below and above, that they endeavor to suppress these demonstrations when the votes are given. I make it as an earnest request.

Order being restored, the Secretary stated that, in addition to the vote of California already announced, that State gave three votes for Pendleton. (Cheers).

The call of the roll then proceeded.

Connecticut. — Three for Pendleton, three for Hendricks.
Delaware. — Three for Pendleton.
Florida. — Three for Hendricks.
Georgia. — Nine for Pendleton.
Illinois. — Sixteen for Pendleton.
Indiana. — Nine and a half votes for Hendricks, three for Pendleton, one-half declining.
Iowa. — Eight for Pendleton.
Kansas. — Two for Pendleton, one-half for Hendricks, one-half for Blair.
Kentucky. — Eleven for Pendleton.
Louisiana. — Seven votes for Pendleton.
Maine. — Four and a half for Hancock, one and a half for Pendleton, and one for Hendricks.

Maryland. — Four and a half for Pendleton, two and a half for Hendricks
Massachusetts. — Eleven for Hancock, and one for Pendleton.
Michigan. — Eight for Hendricks.
Minnesota. — Four for Pendleton.
Mississippi. — Seven for Pendleton.
Missouri. — Four for Pendleton, seven for Hendricks.
Nebraska. — Three for Pendleton.
Nevada. — Three for Pendleton.
New Hampshire. — One-half for Doolittle, one for Hendricks, one and a half for Pendleton; and two for Hancock.
New Jersey. — Seven for Parker.
New York. — Thirty-three for Hendricks.
North Carolina. — Nine for Hendricks.
Ohio. — Twenty-one for Pendleton.
Oregon. — Three for Pendleton.
Pennsylvania. — Twenty-six for Packer.
Rhode Island. — Four for Hancock.
South Carolina. — Six for Hancock.
Tennessee. — Four and a half for Johnson, four and a half for Pendleton, and one for McClellan. (Cheers and great applause.)
Texas. — Six for Hancock.
Vermont. — Five for Hendricks.
Virginia. — Nine and a half for Pendleton, and one-half for Hancock.
West Virginia. — Five for Pendleton,
Wisconsin. — Eight for Doolittle.

Mr. WOODWARD, of Pennsylvania. — The Pennsylvania delegation ask leave to retire.

There being no objection, leave was granted.

NATIONAL DEMOCRATIC CONVENTION.

The Secretary announced the result of the vote, as follows, —

The whole number of votes cast	316½
W. S. Hancock	30
George H. Pendleton	145½
Joel Parker	7
Asa Packer	26
Andrew Johnson	4½
James R. Doolittle	12½
Thomas A. Hendricks	89
Frank P. Blair	½
S. P. Chase	½
G. B. McClellan	1

TWELFTH BALLOT — RECAPITULATION.

STATES.	WHOLE NO.	HANCOCK.	PENDLETON.	PARKER.	PACKER.	A. JOHNSON.	DOOLITTLE.	HENDRICKS.	BLAIR.	CHASE.	McCLELLAN.
Alabama	8	..	8	..	..	..	..	..	..	..	..
Arkansas	5	..	..	..	..	..	..	5	..	..	..
California	5	..	3	..	..	..	..	1½	..	½	..
Connecticut	6	..	3	..	..	..	..	3	..	..	..
Delaware	3	..	3	..	..	..	..	..	..	..	..
Florida	3	..	..	..	..	..	..	3	..	..	..
Georgia	9	..	9	..	..	..	..	..	..	..	..
Illinois	16	..	16	..	..	..	..	..	..	..	..
Indiana*	13	..	3	..	..	..	..	9½	..	..	..
Iowa	8	..	8	..	..	..	..	..	..	..	..
Kansas	3	..	2	..	..	..	..	½	½	..	..
Kentucky	11	..	11	..	..	..	..	..	..	..	..
Louisiana	7	..	7	..	..	..	..	..	..	..	..
Maine	7	4½	1½	..	..	..	..	1	..	..	..
Maryland	7	..	4½	..	..	..	..	2½	..	..	..
Massachusetts	12	11	1	..	..	..	..	..	..	..	..
Michigan	8	..	..	..	..	..	..	8	..	..	..
Minnesota	4	..	4	..	..	..	..	..	..	..	..
Mississippi	7	..	7	..	..	..	..	..	..	..	..
Missouri	11	..	4	..	..	..	..	7	..	..	..
Nebraska	3	..	3	..	..	..	..	..	..	..	..
Nevada	3	..	3	..	..	..	..	..	..	..	..
New Hampshire	5	2	1½	..	..	..	½	1	..	..	..
New Jersey	7	..	..	7	..	..	..	..	..	..	..
New York	33	..	..	..	..	..	..	33	..	..	..
North Carolina	9	..	..	..	..	..	..	9	..	..	..
Ohio	21	..	21	..	..	..	..	..	..	..	..
Oregon	3	..	3	..	..	..	..	..	..	..	..
Pennsylvania	26	..	..	..	26	..	..	..	..	..	..
Rhode Island	4	..	..	..	..	..	4	..	..	..	..
South Carolina	6	6	..	..	..	..	..	..	..	..	..
Tennessee	10	..	4½	..	..	4½	..	..	..	..	1
Texas	6	6	..	..	..	..	..	..	..	..	..
Vermont	5	..	..	..	..	..	..	5	..	..	..
Virginia	10	½	9½	..	..	..	..	..	..	..	..
West Virginia	5	..	5	..	..	..	..	..	..	..	..
Wisconsin	8	..	..	..	..	..	8	..	..	..	..
Total	317	30	145½	7	26	4½	12½	89	½	½	1

* ½ not voting.

Mr. WHITE, of Maryland. — I move that the Convention take a recess for fifteen minutes for consultation.

Mr. VALLANDIGHAM. — I move to amend by making the recess thirty minutes.

The amendment was carried, and the Convention took a recess of thirty minutes.

During the recess the audience in the gallery recognized the Hon. D. W. Voorhies on the floor, and began calling for him.

Mr. VOORHIES appeared on the platform, and was greeted with loud cheers. He said, —

Gentlemen of the Convention, it would be so manifestly improper at this time to indulge in any remarks to you, that I only appear before you to bow my acknowledgments in return for the compliment of your call.

Cries of "Good! good!" from delegates, and cheers.

Thirteenth Ballot.

After the recess, the Convention proceeded to vote on the thirteenth ballot, with the following result, —

Alabama. — Eight for Pendleton.
Arkansas. — Five for Hendricks.
California. — The Chairman of the Delegation: Pass California for the present.
Connecticut. — The Chairman of the Delegation: Pass Connecticut.
Delaware. — Three for Pendleton.
Florida. — Three for Hendricks.
Georgia. — The Chairman of the Delegation: Pass Georgia for the present.
Illinois. — Sixteen for Pendleton.
Indiana. — Nine and a half for Hendricks, and three for Pendleton.
Iowa. — Eight for Pendleton.
Kansas. — Two votes for Pendleton, one-half vote for Hendricks, and one-half vote for Blair.
Kentucky. — Eleven for Pendleton.
Louisiana. — Seven for Pendleton.
Maine. — Four and a half for Hancock, one and a half for Pendleton, and one for Hendricks.
Maryland. — Four and a half for Pendleton, and two and a half for Hendricks.
Massachusetts. — Eleven for Hancock, and one for Pendleton.
Michigan. — Eight votes for Hendricks.
Minnesota. — Four votes for Pendleton.
Mississippi. — Seven votes for Pendleton.
Missouri. — The Chairman of the Delegation: Pass Missouri.
Nebraska. — Three for Pendleton.
Nevada. — Three for Pendleton.
New Hampshire. — There being no response to the call, New Hampshire was passed.
New Jersey. — Seven for Parker.

New York. — Thirty-three for Hendricks.
North Carolina. — Nine for Hancock.
Ohio. — Twenty-one for Pendleton.
Oregon. — Three for Pendleton.
Pennsylvania. — Twenty-six for Packer.
Rhode Island. — Four for Doolittle.
South Carolina. — Six for Hancock.
Tennessee. — Four and a half for Johnson, four and a half for Pendleton, and one for Franklin Pierce.
Texas. — Six for Hancock.
Vermont. — Five for Hendricks.
Virginia. — Ten for Hancock. (Applause.)
West Virginia. — Four for Pendleton, and one for Hendricks. (Applause.)
Wisconsin. — Eight for Doolittle.
California. — One-half for Chase, three for Pendleton, one and a half for Hendricks. (Applause.)
Connecticut. Three for Pendleton, three for Hendricks.
Georgia. — Seven and a half for Pendleton, one and a half for Hendricks.
Missouri. — Five for Pendleton, six for Hendricks.
New Hampshire. — One-half for Hendricks, one for Doolittle, one and a half for Pendleton, two for Hancock.

The Secretary announced the result of the vote, as follows, —

The whole number of votes cast.......................... 316½
W. S. Hancock... 48½
George H. Pendleton..................................... 134½
Joel Parker... 7
Asa Packer.. 26
Andrew Johnson.. 4½
James R. Doolittle...................................... 13
Thomas A. Hendricks..................................... 81
Frank P. Blair.. ½
S. P. Chase... ½
Franklin Pierce... 1

THIRTEENTH BALLOT—RECAPITULATION.

STATES.	WHOLE NO.	HANCOCK.	PENDLETON.	PARKER.	PACKER.	A. JOHNSON.	DOOLITTLE.	HENDRICKS.	BLAIR.	CHASE.	F. PIERCE.
Alabama................	8	..	8	..	..	..	..	..	..	..	..
Arkansas...............	5	..	..	..	..	..	..	5	..	..	..
California.............	5	..	3	..	..	..	..	1½	..	½	..
Connecticut............	6	..	3	..	..	..	..	3	..	..	..
Delaware...............	3	..	3	..	..	..	..	..	..	..	..
Florida................	3	..	..	..	..	..	..	3	..	..	..
Georgia................	9	..	7½	..	..	..	..	1½	..	..	..
Illinois...............	16	..	16	..	..	..	..	..	..	..	..
Indiana*...............	13	..	3	..	..	..	..	9½	..	..	..
Iowa...................	8	..	8	..	..	..	..	..	..	..	..
Kansas.................	3	..	2	..	..	..	..	½	½	..	..
Kentucky...............	11	..	11	..	..	..	..	..	..	..	..
Louisiana..............	7	..	7	..	..	..	..	..	..	..	..
Maine..................	7	4½	1½	..	..	..	..	1	..	..	..
Maryland...............	7	..	4½	..	..	..	..	2½	..	..	..
Massachusetts..........	12	11	1	..	..	..	..	..	..	..	..
Michigan...............	8	..	..	..	..	..	..	8	..	..	..
Minnesota..............	4	..	4	..	..	..	..	..	..	..	..
Mississippi............	7	..	7	..	..	..	..	..	..	..	..
Missouri...............	11	..	5	..	..	..	..	6	..	..	..
Nebraska...............	3	..	3	..	..	..	..	..	..	..	..
Nevada.................	3	..	3	..	..	..	..	..	..	..	..
New Hampshire..........	5	2	1½	..	..	..	1	½	..	..	..
New Jersey.............	7	..	..	7	..	..	..	..	..	..	..
New York...............	33	..	..	..	..	..	..	33	..	..	..
North Carolina.........	9	9	..	..	..	..	..	..	..	..	..
Ohio...................	21	..	21	..	..	..	..	..	..	..	..
Oregon.................	3	..	3	..	..	..	..	..	..	..	..
Pennsylvania...........	26	..	..	..	26	..	..	..	..	..	..
Rhode Island...........	4	..	..	..	..	..	4	..	..	..	..
South Carolina.........	6	6	..	..	..	..	..	..	..	..	..
Tennessee..............	10	..	4½	..	..	4½	..	..	..	..	1
Texas..................	6	6	..	..	..	..	..	..	..	..	..
Vermont................	5	..	..	..	..	..	..	5	..	..	..
Virginia...............	10	10	..	..	..	..	..	..	..	..	..
West Virginia..........	5	..	4	..	..	..	..	1	..	..	..
Wisconsin..............	8	..	..	..	..	..	8	..	..	..	..
Total..................	317	48½	134½	7	26	4½	13	81	½	½	1

* ½ not voting.

NATIONAL DEMOCRATIC CONVENTION. 125

Fourteenth Ballot.

The SECRETARY.— The Convention will now proceed with the fourteenth ballot.

The roll was called as follows, —

Alabama. — Eight for Pendleton.
Arkansas. — Five for Hendricks.
California. — Four for Pendleton, one for Hendricks.
Connecticut. — Three for Pendleton, three for Hendricks.
Delaware. — Three for Pendleton.
Florida. — Three for Hendricks.
Georgia. — The Chairman of the Delegation: Pass Georgia.
Illinois. — Sixteen for Pendleton.
Indiana. — Nine and a half for Hendricks, three for Pendleton.
Iowa. — Eight for Pendleton.
Kansas. — Two and a half for Hendricks, and one-half for Pendleton.
Kentucky. — Eleven for Pendleton.
Louisiana. — Seven for Pendleton.
Maine. — Four and a half for Hancock, one and a half for Pendleton, and one for Hendricks.
Maryland. — Five for Pendleton, and two for Hendricks.
Massachusetts. — Eleven for Hancock, and one for Pendleton.
Michigan. — Eight for Hendricks.
Minnesota. — Four for Pendleton.
Mississippi. — Seven for Pendleton.
Missouri. — Four for Pendleton, five for Hendricks, and two for Hancock.
Nebraska. — The Chairman of the Delegation: Pass Nebraska.
Nevada. — Three for Pendleton.
New Hampshire. — One-half for Hendricks, one for Doolittle, one and a half for Pendleton, and two for Hancock.
New Jersey. — Seven for Parker.
New York. — Thirty-three for Hendricks.
North Carolina. — Nine for Hancock.
Ohio. — Twenty-one for Pendleton.
Oregon. — Three for Pendleton.
Pennsylvania. — Twenty-six for Packer.
Rhode Island. — Four for Doolittle.
South Carolina. — Six for Hancock.
Tennessee. — Five and a half for Hancock, and five and a half for Pendleton.
Texas. — Six for Hancock.
Vermont. — Five for Hendricks.
Virginia. — Ten for Hancock.
West Virginia. — Four for Pendleton, and one for Hendricks.
Wisconsin. — Eight for Doolittle.
Georgia. — Seven for Pendleton, and two for Hendricks.
Nebraska. — Three for Hendricks.

The Secretary announced the result, as follows,—

Total number of votes cast.......................... 316½
W. S. Hancock...................................... 56
George H. Pendleton 130
Joel Parker... 7
Asa Packer 26
James R. Doolittle 13
Thomas A. Hendricks 84½

FOURTEENTH BALLOT—RECAPITULATION.

STATES.	WHOLE NO.	HANCOCK.	PENDLETON.	PARKER.	PACKER.	DOOLITTLE.	HENDRICKS.
Alabama	8	..	8	..	..	..	..
Arkansas	5	..	..	..	..	..	5
California	5	..	4	..	..	..	1
Connecticut	6	..	3	..	..	..	3
Delaware	3	..	3	..	..	..	..
Florida	3	..	..	..	..	..	3
Georgia	9	..	7	..	..	..	2
Illinois	16	..	16	..	..	..	..
Indiana*	13	..	3	..	..	..	9½
Iowa	8	..	8	..	..	..	..
Kansas	3	..	½	..	..	..	2½
Kentucky	11	..	11	..	..	..	..
Louisiana	7	..	7	..	..	..	..
Maine	7	4½	1½	..	..	..	1
Maryland	7	..	5	..	..	..	2
Massachusetts	12	11	1	..	..	..	..
Michigan	8	..	..	..	..	..	8
Minnesota	4	..	4	..	..	..	..
Mississippi	7	..	7	..	..	..	..
Missouri	11	2	4	..	..	..	5
Nebraska	3	..	..	..	..	..	3
Nevada	3	..	3	..	..	..	..
New Hampshire	5	2	1½	..	..	1	¼
New Jersey	7	..	..	7	..	..	..
New York	33	..	..	..	..	..	33
North Carolina	9	9	..	..	..	..	..
Ohio	21	..	21	..	..	..	..
Oregon	3	..	3	..	..	..	..
Pennsylvania	26	..	..	..	26	..	..
Rhode Island	4	..	..	..	..	4	..
South Carolina	6	6	..	..	..	..	..
Tennessee	10	5½	4½	..	..	..	..
Texas	6	6	..	..	..	..	..
Vermont	5	..	..	..	..	..	5
Virginia	10	10	..	..	..	..	..
West Virginia	5	..	4	..	..	..	1
Wisconsin	8	..	..	..	..	8	..
Total	317	56	130	7	26	13	84½

* ½ not voting.

The Fifteenth Ballot.

The Secretary called the roll of States for the fifteenth ballot, with the following result, —

Alabama. — Eight for Pendleton.
Arkansas. — Five for Hendricks.
California. — Three for Pendleton, one and a half for Hendricks, one-half not voting.
Connecticut. — Three for Pendleton, three for Hancock.
Delaware. — Three for Pendleton.
Florida. — Three for Hendricks.
Georgia. — Seven for Pendleton, two for Hendricks.
Illinois. — Sixteen for Pendleton.
Indiana. — Nine and a half for Hendricks, three for Pendleton, one-half not voting.
Iowa. — Eight for Pendleton.
Kansas. — Two and a half votes for Hendricks, one-half for Pendleton.
Kentucky. — Eleven for Pendleton.
Louisiana. — Seven for Pendleton.
Maine. — Four and a half for Hancock, one and a half for Pendleton, one for Hendricks.
Maryland. — Four and a half for Pendleton.
Massachusetts. — Two and a half for Hendricks, eleven for Hancock, one for Pendleton.
Michigan. — Eight for Hendricks.
Minnesota. — Four for Pendleton.
Mississippi. — The Chairman of the Delegation: The delegation from Mississippi asks time for consultation.
The PRESIDENT. — If there is no objection it will be granted.
Missouri. — Five for Pendleton, five for Hendricks, two for Hancock.
Nebraska. — Three for Hendricks.
Nevada. — Three for Pendleton.
New Hampshire. — One-half for Hendricks, eleven and a half for Pendleton, and three for Hancock. (Applause.)
New Jersey. — Seven for Parker.
New York. — Thirty-three for Hendricks.
North Carolina. — Nine for Hancock.
Ohio. — Twenty-one for Pendleton.
Oregon. — Three for Pendleton.
Pennsylvania. — Pennsylvania was out for consultation.
Rhode Island. — Four for Doolittle.
North Carolina. — Six for Hancock. (Applause.)
Tennessee. — Five and a half for Johnson, and four and a half for Pendleton.
Texas. — Six for Hancock.
Vermont. — Five for Hendricks.
Virginia. — Ten for Hancock.
West Virginia. — Four for Pendleton, and one for Hendricks.
Wisconsin. — Eight for James R. Doolittle.
Mississippi. — Seven for Pendleton.

At this point the Pennsylvania delegation returned.

The CHAIRMAN of the Delegation.—The delegation from Pennsylvania, having supported the man of their choice in several unsuccessful ballots, have instructed their chairman to cast the twenty-six votes of the State of Pennsylvania for Gen. Winfield Scott Hancock.

Vociferous applause in the galleries.

NATIONAL DEMOCRATIC CONVENTION.

The Secretary announced the result, as follows, —

Total number of votes cast	316
W. S. Hancock	79½
George H. Pendleton	129½
Joel Parker	7
Andrew Johnson	5½
James R. Doolittle	12
Thomas A. Hendricks	82¼

FIFTEENTH BALLOT — RECAPITULATION.

STATES.	WHOLE NO.	HANCOCK.	PENDLETON.	PARKER.	A. JOHNSON.	DOOLITTLE.	HENDRICKS.
Alabama	8	..	8	..	..	..	..
Arkansas	5	..	..	..	..	..	5
California*	5	..	3	..	..	..	1¼
Connecticut	6	3	3	..	..	..	..
Delaware	3	..	3	..	..	..	..
Florida	3	..	..	..	..	..	3
Georgia	9	..	7	..	..	..	2
Illinois	16	..	16	..	..	..	..
Indiana*	13	..	3	..	..	..	9½
Iowa	8	..	8	..	..	..	..
Kansas	3	..	½	..	..	..	2½
Kentucky	11	..	11	..	..	..	..
Louisiana	7	..	7	..	..	..	..
Maine	7	4½	1½	..	..	..	1
Maryland	7	..	4½	..	..	..	2½
Massachusetts	12	11	1	..	..	..	..
Michigan	8	..	..	..	..	..	8
Minnesota	4	..	4	..	..	..	..
Mississippi	7	..	7	..	..	..	..
Missouri	11	1	5	..	..	..	5
Nebraska	3	..	..	..	..	..	3
Nevada	3	..	3	..	..	..	..
New Hampshire	5	3	1½	..	..	..	½
New Jersey	7	..	..	7	..	..	..
New York	33	..	..	..	..	..	33
North Carolina	9	9	..	..	..	..	..
Ohio	21	..	21	..	..	..	..
Oregon	3	..	3	..	..	..	..
Pennsylvania	26	26	..	..	..	..	..
Rhode Island	4	..	..	..	..	4	..
South Carolina	6	6	..	..	..	..	..
Tennessee	10	..	4½	..	5½	..	..
Texas	6	6	..	..	..	..	..
Vermont	5	..	..	..	..	..	5
Virginia	10	10	..	..	..	..	..
West Virginia	5	..	4	..	..	..	1
Wisconsin	8	..	..	..	..	8	..
Total	317	79½	129½	7	5½	12	82¼

* ¼ not voting.

Sixteenth Ballot.

The Secretary then called the roll, as follows,—

Alabama. — Eight for Pendleton.

Arkansas. — Five for Hancock.

California. — Three for Pendleton, one and a half for Hendricks; one-half not voting.

Connecticut. — Three for Pendleton, and three for Hancock.

Delaware. — Three for Pendleton.

Florida. — Two for Hendricks and one for Pendleton.

Georgia. — Two and a half for Pendleton, six and a half for Hancock.

Illinois. — The Chairman of the Delegation: Illinois casts her sixteen votes for Pendleton, and requests leave to retire for deliberation.

Permission being granted, the delegation withdrew from the hall.

Indiana. — Nine and a half for Hendricks, three and a half for Pendleton.

Iowa. — Eight for Pendleton.

Kansas. — Two for Hendricks, and one for Hancock.

Kentucky. — Eleven for Pendleton.

Louisiana. — Seven for Hancock. (Cheers.)

Maine. — Four and a half for Hancock, one and a half for Pendleton, one for Hendricks.

Maryland.—The Chairman of the Delegation: Pass Maryland for the present.

Massachusetts. — Eleven votes for Hancock, and one for Pendleton.

Michigan. — Eight for Hendricks.

Minnesota. — Four for Pendleton.

Mississippi. — Seven for Hancock. (Cheers.)

Missouri. — Five for Pendleton, three for Hendricks, and three for Hancock. (Applause.)

Nebraska. — Three for Thomas A. Hendricks.

Nevada. — Three for Pendleton.

New Hampshire. — One-half for Hendricks, one and a half for Pendleton, three for Hancock. (Applause.)

New Jersey. — The Chairman of the Delegation: New Jersey still casts her seven votes for Joel Parker. (Laughter.)

New York. — The Chairman of the Delegation: New York casts her thirty-three votes for Hendricks.

North Carolina. — Nine for Hancock.

Ohio. — Twenty-one votes for Pendleton.

Oregon. — Three for Pendleton.

Pennsylvania. — Twenty-six for Hancock. (Applause.)

Rhode Island. — Four for Doolittle.

South Carolina. — Six for Hancock.

Tennessee. — Five and a half for Johnson, four and a half for Pendleton.

Texas. — Six for Hancock.

Vermont. — Five for Hendricks.

Virginia. — Ten for Hancock.

West Virginia. — Three and a half for Pendleton, one and a half for Hendricks.

Wisconsin. — Eight for Doolittle.

Maryland. — One-half for Hendricks, one for Pendleton, five and a half for Hancock. (Cheers.)

The Secretary announced the result of the vote, as follows,—

The whole number of votes cast	316
W. S. Hancock	113½
George H. Pendleton	107½
Joel Parker	7
Asa Packer	—
Andrew Johnson	5½
James R. Doolittle	12
Thomas A. Hendricks	70½
Frank P. Blair	—
S. P. Chase	—

SIXTEENTH BALLOT—RECAPITULATION.

STATES.	WHOLE NO.	HANCOCK.	PENDLETON.	PARKER.	PACKER.	A. JOHNSON.	DOOLITTLE.	HENDRICKS.	BLAIR.	CHASE.
Alabama	8	..	8	..	..	..	..	..	..	..
Arkansas	5	5	..	..	..	..	..	..	..	..
California*	5	..	3	..	..	..	..	1½	..	..
Connecticut	6	3	3	..	..	..	..	..	..	..
Delaware	3	..	3	..	..	..	..	..	..	..
Florida	3	..	1	..	..	..	..	2	..	..
Georgia	9	6½	2½	..	..	..	..	..	..	..
Illinois	16	..	16	..	..	..	..	..	..	..
Indiana*	13	..	3	..	..	..	..	9½	..	..
Iowa	8	..	8	..	..	..	..	..	..	..
Kansas	3	1	..	..	..	..	..	2	..	..
Kentucky	11	..	11	..	..	..	..	..	..	..
Louisiana	7	7	..	..	..	..	..	..	..	..
Maine	7	4½	1½	..	..	..	..	1	..	..
Maryland	7	5¼	1	..	..	..	..	½	..	..
Massachusetts	12	11	1	..	..	..	..	..	..	..
Michigan	8	..	..	..	..	..	..	8	..	..
Minnesota	4	..	4	..	..	..	..	..	..	..
Mississippi	7	7	..	..	..	..	..	..	..	..
Missouri	11	3	5	..	..	..	..	3	..	..
Nebraska	3	..	..	..	..	..	..	3	..	..
Nevada	3	..	3	..	..	..	..	..	..	..
New Hampshire	5	3	1½	..	..	..	..	½	..	..
New Jersey	7	..	..	7	..	..	..	..	..	..
New York	33	..	..	..	..	..	..	33	..	..
North Carolina	9	9	..	..	..	..	..	..	..	..
Ohio	21	..	21	..	..	..	..	..	..	..
Oregon	3	..	3	..	..	..	..	..	..	..
Pennsylvania	26	26	..	..	..	..	..	..	..	..
Rhode Island	4	..	..	..	..	..	4	..	..	..
South Carolina	6	6	..	..	..	..	..	..	..	..
Tennessee	10	..	4½	..	..	5½	..	..	..	..
Texas	6	6	..	..	..	..	..	..	..	..
Vermont	5	..	..	..	..	..	..	5	..	..
Virginia	10	10	..	..	..	..	..	..	..	..
West Virginia	5	..	3½	..	..	..	..	1½	..	..
Wisconsin	8	..	..	..	..	..	8	..	..	..
Total	317	113½	107½	7	..	5½	12	70½	..	..

* ½ not voting.

Mr. STANTON, of Kentucky. — The delegation from Kentucky asks leave to retire for consultation.

Mr. BLANCHARD. — I move that the Convention now take a recess until five o'clock.

Cries of "No, no." Lost.

Mr. TILDEN, of New York. — The New York delegation ask leave to go out to consult.

The PRESIDENT. — As three delegations are out, it is useless to weary the Secretary with calling the roll until they return.

The SECRETARY. — By announcement of the President, the business of the Convention will now be suspended until the three delegations from Kentucky, Illinois, and New York return.

A DELEGATE. — Fix the time.

Another DELEGATE. — Make it ten minutes.

The SECRETARY. — A recess of ten minutes is called for.

Cries of "No, no."

The PRESIDENT. — The Chair will remind the delegates, who are tenacious that something should be done, to remember the Secretaries, whose duties are very onerous: a recess of ten minutes will be allowed for them to rest.

The Convention took a recess for ten minutes, after which the Secretary announced that they would proceed to vote on the

Seventeenth Ballot.

Alabama. — Eight for Hancock. (Loud Applause.)

Arkansas. — Five for Hancock. (Applause.)

California. — Three for Pendleton, one and a half for Hancock, and one-half for Chase. (Laughter and cheers.)

Connecticut. — Three for Pendleton, three for Hancock. (Applause.)

Delaware. —Three for Pendleton.

Florida. — Three for Hendricks.

Georgia. — Nine for Gen. Hancock. (Applause.)

The Secretary of the Convention said that the delegation from Illinois was out, and proceeded to the roll-call.

Indiana. — Ten for Hendricks, and three for Pendleton.

Iowa. — Eight votes for Pendleton.

Kansas. — Two for Hendricks, one for Hancock.

The Kentucky delegation being out, the ballot continued.

Louisiana. — Seven for Hancock. (Applause.)

Maine. — Four and a half for Hancock, one and a half for Pendleton, one for Hendricks.

Maryland. — Hendricks one, Hancock six. (Applause.)

Massachusetts. — Eleven for Hancock and one for Pendleton (Cheers.)

Michigan. — Eight for Hendricks.

Minnesota. — Two for Pendleton and two for Hancock. (Applause.)

Mississippi. — Seven for Hancock.

Missouri. — Missouri did not respond; the Secretary passed to the next State on the list.

Nebraska nominates John T. Hoffman.

Nebraska. — Chairman of the Delegation: I am instructed by the Nebraska delegation to cast her vote for that gallant Chief of the Tammany Democracy, John T. Hoffman, of New York. (Loud cheers.)

Nevada. — Three for Pendleton.

New Hampshire. — Five for Hancock.

New Jersey. — Seven for Parker. (Laughter.)

New York. — Thirty-three for Hendricks. (Applause.)

North Carolina. — Nine for Hancock. (Applause.)

Ohio. — Twenty-one for Pendleton.

Oregon. — Twenty-one for Pendleton. (Loud laughter.)

The SECRETARY of the Convention — The State of Oregon casts her three votes — instead of twenty-one — for Pendleton. (Laughter.)

Pennsylvania. — Twenty-six for Hancock. (Applause.)

Rhode Island. — Four for Doolittle.

South Carolina. — Six for Hancock.

Tennessee. — Five and a half for Johnson, four and a half for Pendleton.

Texas. — Six for Hancock.

Vermont. — Five for Hendricks.

Virginia. — Ten for Hancock.

West Virginia. — Three for Hancock, one for Pendleton, one for Hendricks.

Wisconsin. — Eight for Doolittle.

Illinois. — Eight and a half for Pendleton, one-half for Andrew Johnson, and seven for Hendricks.

Kentucky and Missouri. — The Secretary called the States of Kentucky and Missouri, but their delegations had not yet returned, having retired for consultation.

Mr. TILDEN, of New York. — The Convention, in prosecution of its monotonous duties, has reached a point where it is evident to all the members entrusted with this important work, that they should pause and consider.

NUMEROUS DELEGATES. — No! No!

Mr. TILDEN. — A little time is but of little moment. It is of vast moment that we act wisely and well in the position to which we have arrived. I therefore move, for the purpose of enabling the delegates to have an opportunity for consultation and reflection, that the Convention do now adjourn.

Mr. VALLANDIGHAM, of Ohio. — I second the motion to adjourn.

A DELEGATE. — What becomes of the vote which has just been taken?

The PRESIDENT. — The proposition is that the Convention adjourn when the Kentucky and Missouri delegations return and vote, and the vote is announced.

Mr. CLYMER, of Pennsylvania. — On that motion I call for a vote by States.

The PRESIDENT. — Those in favor of the motion to adjourn when the delegations from Kentucky and Missouri return, will, when their names are called, answer in the affirmative; those opposed, in the negative.

A DELEGATE. — It will require five minutes at least for the different delegations to decide how they will vote.

The PRESIDENT. — The delegates are allowed five minutes to consult with each other under the rule.

Missouri. — The Missouri delegation having returned to the hall, the chairman of the delegation voted seven for Hendricks and four for Hancock.

Kentucky. — The Kentucky delegation having returned, the chairman of the delegation voted five votes for Geo. H. Pendleton, five for Gen. Hancock, one-half for Hendricks, and one-half not voting.

The Secretary announced the result, as follows,—

Total number of votes cast	316½
W. S. Hancock	137½
George H. Pendleton	70½
Joel Parker	7
Andrew Johnson	6
James R. Doolittle	12
Thomas A. Hendricks	80
S. P. Chase	½
John T. Hoffman	3

SEVENTEENTH BALLOT — RECAPITULATION.

STATES.	WHOLE NO.	HANCOCK.	PENDLETON.	PARKER.	A. JOHNSON.	DOOLITTLE.	HENDRICKS.	CHASE.	HOFFMAN.
Alabama	8	8							
Arkansas	5	5							
California	5		3				1½	½	
Connecticut	6	3	3						
Delaware	3		3						
Florida	3						3		
Georgia	9	9							
Illinois	16		8½		½		7		
Indiana	13		3				10		
Iowa	8		8						
Kansas	3	1					2		
Kentucky*	11	5	5				½		
Louisiana	7	7							
Maine	7	4½	1½				1		
Maryland	7	6					1		
Massachusetts	12	11	1						
Michigan	8						8		
Minnesota	4	2	2						
Mississippi	7	7							
Missouri	11	4					7		
Nebraska	3								3
Nevada	3		3						
New Hampshire	5	5							
New Jersey	7			7					
New York	33						33		
North Carolina	9	9							
Ohio	21		21						
Oregon	3		3						
Pennsylvania	26	26							
Rhode Island	4					4			
South Carolina	6	6							
Tennessee	10		4½		5½				
Texas	6	6							
Vermont	5						5		
Virginia	10	10							
West Virginia	5	3	1				1		
Wisconsin	8					8			
Total	317	137½	70½	7	6	12	80	½	3

*½ not voting.

The vote was then taken by States on the motion of Mr. Tilden to adjourn, and it was lost by the following vote, —

	Yeas.	Nays.		Yeas.	Nays.
Alabama 8	—	8	Nebraska 3	3	—
Arkansas........... 5	5	—	Nevada 3	3	—
California 5	5	—	New Hampshire...... 5	—	5
Connecticut 6	—	6	New Jersey 7	—	7
Delaware............ 3	1½	1½	New York............33	33	—
Florida.............. 3	—	3	North Carolina....... 9	—	9
Georgia 9	—	9	Ohio.................21	21	—
Illinois..............16	—	16	Oregon 3	3	—
Indiana.............13	13	—	Pennsylvania.........26	—	26
Iowa................ 8	8	—	Rhode Island......... 4	4	—
Kansas 3	—	3	South Carolina 6	—	6
Kentucky............11	11	—	Tennessee 10	—	10
Louisiana 7	—	7	Texas................ 6	—	6
Maine............... 7	2	5	Vermont............. 5	4	1
Massachusetts.......12	—	12	Virginia 10	10	—
Maryland............ 7	—	7	West Virginia........ 5	—	5
Michigan............ 8	8	—	Wisconsin 8	8	—
Minnesota 4	—	4			
Mississippi 7	—	7	Total 142½		174½
Missouri 11	—	11			

Mr. LATROOP, of New Jersey, moved that the Convention take a recess until seven o'clock.

The motion was lost.

The PRESIDENT. — We will now proceed with the eighteenth ballot.

Eighteenth Ballot.

Alabama. — Eight for Hancock. (Applause.)

Arkansas. — Five for Hancock.

California. — Three for Pendleton, one and a half for Hancock, one-half for Chase.

Connecticut. — Three for Pendleton, three for Hancock.

Delaware. — Two for Pendleton, one for Hancock. (Applause.)

Illinois. — Mr. RICHARDSON: Mr. President, the State of Illinois instructed her delegates to cast their vote as a unit. On the last ballot, I yielded to the casting of their individual votes. The vote is adverse to my opinion; but I nevertheless cast her sixteen votes for Mr. Hendricks. (Applause.)

Mr. MALONEY, of Illinois. — I want that corrected. I want to give my vote for Pendleton.

The PRESIDENT. — We will pass Illinois for the present.

Indiana. — Ten for Hendricks, three for Pendleton.

Iowa. — Eight for Pendleton.

Kansas. — Two for Hendricks, one for Hancock.

Kentucky. — Four and a half for Pendleton, four and a half for Hancock, two for Hendricks.

Louisiana. — Seven for Hancock.

Maine. — Four and a half for Hancock, one and a half for Pendleton, one for Hendricks.

Maryland. — Six and a half for Hancock, one and a half for Hendricks.

Massachusetts. — Eleven for Hancock, one for Pendleton.

Michigan. — Eight for Hendricks.

Minnesota. — Two for Pendleton, two for Hancock.
Mississippi. — Seven for Hancock.
Missouri. — Four for Hendricks, seven for Hancock. (Applause.)
Nebraska. — Three for Hoffman.
Nevada. — Three for Pendleton.
New Hampshire. — One-half for Hendricks, one for Pendleton, and three and a half for Hancock.
New Jersey. — Three and a half for Parker, three for Hancock, and one-half for Pendleton.
New York. — Thirty-three for Hendricks.
North Carolina. — Nine for Hancock.
Ohio. — Twenty-one for Pendleton.
Pennsylvania. — Twenty-six for Hancock. (Cheers.)
Rhode Island. — Four for Doolittle.
South Carolina. — Six for Hancock.
Tennessee. — The Chairman of the Delegation: The State of Tennessee, faithful to him who has ever been faithful to our country, casts her united vote for Andrew Johnson. (Cheers.)
Texas. — Six for Hancock.
Vermont. — Five for Hendricks.
Virginia. — Ten for Hancock.
West Virginia. — Five for Hendricks.
Wisconsin. — Eight for Doolittle.
Illinois. — Sixteen for Hendricks.

Mr. MALONY, of Illinois. — I want to correct that vote. I want my vote cast for George H. Pendleton, of Ohio.

The PRESIDENT. — That is a question you must settle among yourselves.

ANOTHER DELEGATE. — There is among the delegates from Illinois —

Cries of "Order!"

The gentleman made a further effort to speak, but his voice was drowned by cries of "Order!"

Mr. MALONY, of Illinois. — Mr. President: I offer, sir, one-half of the votes of the second district of Illinois (Cries of "Order"!) for the able, defender (Cheers and cries of "Order"!) of the Constitution and of the Union. The chairman of the Illinois delegation is not authorized to speak for me here, or for my district.

The PRESIDENT. — The Secretary will now announce the result of the last ballot.

NATIONAL DEMOCRATIC CONVENTION.

The Secretary announced the result of the vote, as follows, —

The whole number of votes cast	317
W. S. Hancock	144½
George H. Pendleton	56½
Joel Parker	3½
Andrew Johnson	10
James R. Doolittle	12
Thomas A. Hendricks	87
John T. Hoffman	3
S. P. Chase	½
Asa Packer	—

EIGHTEENTH BALLOT—RECAPITULATION.

STATES.	WHOLE NO.	HANCOCK.	PENDLETON.	PARKER.	A. JOHNSON.	DOOLITTLE.	HENDRICKS.	HOFFMAN.	CHASE.	PACKER.
Alabama	8	8	..	..	..	..	..	..	..	..
Arkansas	5	5	..	..	..	..	..	..	..	..
California	5	1½	3	..	..	..	..	..	½	..
Connecticut	6	3	3	..	..	..	..	..	..	..
Delaware	3	1	2	..	..	..	..	..	..	..
Florida	3	3	..	..	..	..	..	..	..	..
Georgia	9	9	..	..	..	..	..	..	..	..
Illinois	16	..	..	..	..	..	16	..	..	..
Indiana	13	..	3	..	..	..	10	..	..	..
Iowa	8	..	8	..	..	..	..	..	..	..
Kansas	3	1	..	..	..	..	2	..	..	..
Kentucky	11	4½	4½	..	..	..	2	..	..	..
Louisiana	7	7	..	..	..	..	..	..	..	..
Maine	7	4½	1½	..	..	..	1	..	..	..
Maryland	7	6½	..	..	..	..	..	½	..	..
Massachusetts	12	11	1	..	..	..	..	..	..	..
Michigan	8	..	..	..	..	..	8	..	..	..
Minnesota	4	2	2	..	..	..	..	..	..	..
Mississippi	7	7	..	..	..	..	..	..	..	..
Missouri	11	7	..	..	..	..	4	..	..	..
Nebraska	3	..	..	..	..	..	..	3	..	..
Nevada	3	..	3	..	..	..	..	..	..	..
New Hampshire	5	3½	1	..	..	..	..	½	..	..
New Jersey	7	3	..	½	3½	..	..	..	..	..
New York	33	..	..	..	..	..	33	..	..	..
North Carolina	9	9	..	..	..	..	..	..	..	..
Ohio	21	..	21	..	..	..	..	..	..	..
Oregon	3	..	3	..	..	..	..	..	..	..
Pennsylvania	26	26	..	..	..	..	..	..	..	..
Rhode Island	4	..	..	..	..	4	..	..	..	..
South Carolina	6	6	..	..	..	..	..	..	..	..
Tennessee	10	..	..	..	10	..	..	..	..	..
Texas	6	6	..	..	..	..	..	..	..	..
Vermont	5	..	..	..	..	..	5	..	..	..
Virginia	10	10	..	..	..	..	..	..	..	..
West Virginia	5	..	..	..	..	..	5	..	..	..
Wisconsin	8	..	..	..	..	8	..	..	..	..
Total	317	144½	56½	3½	10	12	87	3	½	..

Mr. MALONY, of Illinois. — Mr. President: I have a proposition to make, — a motion to submit to the Convention. My motion is this: That every gentleman who has credentials entitling him to a seat on this floor shall be entitled to represent, by vote and voice, the district that in part sent him here.

Applause, and cries of " Take your seat! " and " Order! "

The PRESIDENT. — The gentleman from Illinois (Mr. Malony), if the Chair understands his proposition, moves that each delegate shall have a right to vote as he sees fit upon each nomination. The rule already adopted by the Convention is this: That when the nominations are made, each delegation is to vote through its chairman. That is now the rule of the Convention. The motion, therefore, of the gentleman from Illinois is a motion to change the rules of the Convention and the order of its proceedings. This can be done only upon one day's notice, if any objections are made to such change. More than that, the Chair will state that it understands (and I think in every Convention I have attended), when the question has been raised touching the votes of the delegates, it has always been decided that each delegation has a right to decide for itself how it would act as a whole. That was the decision of the Convention which met in Baltimore.

A DELEGATE from California. — I object to the proposed change.

Mr. MALONY. — Do I understand the Chair, then, to decide that I, who differ from the expressed vote of the chairman of the Illinois delegation, must permit his vote to be taken here and not mine?

The PRESIDENT. — The rule already adopted by the Convention will be read by the Secretary, whose voice is so much clearer than my own, that the Convention will better understand it than if I state it.

Mr. BAYARD, of Delaware. — I understand the rule of the Convention to be that the chairman is to announce the vote of each delegation.

The PRESIDENT. — It is.

Mr. BAYARD. — Does that involve the principle that individual members are to be here as mere agents of the majority and not of the people they represent? I think not. I suppose this to be a deliberative body, as much so as is the House of Representatives; and I should think it just as rational that a majority of the members of the House of Representatives should undertake to control the individual opinions of the representatives, as that a majority of a delegation should undertake here to control the individual opinion of any member of this Convention. Such delegation is no longer a representative of the sentiment of the people of the State, if such a principle is permitted to govern its action. It would be nothing more than a mode by which faction and personal combinations might override public sentiment.

The Clerk then read the rule already adopted by the Convention, as follows, —

Resolved, That, in casting their votes for President and Vice-President, each chairman of each delegation shall rise in his place and name how the delegation votes.

Mr. CLYMER. — Mr. President, this Convention adopted the rules which governed the Convention at Chicago; that Convention adopted the rules of the Conventions which sat at Charleston and at Baltimore. At Charleston there was a rule reported for the government of the Convention upon this subject, which was adopted by the Convention, and that rule is this, —

"That in any State which has not provided or directed by its State Convention how its vote shall be given, the Convention will recognize the right of each delegate to cast his individual vote."

I have thought it my duty to bring to the knowledge of the President of the Convention this rule.

Mr. MALONY. — Mr. President, I surrendered the floor only out of compliment to the gentleman from Pennsylvania, and I now claim my right to be heard.

Cries of "Order!"

The PRESIDENT. — The Clerk will first read the rule submitted by the gentleman from Pennsylvania.

The Clerk again read the rule to which attention was called by Mr. Clymer.

Mr. MALONY. — Mr. President: Under that rule, which vindicates the right of every district in this broad country to give an expression, through its delegates sent here, of its wishes in regard to the nominations made, and in defiance of the attempt of the chairman of the Illinois delegation to gag down my district, I give one-half vote for the ablest defender of the Constitution, for the man who has done more to vindicate the unity of our government, and the polity and sovereignty of its States under the Constitution of our country than any other living man. (Great applause.)

The PRESIDENT. — The Chair wishes to inquire of the chairman of the Illinois delegation what instruction, if any, was given that delegation by the State Convention.

Mr. RICHARDSON, of Illinois. — The Convention of Illinois instructed her delegates to vote as a unit. They instructed them to vote for Mr. Pendleton. A majority of the delegation, not in accordance with my wish, but overthrowing that wish of mine, chose to go for another distinguished gentleman. I thought it my duty, sir, I still think it was my duty, to cast her whole vote for that other gentleman. (Applause.) I have disregarded —

Mr. MALONY. — Mr. President —

The PRESIDENT. — I beg the gentleman from Illinois to take his seat and allow the Convention to proceed to another vote, and then, if he has any objection to make, it will come up in its order.

Mr. ABBOTT, of Massachusetts. — I move that this Convention do now adjourn.

A vote was taken on the motion to adjourn, and it was carried.

The President then announced, at five minutes past four o'clock, that the Convention stood adjourned until ten o'clock on Thursday morning.

FIFTH DAY.

July 9, 1868.

The Convention met pursuant to adjournment, Hon. THOMAS L. PRICE, of Missouri, in the chair.

The following prayer was offered by Rev. D. PLUMMER, of South Carolina, —

Prayer.

Holy, Holy, Holy, Lord God of Hosts! Creation abounds in the monuments and memorials of Thy being, wisdom, power, glory, justice, goodness, and truth. Thy nature is infinite, eternal, and unchangeable. Thou hast supreme claims to our love and homage — our submission and thanksgiving. Thou hast done great things for us, whereof we would make adoring mention. Thou madest man a little lower than the angels; and when he had sinned Thou didst provide a Redeemer. Thou hast also greatly favored our country. In days gone by Thou didst bring a vine out of a distant land. Thou didst cast out the heathen. Thou preparedst room before it, and didst cause it to take deep root, and it filled the land. The hills were covered with the shadow of it, and the boughs thereof were like the goodly cedars. She sent out her boughs into the sea and her branches into the river. Why, then, hast Thou broken down her hedges, so that all they who pass by the way do pluck her? The boar out of the wood doth waste it, and the wild beast of the field doth devour it. Return, we beseech Thee, O God of Hosts; look down from Heaven and visit this vine. Thou hast for some time sorely afflicted us. The grievousness of war was long upon us; countless myriads of our people, as loving and magnanimous as those who survive them, permaturely sleep the long sleep of death. If we went into the field, behold the slain! If we went into the city, behold Rachael weeping for her children, and refusing to be comforted because they were not. Our great men have conceived chaff and brought forth stubble. Our land is full of widows and orphans. Even stout hearts among us have often been ready to fail for looking after those things which were thought to be coming upon us. We have hoped for succor, and behold sadness; for salvation, and behold perplexity. Thou that dwellest between the cherubim, shinest forth before all our tribes, stir up Thy strength and come and save us. Feed us no longer with the bread of tears. Let the love and fear of God rule all hearts. Let us cease from man, whose breath is in his nostrils. Let us no more pervert our blessings to the nourishing of our personal or national vanity, nor to malevolence, worldliness, or ungodliness. Compass our land with Thy power, as with a shield. Let not our bruise be incurable, nor our wound immedicable. Let our children be as aforetime, and our people be established before Thee. Be not Thou as a man as to need, as a mighty man that cannot save. Implant and nourish in all our people a genuine love of country. Purely purge away our dross, and take away our sin. Thou only canst heal our breaches, or make us dwell in safety. Let not lots again be cast for our honorable men, nor our great men be bound with chains. Feed our hungry, clothe our naked; make the widow's heart to sing for joy; in Thee let the fatherless find mercy; pity all who are tossed with tempest and not comforted; let not the rod of the wicked rest upon the lot of the righteous. Thou, blessed and only Potentate, canst make men to be of one mind and of the same judgment. O Thou, which has showed us great and sore troubles, wilt Thou not quicken us again, and bring us up again from these low depths? Do Thou, the glorious Lord, be unto us a place of broad rivers and streams, wherein shall go no galley with oars, neither shall gallant ship pass thereby. Let the future history of our government be as a morning without clouds. Let our sun no more go down, nor our moon refuse to give her light. Let North and South, East and West, henceforth see eye to eye, feel heart to heart, and join inseparable bonds in love and peace, with joy and singing. And to the King eternal, immortal, invisible, the only wise God, our Saviour, be honor and glory, dominion and power, salvation and blessing, through Jesus Christ, forever and ever. Amen and Amen.

The PRESIDENT *pro tem.* — The first business in order is the reading of the proceedings of yesterday.

Mr. BLACK, of Indiana. — I move that the reading of the journal be dispensed with.

The PRESIDENT *pro tem.* — It will be so ordered unless objection is made.

It was so ordered.

Mr. SLADE, of Missouri. — I rise to a privileged question. This Convention has adopted a resolution inviting the delegates to the Soldiers and Sailors' Convention to seats upon this floor. Numerous complaints, however, have been made in my hearing, and some of them personally to myself, that that rule is disregarded, and some of the delegates are refused admission.

The PRESIDENT *pro tem.* — The Secretary will state the proceedings in regard to the delegates to the Soldiers and Sailors' Convention.

The SECRETARY. — In conformity with the resolution of the Convention inviting the delegates to the Soldiers and Sailors' Convention to seats upon this floor, tickets have been issued by the National Executive Committee to their officers and sent to their hall for distribution. This hall is limited in capacity, and the Committee have endeavored to extend the courtesy just as far as the seats will permit.

Mr. SLADE. — I learn that delegates have presented their tickets and have been refused admission.

The PRESIDENT *pro tem.* — Those were the tickets that were issued for a previous day. The tickets were changed yesterday, and new tickets were sent to the officers of that Convention.

Mr. SLADE. — I move that the explanation be entered upon the record.

The PRESIDENT *pro tem.* — It will be so ordered unless there is objection.

It was so ordered.

Missouri nominates F. P. Blair.

Mr. BRODHEAD, of Missouri. — We have reached the fifth day of our session without any successful result. I now ask leave to present to the Convention another name for their consideration. I will nominate Gen. FRANCIS P. BLAIR, of Missouri. It is not necessary, in this Convention, that I should attempt to repeat his honorable services as a soldier or a statesman, for they are known to the whole country. Without desiring to disparage the qualifications of any other of the distinguished gentlemen whose names are presented for the consideration of this Convention, I will only say that Gen. BLAIR is eminently possessed of those qualities most needed at this time, — firmness of purpose, moral courage, and indomitable will. He will not be readily turned from a purpose once deliberately formed, although another co-ordinate department of the government may place itself in the way of its performance; and, as President of the United States, he would preserve, protect, and defend the Constitution; and he would give to it a living meaning which, in the absence of any judicial interpretation to the contrary, gives to the President the right and imposes upon him the duty of refusing to execute unconstitutional laws. (Applause.) If we would meet the demands of this crisis, if we would not shirk from the issues of this hour, we must, by some tangible form of action, maintain the independence of the Executive. Congressional despotism is the great evil against which we have to contend. It is the fruitful source of all our troubles. It is that which is riving asunder the framework of our government, and substituting the views of faction for the requirements of the Constitution. We want a man at the head of the government who knows the duties of the executive station, and knowing, dares maintain them. Such a man is the gentleman whose name I now present to the consideration of this Convention.

The PRESIDENT, pro tem. — Mr. Brodhead, of the Missouri delegation, in behalf of that delegation, puts in nomination for President FRANCIS P. BLAIR, Jr., of Missouri.

Mr. MILLER, of Pennsylvania. — I rise, sir, to a privileged question. I notice, sir, by the report of the proceedings of this Convention yesterday, that it is rather made a matter of congratulation by a portion of the press, that by the superior shrewdness or "sharpness" (for I believe that is the word used) of certain politicians, the rules of this Convention can be utterly ignored. Now, sir, I allude to the announcement of the change in the vote of the delegation from New York, and I insist upon it, sir, that upon a delegation voting for its candidate, or in changing its vote, even if its vote is changed from Andrew Johnson or Salmon P. Chase (applause), it shall content itself with simply voting. In order that the Chairman give the lie to the intimations that shrewdness and sharpness, emanating from where it may, can override the prevailing order of this Convention —

Cries of "Order!"

The PRESIDENT. — Will the gentleman submit his motion?

Mr. MILLER. — I make no motion; I simply rise to a privileged question to call attention to the fact that it is alleged that the orders of this Convention cannot be enforced because some people are smart enough to avoid them.

Cries of "Order!"

The PRESIDENT. — The first business in order will be the calling of the roll for the nineteenth ballot.

California nominates Judge Field.

Mr. ROSE, of California. — Mr. President, I rise for the purpose of placing before the Convention the name of an eminent gentleman and statesman, — a gentleman of accomplished education; of brilliant talents; one who has distinguished himself in the service of his State and the nation; a gentleman who has occupied the highest position of the judiciary of California; who from that position was transferred to the Supreme Court of the United States. Occupying that position, it was his province to stand up like a wall of fire against the encroachments of Radical domination, and stand as the guardian of the Constitution of his country against all the power of the Radical party at Washington; to vindicate the charter of our liberties at a time when it required some one of ability to raise his voice and his pen against Radical misrule. I allude, sir, to STEPHEN J. FIELD, of the Supreme Court. (Great applause.)

A DELEGATE. — Mr. Chairman, —

The PRESIDENT. — The Clerk will announce the nomination.

SECRETARY. — Mr. Rose, of California, places in nomination for President, STEPHEN J. FIELD, of California. (Cheers.)

Withdrawal of George H. Pendleton.

Mr. VALLANDIGHAM, of Ohio. — I have a communication in writing to make to this Convention. By permission of the Chair, I will read it from the stand.

Applause, during which Mr. Vallandigham made his way to the rostrum.

The PRESIDENT. — Mr. Vallandigham, of Ohio, will make a communication to the Convention.

Mr. VALLANDIGHAM. — The following is the communication to which I refer, —

CINCINNATI, July 2, 1868.

Washington McLean, Fifth Avenue Hotel, New York:

MY DEAR SIR, — You know better than any one the feelings and principles which have guided my conduct since the suggestion of my name for the Presidential nomination.

You know that while I covet the good opinion of my countrymen, and would feel an honest pride in so distinguished a mark of their confidence, I do not desire it at the expense of one single electoral vote (Great applause), or of the least disturbance of the harmony of our party. I consider the success of the Democratic party in the next election of far greater importance than the gratification of any personal ambition, however pure and lofty it might be. (Loud cheers.)

If, therefore, at any time, a name shall be suggested, which, in the opinion of yourself and those friends who have shared our confidence, shall be stronger before the country, or which can more thoroughly unite our own party, I beg that you will instantly withdraw my name, and pledge to the Convention my hearty and zealous and active support for its nominee.

Very truly yours,
GEORGE H. PENDLETON.

Great cheering.

Mr. VALLANDIGHAM. — At the request of the gentleman to whom this letter is addressed, I submit it to this Convention. It was his desire that it should have been done very early in the afternoon of yesterday, but the earnest zeal and fidelity of the Ohio delegation, for the distinguished son of Ohio whom they had presented to the Convention for the office of President, precluded their consent to any such proposition. This morning his request has been renewed, and in conformity with it I have produced and read the letter, and submit that its spirit of magnanimity, unselfishness, and patriotic devotion to the interests of the country speak in terms of far higher eulogy in behalf of this distinguished gentleman than any words I could utter. (Great applause.) Pursuant, therefore, to the authority of Mr. McLean, and acting under the advice of Mr. Pendleton, I withdraw his name, with hearty thanks to the multitude of earnest, zealous and devoted friends who have adhered to him with so great fidelity.

Applause long and continued, and cheers for Pendleton.

The PRESIDENT. — Mr. Vallandigham, by the instructions of the Ohio delegation, withdraws the name of George H. Pendleton as a candidate for the Presidency, before this Convention, and he does so by the direction of Mr. Pendleton himself. (Cheers.)

We will now proceed with the nineteenth ballot.

Nineteenth Ballot.

The Secretary called the roll, with the following result, —

Alabama. — Eight for Gen. Hancock. (Applause.)

Arkansas. — Five for Gen. Hancock.

California. — Three for Judge Field, one and a half for Hendricks, and one-half for Salmon P. Chase.

Connecticut. — Six for Mr. English.

Delaware. — The Chairman of the Delegation. — As the favorite candidate of the State of Delaware has been withdrawn, Delaware casts her votes for Gen. Hancock. (Applause.)

Florida. — Three for Hendricks.

Georgia. — Nine for Hancock.

Illinois. — Sixteen for Hendricks.

Mr. MALONY, of Illinois — Mr. Chairman —

Cries of "Order!"

The PRESIDENT. — The gentleman must come to order.

Mr. MALONY. — Mr. Chairman, I rise to a privileged question.

Mr. DAWSON of Pennsylvania. — Mr. Chairman, there can be no privileged question while the roll is being called, I insist, therefore, upon the enforcement of the rule. This is no place for mere exhibitions.

The PRESIDENT. — The opinion of the gentleman from Pennsylvania coincides with the opinion of the Chair; and the Chair must consider the gentleman from Illinois (Mr. Malony) out of order.

A delegate moved that Mr. Malony have permission to make an explanation.

Cries of "No! No!"

The PRESIDENT. — The gentleman from Illinois cannot proceed without suspending the rule of this Convention. I therefore hope he will take his seat and let us proceed with the balloting. The Clerk will proceed.

Indiana. — Thirteen for Hendricks.

Iowa — requests to be passed by for the present.

Kansas. — Two for Hendricks, and one for Hancock.

Kentucky — asks time.

Louisiana. — Seven for Hancock.

Maine. — Four and a half for Hancock, two and a half for Hendricks. (Applause.)

Maryland. — Three for Blair, three for Hancock, one for Hendricks.

Massachusetts. — Twelve for Gen. Winfield Scott Hancock. (Applause.)

Michigan. — Eight for Thomas A. Hendricks.

Minnesota. — Two and a half for Hendricks, one for Hancock and one-half for Thomas H. Seymour, of Connecticut. (Applause; three cheers proposed for Thomas H. Seymour, but were not given.)

Mississippi. — Seven for Hancock.

Missouri. — Ten and a half for Blair, one-half for Hancock.

Nebraska. — Three for Hendricks.

Nevada. — Three for Judge Field.

New Hampshire. — One-half for Thomas A. Hendricks, and four and a half for Gen. Hancock. (Applause.)

New Jersey. — Seven for Judge Field, of California.

New York. — Thirty-three for Thomas A. Hendricks. (Great applause.)
North Carolina.— Nine for Gen. Hancock. (Applause.)
Ohio. — Twenty-one for Judge Packer, of Pennsylvania.
Oregon. — Two for Field and one for Packer.
Pennsylvania. — Mr. WOODWARD: Mr. President, I beg that the vote of Pennsylvania may be passed for the present, and that her delegation have leave to retire.

Leave was granted.

Rhode Island. — Four for James R. Doolittle.
South Carolina. — Six for Gen. Hancock. (Applause.)
Tennessee. — Ten for Hancock. (Applause.)
Texas. — Six for Hancock.
Vermont. — Five for Thomas A. Hendricks.
Virginia. — Ten for Hancock. (Applause.)
West Virginia. — Five for Hendricks.
Wisconsin. — Eight for Doolittle.
Iowa. — Eight for Thomas A. Hendricks, of Indiana. (Applause.)
Kentucky. — Three and a half votes for Hendricks, three votes for Gen. Hancock, three and a half votes for Thomas H. Seymour, of Connecticut, one vote not voting.

Pennsylvania. — Mr. WOODWARD: Pennsylvania casts twenty-six votes for Gen. Hancock. (Loud Applause.)

The Secretary announced the result of the vote, as follows, —

The whole number of votes cast	316
W. S. Hancock	135¼
James R. Doolittle	12
Thomas A. Hendricks	107½
James E. English	6
Frank P. Blair	13½
S. T. Field	15
S. P. Chase	½
Asa Packer	22
T. H. Seymour	4

NINETEENTH BALLOT—RECAPITULATION.

STATES.	WHOLE NO.	HANCOCK.	DOOLITTLE.	HENDRICKS.	ENGLISH.	BLAIR.	FIELD.	CHASE.	PACKER.	T.H.SEYMOUR
Alabama	8	8	..	..	..	..	..	..	..	..
Arkansas	5	5	..	..	..	..	..	..	..	..
California	5	..	..	1½	..	..	3	½	..	..
Connecticut	6	..	..	..	6	..	..	..	..	..
Delaware	3	3	..	..	..	..	..	..	..	..
Florida	3	..	..	3	..	..	..	..	..	..
Georgia	9	9	..	..	..	..	..	..	..	..
Illinois	16	..	..	16	..	..	..	..	..	..
Indiana	13	..	..	13	..	..	..	..	..	..
Iowa	8	..	..	8	..	..	..	..	..	..
Kansas	3	1	..	2	..	..	..	..	..	..
Kentucky*	11	3	..	3½	..	..	..	..	..	3½
Louisiana	7	7	..	..	..	..	..	..	..	..
Maine	7	4½	..	2½	..	..	..	..	..	..
Maryland	7	3	..	1	..	3	..	..	..	..
Massachusetts	12	12	..	..	..	..	..	..	..	..
Michigan	8	..	..	8	..	..	..	..	..	..
Minnesota	4	1	..	2½	..	..	..	..	..	½
Mississippi	7	7	..	..	..	..	..	..	..	..
Missouri	11	½	..	..	..	10½	..	..	..	..
Nebraska	3	..	..	3	..	..	..	..	..	..
Nevada	3	..	..	..	..	..	3	..	..	..
New Hampshire	5	4½	..	½	..	..	..	..	..	..
New Jersey	7	..	..	..	..	..	7	..	..	..
New York	33	..	..	33	..	..	..	..	..	..
North Carolina	9	9	..	..	..	..	..	..	..	..
Ohio	21	..	..	..	..	..	..	..	21	..
Oregon	3	..	..	..	..	..	..	2	1	..
Pennsylvania	26	26	..	..	..	..	..	..	..	..
Rhode Island	4	..	4	..	..	..	..	..	..	..
South Carolina	6	6	..	..	..	..	..	..	..	..
Tennessee	10	10	..	..	..	..	..	..	..	..
Texas	6	6	..	..	..	..	..	..	..	..
Vermont	5	..	..	5	..	..	..	..	..	..
Virginia	10	10	..	..	..	..	..	..	..	..
West Virginia	5	..	..	5	..	..	..	..	..	..
Wisconsin	8	..	8	..	..	..	..	..	..	..
Total	317	135½	12	107½	6	13½	15	½	22	4

*1 not voting.

Twentieth Ballot.

The Secretary then proceeded with the call of the States for the twentieth ballot, as follows, —

Alabama. — Eight votes for Hancock.
Arkansas. — One vote for Hancock, four for Hendricks,
California. — Three votes for Field, one and a half for Hendricks, and one-half for Hancock.
Connecticut. — Six votes for English.
Delaware. — Three votes for Hancock.
Florida. — Three votes for Hendricks.
Georgia. — Nine votes for Hancock.
Illinois. — Sixteen votes for Hendricks.
Indiana. — Thirteen votes for Hendricks.
Iowa. — Eight votes for Hendricks.
Kansas. — Two votes for Hancock, one for Hendricks.
Louisiana. — Seven votes for Hancock.
Maine. — Four and a half votes for Hancock, and two and a half for Hendricks.
Maryland. — Three votes for Blair, three for Hancock, and one for Hendricks.
Michigan. — Eight votes for Hendricks.
Minnesota. — Three and a half votes for Hendricks, one-half for Hancock.
Mississippi. — Seven votes for Hancock.
Missouri. — Three votes for Hendricks.
Nevada. — Three votes for Field.
New Hampshire. — One-half vote for Hendricks, four and a half for Hancock.
New Jersey. — Seven votes for Hendricks.
New York. — Thirty-three votes for Hendricks. (Cheers.)
North Carolina. — Nine votes for Hancock.
Ohio. — Passed at the request of the Chair.
Oregon. — Three votes for Field.
Pennsylvania. — Twenty-six votes for Hancock. **(Cheers.)**
Rhode Island. — Four votes for Doolittle.
South Carolina. — Six votes for General Hancock.
Tennessee. — Ten votes for Hancock.
Texas. — Six votes for Hancock.
Vermont. — Five votes for Hendricks.
Virginia. — Ten votes for Hancock.
West Virginia. — Five votes for Hendricks.
Missouri. — Eight votes for Doolittle.
Kentucky. — Three and a half votes for Thomas H. Seymour, one-half not voting.
Massachusetts. — The Chairman of the Delegation: The State of Massachusetts asks leave to retire for fifteen minutes for consultation. It is the first time we have made the request. I believe we have always been ready to vote when called upon.

The PRESIDENT. — There being no objection, the request is granted.

Ohio. — Ten votes for James E. English, eleven for General Hancock. (Applause.)

The SECRETARY. — The call will be suspended fifteen minutes, waiting for the Massachusetts delegation.

General McCOOK. — I ask the same leave for Ohio.

The PRESIDENT. — Leave is granted. I would suggest that, inasmuch as two large delegations have retired for fifteen minutes, we take a recess for fifteen minutes.

A recess for fifteen minutes was accordingly taken by the Convention.

On the return from recess, and when order was restored, the Secretary proceeded with the call.

Massachusetts. — Eleven votes for General Hancock, one voter declining to vote. (Applause.)

NATIONAL DEMOCRATIC CONVENTION.   149

The Secretary announced the result, as follows, —

Total number of votes cast	315½
W. S. Hancock	142½
James E. English	16
James R. Doolittle	12
Thomas A. Hendricks	121
Frank P. Blair	13
S. T. Field	9
T. H. Seymour	2
John T. Hoffman	—

TWENTIETH BALLOT — RECAPITULATION.

STATES.	WHOLE NO.	HANCOCK.	ENGLISH.	DOOLITTLE.	HENDRICKS.	BLAIR.	FIELD.	T.H.SEYMOUR.	HOFFMAN.
Alabama	8	8	..	..	..	..	..	..	..
Arkansas	5	1	..	..	4	..	..	..	..
California	5	½	..	..	1½	..	3	..	..
Connecticut	6	..	6	..	..	..	..	..	..
Delaware	3	3	..	..	..	..	..	..	..
Florida	3	..	..	..	3	..	..	..	..
Georgia	9	9	..	..	..	..	..	..	..
Illinois	16	..	..	..	16	..	..	..	..
Indiana	13	..	..	..	13	..	..	..	..
Iowa	8	..	..	..	8	..	..	..	..
Kansas	3	1	..	..	2	..	..	..	..
Kentucky*	11	3½	..	..	5	..	..	2	..
Louisiana	7	7	..	..	..	..	..	..	..
Maine	7	4½	..	..	2½	..	..	..	..
Maryland	7	3	..	..	1	3	..	..	..
Massachusetts†	12	11	..	..	..	..	..	..	..
Michigan	8	..	..	..	8	..	..	..	..
Minnesota	4	½	..	..	3½	..	..	..	..
Mississippi	7	7	..	..	..	..	..	..	..
Missouri	11	1	..	..	..	10	..	..	..
Nebraska	3	..	..	..	3	..	..	..	..
Nevada	3	..	..	..	..	..	..	3	..
New Hampshire	5	4½	..	..	1½	..	..	..	..
New Jersey	7	..	..	..	7	..	..	..	..
New York	33	..	..	..	33	..	..	..	..
North Carolina	9	9	..	..	..	..	..	..	..
Ohio	21	11	10	..	..	..	..	..	..
Oregon	3	..	..	..	..	..	3	..	..
Pennsylvania	26	26	..	..	..	..	..	..	..
Rhode Island	4	..	..	4	..	..	..	..	..
South Carolina	6	6	..	..	..	..	..	..	..
Tennessee	10	10	..	..	..	..	..	..	..
Texas	6	6	..	..	..	..	..	..	..
Vermont	5	..	..	..	5	..	..	..	..
Virginia	10	10	..	..	..	..	..	..	..
West Virginia	5	..	..	..	5	..	..	..	..
Wisconsin	8	..	..	8	..	..	..	..	..
Total	317	142½	16	12	121	13	9	2	..

* ½ not voting.   † 1 not voting.

Twenty-first Ballot.

The SECRETARY. — The Convention will now proceed to take the twenty-first ballot.

Alabama. — Eight votes for General Hancock. (Applause.)
Arkansas. — Five votes for Thomas A. Hendricks. (Applause.)
California. — Three votes for Field, one for Hendricks, and one for English.
Connecticut. — Six votes for English.
Delaware. — Three votes for General Hancock. (Applause.)
Florida. — Three votes for Thomas A. Hendricks. (Applause.)
Georgia. — Nine votes for Hancock. (Applause.)
Illinois. — Sixteen votes for Hendricks. (Applause.)
Indiana. — Thirteen votes for Hendricks. (Applause.)
Iowa. — Eight votes for Hendricks. (Applause.)
Kansas. — Two votes for Hendricks, and one for General Hancock.
Kentucky. — The Chairman of the Delegation: Pass Kentucky; we are not ready.
Louisiana. — Seven votes for Hancock. (Applause.)
Maine. — Four and a half votes for Hancock, and two and a half for Hendricks.
Maryland. — Six votes for Hancock, and one for Hendricks. (Applause.)
Massachusetts.—The Chairman of the Delegation: Massachusetts is not ready.
Michigan. — Eight votes for Thomas A. Hendricks.
Minnesota. — Three and a half votes for Hendricks, and one and a half for Hancock.
Mississippi. — Seven votes for Hancock. (Applause.)
Missouri. — Four for Hendricks, six for Hancock, and one for English (Applause.)
Nebraska. — Three votes for Hendricks.
Nevada. — The Chairman of the Delegation: Pass Nevada.
New Hampshire. — One-half vote for Hendricks, four and a half for Hancock.
New Jersey. — Seven votes for Hendricks.
New York. — Thirty-three votes for Hendricks.
North Carolina. — Eight votes for Hancock, one for Hendricks.
Ohio. — Eleven votes for Hancock, ten for James E. English.
Oregon. — Two votes for Field, one for English.
Pennsylvania. — Twenty-six votes for Hancock.
Rhode Island. — Four votes for James R. Doolittle.
South Carolina. — Six votes for Hancock.
Tennessee. — Five votes for Johnson, two and a half for Hancock, one-half for Hendricks, one-half for McClellan, two and a half not voting.
Texas. — Six votes for Hancock.
Vermont. — Five votes for Hendricks.
Virginia. — Ten votes for Hancock.
West Virginia. — Five votes for Hendricks.
Wisconsin. — Eight votes for Doolittle.
Kentucky. — Three and a half votes for Hancock, seven for Hendricks, and one-half for Hoffman, of New York.
Massachusetts. — Two votes for Hendricks, four for Salmon P. Chase, of Ohio (loud applause, followed by a few hisses); and six for Hancock.
Nevada. — Three votes for Field.

The Secretary announced the result of the vote, as follows, —

The whole number of votes cast	316½
W. S. Hancock	135¼
James R. Doolittle	12
Thomas A. Hendricks	132
James E. English	19
Andrew Johnson	5
S. J. Field	8
S. P. Chase	4
George B. McClellan	½
John T. Hoffman	½

TWENTY-FIRST BALLOT—RECAPITULATION.

STATES.	WHOLE NO.	HANCOCK.	DOOLITTLE.	HENDRICKS.	ENGLISH.	A. JOHNSON.	FIELD.	CHASE.	McCLELLAN.	HOFFMAN.
Alabama	8	8	..	..	..	..	..	..	..	..
Arkansas	5	..	..	5	..	..	..	..	..	..
California	5	..	..	1	1	..	3	..	..	..
Connecticut	6	..	..	..	6	..	..	..	..	..
Delaware	3	3	..	..	..	..	..	..	..	..
Florida	3	..	..	3	..	..	..	..	..	..
Georgia	9	9	..	..	..	..	..	..	..	..
Illinois	16	..	..	16	..	..	..	..	..	..
Indiana	13	..	..	13	..	..	..	..	..	..
Iowa	8	..	..	8	..	..	..	..	..	..
Kansas	3	1	..	2	..	..	..	..	..	..
Kentucky	11	3½	..	7	..	..	..	..	..	½
Louisiana	7	7	..	..	..	..	..	..	..	..
Maine	7	4½	..	2½	..	..	..	..	..	..
Maryland	7	6	..	1	..	..	..	..	..	..
Massachusetts	12	6	..	2	..	..	..	4	..	..
Michigan	8	..	..	8	..	..	..	..	..	..
Minnesota	4	½	..	3½	..	..	..	..	..	..
Mississippi	7	7	..	..	..	..	..	..	..	..
Missouri	11	6	..	4	1	..	..	..	..	..
Nebraska	3	..	..	3	..	..	..	..	..	..
Nevada	3	..	..	..	..	..	3	..	..	..
New Hampshire	5	4½	..	½	..	..	..	..	..	..
New Jersey	7	..	..	7	..	..	..	..	..	..
New York	33	..	..	33	..	..	..	..	..	..
North Carolina	9	8	..	1	..	..	..	..	..	..
Ohio	21	11	..	..	10	..	..	..	..	..
Oregon	3	..	..	..	1	..	2	..	..	..
Pennsylvania	26	26	..	..	..	..	..	..	..	..
Rhode Island	4	..	4	..	..	..	..	..	..	..
South Carolina	6	6	..	..	..	..	..	..	..	..
Tennessee*	10	2½	..	1½	..	5	..	..	½	..
Texas	6	6	..	..	..	..	..	..	..	..
Vermont	5	..	..	5	..	..	..	..	..	..
Virginia	10	10	..	..	..	..	..	..	..	..
West Virginia	5	..	..	5	..	..	..	..	..	..
Wisconsin	8	..	8	..	..	..	..	..	..	..
Total	317	135½	12	132	19	5	8	4	½	½

* ½ not voting.

Mr. HUNTER, of Missouri. — I desire to offer a resolution in reference to an adjournment to St. Louis, in September next. I will send it to the desk to be read. I rather think sometimes that I have not got into a Democratic Convention. I therefore present the resolution, in order that it may be read.

The PRESIDENT. — The resolution is not now in order. The Clerk will proceed to call the roll.

Twenty-Second Ballot.

Alabama. — Eight votes for Hancock.
Arkansas. — Five votes for Hendricks.
California. — Five votes for Hendricks. (Applause.)
Connecticut. — Six votes for English.
Delaware. — Three votes for Hancock.
Florida. — Three votes for Hendricks.
Georgia. — Nine votes for Hancock. (Applause.)
Illinois. — Sixteen votes for Hendricks. (Applause.)
Indiana. — Thirteen votes for Hendricks.
Iowa. — Eight votes for Hendricks.
Kansas. — Two votes for Hendricks, one for Hancock.
Kentucky. — The Chairman of the Delegation: Pass Kentucky.
Louisiana. — Seven votes for Hancock.
Maine. — Four and a half votes for Hancock, two and a half for Hendricks.
Maryland. — Six votes for Hancock, one for Hendricks.
Massachusetts. — The Chairman of the Delegation: Pass Massachusetts.
Michigan. — Eight votes for Hendricks.
Minnesota. — Four votes for Hendricks.
Mississippi. — Seven votes for Hancock.
Missouri. — Two votes for Hancock, eight for Hendricks, and one for English.
Nebraska. — Three votes for Hendricks.
Nevada. — Three votes for Hendricks.
New Hampshire. — One-half vote for Hendricks, four and a half for Hancock.
New Jersey. — Seven votes for Hendricks.
New York. — Thirty-three votes for Hendricks. (Cheers.)
North Carolina. — Nine votes for Hendricks.

Ohio was called.

Ohio nominates Horatio Seymour.

General MCCOOK, of Ohio. — Mr. Chairman, I arise at the unanimous request and demand of the delegation from Ohio, and with the consent and approval of every public man in the State, including the Hon. George H. Pendleton, to again place in nomination, against his inclination, but no longer against his honor, the name of HORATIO SEYMOUR, of New York. (Rousing cheers and long-continued applause.) Let us vote, Mr. Chairman and gentlemen of the Convention, for a man whom the Presidency has sought, but who has not sought the Presidency. (Applause.) I believe in my heart that it is the solution of the problem which has been engaging the minds of the Democrats and conservative men of this nation for the last six months. ("Good! good!") I believe it is the solution which will drive from power the Vandals who now possess the Capitol of the nation. (Applause.) I believe it will receive the unanimous assent and approval of the great belt of States, from the Atlantic — New York, New Jersey, Pennsylvania, Ohio, Indiana, Michigan, Illinois, and Missouri, and away west to the Pacific Ocean. (Applause.) I say that he has not sought the Presidency, and I ask that this Convention shall demand of him that, sinking his own inclination and his own well-known desires, he shall yield to what we believe to be the almost unanimous wish and desire of the delegates to this Convention. (Great applause, and three cheers.) In my earnestness and enthusiasm, I had almost forgotten to cast the twenty-one votes of Ohio for Horatio Seymour. (Tremendous excitement, and nine cheers for Horatio Seymour.)

The President (Hon. Horatio Seymour) here advanced to the front of the stage, and as soon as the enthusiasm would permit of his being heard, addressed the Convention.

Speech of Governor Seymour.

GENTLEMEN OF THE CONVENTION, — (Cheers). The motion just made by the gentleman from Ohio excites in my mind the most mingled emotions. (Applause.) I have no terms in which to express my gratitude (Cheers) for the magnanimity of his State, and for the generosity of this Convention. (Cheers.) I have no terms in which to tell of my regret that my name has been brought before this Convention. God knows that my life and all that I value most in life I would give for the good of my country, which I believe to be identified with that of the Democratic party. (Applause, and cries of "Take the nomination then.") I do not stand here as a man proud of his opinions, or obstinate in his purposes; but upon a question of duty and of honor I must stand upon my own convictions against the world. (Applause, and a voice, "God bless you, Horatio Seymour.") Gentlemen, when I said here at an early day, that honor forbade my accepting a nomination by this Convention, I *meant* it. When, in the course of my intercourse with those of my own delegation and my friends, I said to them that I could not be a candidate, I *meant* it. And now permit me here to say that I know, after all that has taken place, I could not receive the nomination without placing, not only myself, but the great Democratic party, in a false position. But, gentlemen of the Convention, more than that, we have had to-day an exhibition, from the distinguished citizen of Ohio, that has touched my heart, as it has touched yours. (Cheers.) I thank God and I congratulate this country, that there is in the great State of Ohio, whose magnificent position gives it so great a control over the action of our country, a young man, rising fast into fame, whose future is all glorious, who has told the world that he could tread beneath his feet every other consideration than that of duty; and when he expressed to his delegation, and expressed in more direct terms, that he was willing that I should be nominated, who had stood in such a position of marked opposition to his own nomination, I should feel a dishonored man if I could not tread, in the far distance, and in a feeble way, the same honorable pathway which he has marked out. (Great applause.) Gentlemen, I thank you, and may God bless you for your kindness to me; but your candidate I cannot be. (Three cheers for Horatio Seymour.)

Hon. THOMAS L. PRICE, of Missouri, here assumed the chair.

Mr. VALLANDIGHAM, of Ohio.—Mr. President: In times of great public exigency, and especially in times of great public calamity, every personal consideration must be yielded to the public good. (Applause.) The safety of the people is the supreme law, and the safety of the American Republic demands the nomination of Horatio Seymour, of New York. (Cheers.) Ohio cannot—Ohio will not accept his declination, and her twenty-one votes shall stand recorded in his name. (Cries of "Good, good!" and cheers.) And now I call upon the delegations from all the States represented on this floor; upon the delegations from all the States of this Union, from the Atlantic to the Pacific, from the great lakes to the gulf, disregarding those minor considerations which justly it may be, properly I know, tend to sway them in casting their ballots, to make this nomination unanimous; and, before God, I believe that in November the judgment of this Convention will be confirmed and ratified by the people of all the United States. (Applause.) Let the vote of Ohio stand recorded then—twenty-one votes for Horatio Seymour. (Immense and continued applause.)

Mr. KERNAN, of New York.—Mr. President: Belonging to the delegation from the State of New York, and coming from the district where the President of this Convention lives, I cannot, as an individual delegate, refrain from asking the indulgence of this Convention in making one or two observations. And in order that we may relieve everybody, in order that we may relieve our Chairman from every bit of sensitiveness on the question of honor, I desire to say, on behalf of the delegation from the State of New York, that they have had neither lot nor part in the motion, which in our hearts we yet rejoice to hear from the State of Ohio. (Applause.) We heard but recently that some such movement was thought, by wise and good men, necessary for the safety of our country, but our hearts were coerced out of deference to the sensitiveness of the gentleman who presides over this Convention, and we told them we could have neither lot nor part in it, unless others overcame that which we had never been able to do. Now, sir, let me say another word; we have balloted two or three days; we have balloted, thank God, in the best of temper and of spirits; we have resolved, and we required the judgment of two-thirds of the delegates of this Convention for our nominee, to the end that we might be sure, for the sake of our country, that we would have a majority of the electors next November. And, after striving hard, after striving long, and after consulting as well as we could in reference to the various names brought before us, we have not been able yet to convince the judgment of two-thirds of the Convention for the candidates we have supported. New York has steadily voted her judgment, with kind feelings to other candidates. We have pronounced as our second choice for a distinguished citizen of Indiana. But it seems to me that, after this long struggle, and in this crisis of our affairs, and in view of what is so important to every man, woman, and child in this Union, that we should succeed in November,—it seems to me now, in reference to our distinguished Chairman, that his honor is entirely safe. No one can doubt that he has steadily and in good faith declined; but, now that his honor is safe, his duty to his country, his duty to his fellow-citizens, to all that shall come after us, requires that he shall let the judgment of the delegates of this Convention prevail; if they should select him as the standard-bearer most certain, in their opinion, to win a triumph for the country next November. (Applause.) We leave it in the hands of others, as we are constrained to do; but I give it as my judgment, for the past, the present and the future, that if we should select him as the man upon whom we can all unite, New York will fall in and give a majority of a hundred thousand without a canvass. (Great cheers.)

The roll of States continued to be called as follows, —

Oregon. — The Chairman of the Delegation: Three votes for Hendricks.

Pennsylvania. — The Chairman of the Delegation: Twenty-six votes for General Hancock.

Rhode Island. — The Chairman of the Delegation: Rhode Island casts her four votes for Doolittle.

South Carolina. — The Chairman of the Delegation: Six votes for General Hancock.

Tennessee. — The Chairman of the Delegation: Andrew Johnson, four votes, Hendricks one and a half, Hancock three and a half, Seymour one.

Texas. — The Chairman of the Delegation: Six votes for Hancock.

Vermont. — The Chairman of the Delegation: Five votes for Hendricks.

Virginia. — The Chairman of the Delegation: Ten votes for Hancock.

West Virginia. — The Chairman of the Delegation: Five votes for Hendricks.

Wisconsin. — Mr. H. L. Palmer, of Wisconsin: The delegation from Wisconsin have steadily supported a distinguished citizen of that State for the position of President of the United States, but I am now instructed by the delegation of the State to change that vote; and in making this change I am instructed to second the State of Ohio (Applause), and to cast their eight votes for Horatio Seymour. (Tremendous cheering.)

Kentucky. — The Chairman of the Delegation: Kentucky casts her eleven votes for Horatio Seymour. (Wild enthusiasm.)

Massachusetts. — Mr. Abbott, of Massachusetts: The State of Massachusetts instructs me to cast her vote for one, whom Massachusetts, whom all the East, so far as I know, has regarded for years past as the leader of the Democracy, Horatio Seymour, of New York. (Cheering, and waving of hats and handkerchiefs.)

North Carolina. — Mr. Wright, of North Carolina: I am instructed by the delegation from North Carolina to change their vote, and to cast it as they originally cast it, for Horatio Seymour, of New York. (Great cheering.)

The Secretary then announced that the State of North Carolina cast her nine votes for Horatio Seymour.

A scene of the wildest enthusiasm followed, the chairmen of a dozen of the delegations present springing from their seats to obtain a recognition from the *chairman pro tem.* to change their votes to Seymour.

Mr. FEATHERSTONE, of Miss. — I am instructed to change the vote of the State of Mississippi from General Hancock to Horatio Seymour.

The announcement was received throughout the building with uproarious applause, and the rising of delegates to their feet, and calling for recognition by the Chair. The president *pro tem.* insisted upon gentlemen taking their seats.

Mr. WOODWARD, of Pennsylvania, after repeated efforts, made himself heard by the Chair and those immediately surrounding him, that the State of Pennsylvania, having voted uniformly thus far for two of her distinguished sons, had instructed him, through her delegation, to transfer her entire twenty-six votes to Horatio Seymour.

The Secretary, by virtue of the superior strength of his lungs, informed the Convention that the State of Pennsylvania had cast its unanimous vote for Horatio Seymour, of New York.

The wildest enthusiasm continued. Nothing was heard but cheers from the galleries and floor, and cries of "Mr. President" from delegates standing in their seats. Fans, handkerchiefs, and hats were waved, and some took the small banners designating the seats of different delegations, and swayed them in the air.

Seeing no probability of quieting the clamor, the Secretary successively recognized the chairmen of the delegations from Missouri and Virginia, and announced that they had changed their votes to Horatio Seymour.

A scene of still greater excitement and tumultuous enthusiasm followed. All the delegations were standing in their places, and striving for the recognition of the Chair by gesture and by voice, in the midst of which the announcement was made that Maryland, Illinois, Texas, and Delaware, had transferred their united votes to Horatio Seymour.

The announcement of the vote of each State added, if possible, to the tumult.

At this point the cannon outside the building commenced firing, and the discharges were answered by those inside the hall rising to their feet with vociferous cheers and the waving of handkerchiefs.

Mr. SMITH, of Vermont. — Mr. President, Vermont was the first State in this Convention to cast its vote for the distinguished citizen of Indiana (Mr. Hendricks). She now yields to the evident wish of the Convention, and she finds in the distinguished gentleman from New York all she desires as a candidate. She, therefore, changes her vote from Thomas A. Hendricks to Horatio Seymour.

New Jersey, West Virginia, Alabama, Tennessee, Arkansas, Maine, and Georgia, here changed their votes to Seymour, receiving the approval of all who heard the Secretary declare the change.

The CHAIRMAN of the Kansas Delegation. — Kansas casts her three votes for Horatio Seymour.

Mr. BIGLER. — California casts her five votes for Horatio Seymour. (Applause.)

Mr. LAWSON, of Pa. — I am requested to say that it is the unanimous voice of this Convention that the nomination of Horatio Seymour be made by acclamation.

The PRESIDENT *pro tem.* — It cannot be done until all the States have voted on this ballot.

The CHAIRMAN of the Florida Delegation. — Florida wishes to cast her three votes for Horatio Seymour. (Applause.)

The CHAIRMAN of the Minnesota Delegation. — Minnesota, following the lead of Ohio, casts her entire vote for Horatio Seymour.

The CHAIRMAN of the New Hampshire Delegation. — The State of New Hampshire changes her vote, and casts it entire for Horatio Seymour.

The CHAIRMAN of the Georgia Delegation. — The State of Georgia has indicated her choice by casting her vote for the most accomplished soldier of the Union army, he who, when the war was ended, yielded to the supremacy of the Constitution of his country. But, sir, we come here to abide by the choice of the Democratic party, and now join our voice with that of the Democracy, from one end of the country to the other, for Horatio Seymour. (Applause.)

Mr. JONES, of Louisiana. — Louisiana asks leave to change her vote, and vote for Horatio Seymour, and, Mr. Chairman, although we have twenty-five thousand of our white population disfranchised, and although we have fifty-thousand voters unknown to our Constitution and to our laws, yet, Mr. Chairman, I pledge the vote of the State of Louisiana to the nominee. (Applause.)

Mr. STUART, of Michigan. — Mr. Chairman, the delegates from the State of Michigan came to this Convention of all the States in the Union, with but one single purpose in view, and that was to nominate a candidate for the office of President of the United States who could certainly be elected. That position we occupy to-day. And, sir, when we look around in this Convention, and see here, for the first time in eight years, the assembled wisdom of the Democracy of the country, — a country bounded only upon the Atlantic and upon the Pacific, because on the north and on the south America acknowledges as yet no boundary whatever, — when so much wisdom as is here to-day, with a voice so united as this, speaks for the distinguished son of New York, the greatest statesman, in my judgment, now living (Applause), — Michigan cannot consent to withhold her voice in this general expression, not only of confidence in him, but, sir, this expression of patriotic determination to rescue this country from the grasp of the most desperate rebels that ever seized upon the reins of the government. (Voices, "Good! good!") It is a question of Constitution; it is a question of country; it is a question of whether our blessed Union, and the freedom of these millions is to live, or whether it is to be buried deep down in everlasting oblivion and infamy. (A voice, "Good!") Sir, under these circumstances, it is with infinite pleasure that Michigan casts her vote for Horatio Seymour, of New York. (Great applause.)

Mr. JAMES B. CAMPBELL, of South Carolina. — Mr. President, I rise to answer for that State of the Union which bears at this time most heavily the chains and weight of Radical misrule. I did not suppose, sir, that my voice, or that of any of my colleagues, would be heard in this assembly, except in the discharge of the routine business. In the words of the Convention that sent us here, we were instructed to behave with the proprieties which belong to the well-bred guest, and not to assume any of the functions of the symposiarch of the feast. We came here, Mr. President and gentlemen of the Convention, having no favorite candidate, — going not for men but for measures. We have been more than grateful for the declaration of principles and of prospective measures that has been announced by the Convention, not only with unanimity, but with unsurpassed enthusiasm. We were instructed, and the instructions were coincident with the feelings of every honest heart in South Carolina, to accept the nomination of that man who seemed to have the voice of the Convention. Obeying these instructions, South Carolina, with an invocation of God's blessing upon this party wherein is centred the last hopes of the Republic of Washington, nominates and votes for Horatio Seymour, of New York. (Great applause.)

A delegate from California moved that Horatio Seymour be tendered the unanimous vote of the Convention.

VOICES. — "No! no! let the vote be finished."

The CHAIRMAN of the Delaware Delegation. — Delaware would change her vote, if not too late, and casts all her votes for Horatio Seymour. (Applause and laughter.)

Mr. SAMUEL J. TILDEN. — Mr. Chairman —

A DELEGATE from New York. — See if any other State wants to change its vote first.

Mr. TILDEN. — If there is any State which has not yet voted, or that wishes to change its vote, I will yield the floor for that purpose.

DELEGATES. — "No! no!" "Go on!"

Mr. TILDEN. — It is fit that on this occasion New York should wait for the voice of all her sister States. Last evening I should not have believed, did not believe, the event which has just happened to be possible; not because I had not seen here that the underlying choice of almost all of this Convention was that we should do what we now have done. There was but one obstacle, and that was in the repugnance, — which I take upon myself the whole responsibility of declaring to have been earnest, sincere, deep-felt, — on the part of Horatio Seymour to accept this nomination. I did not believe that any circumstance would make it possible, except that Ohio, with whom we have been unfortunately dividing our votes, should herself demand it, and to that I thought New York ought to yield. We were without any connection or any combination that bound our faith or our honor, and I was anxious that when we should leave this Convention there should be underlying our action no heart-burnings, no jealousy, no bitterness of disappointment; and I believe that in this result we have lifted this Convention far above every such consideration. And I believe further, after having surveyed the ground for a long time and meditated most carefully what we ought to do, influenced, I am sure, by no personal partiality, by no other thing than the deliberate conviction of my judgment, — I believe that we have made the nomination most calculated to give us success in the election which approaches. And, sir, having made these observations in behalf of the New York delegation, I now ask that our vote be changed, and be recorded for Horatio Seymour. (Cheers.)

The SECRETARY. — The State of New York changes her vote, and casts her unanimous vote for Horatio Seymour.

Loud and long-continued applause.

Mr. WHITE, of Maryland. — I now propose, Mr. President, that a committee of one from each State be appointed to call upon, —

Loud cries of "No, no!" "Better wait until the vote is taken."

The PRESIDENT, *pro tem.* — The vote has not yet been announced.

Mr. WHITE. — I understood that the chairman of the New York delegation asked if all the States had voted, and it was announced that they had, — that they had all voted for Horatio Seymour, and that he was unanimously nominated.

The PRESIDENT, *pro tem.* — The vote has not been announced.

Mr. WHITE. — I withdraw my motion.

Mr. S. CLARK, of Wisconsin. — I have a proposition to make to this Convention if it is in order to announce it before the vote is announced. I see around me, on the floor and in the galleries, ladies and gentlemen who desire also to be heard, and who should have some voice in this Convention in ratifying the nomination by acclamation. I therefore move that they ratify it by giving three cheers for Horatio Seymour.

The suggestion was immediately acted upon. Every one rose, and amid the waving of hats, handkerchiefs, fans, canes, and parasols, three tremendous cheers were given, which fairly made the building rock.

The PRESIDENT, *pro tem.* — The Convention will come to order.

The SECRETARY. — The following is the result of the twenty-second ballot: All the States having voted, and the vote of the full electoral college having been given, the roll stands for Horatio Seymour three hundred and seventeen votes.

Renewed cheering, the Convention and audience again rising, and another scene of enthusiasm prevailing for five minutes.

The PRESIDENT, *pro tem.* — The Convention will come to order. All business will be suspended until order is restored.

Mr. DAWSON, of Pennsylvania. — Mr. President, —

The PRESIDENT, *pro tem.* — The official announcement has not yet been made. Gentlemen of the Convention will sit down.

Order having been restored, the President *pro tem.* said, —

The Hon. Horatio Seymour having received the unanimous vote of this Convention, I therefore declare him the candidate and the standard-bearer of the Democratic party in the ensuing election.

The announcement was followed by tremendous cheering.

Table of Twenty-second Ballot on First Call.

STATE OF THE BALLOT BEFORE THE STATES CHANGED THEIR VOTES FOR MR. SEYMOUR.

STATES.	WHOLE NO.	HANCOCK.	ENGLISH.	DOOLITTLE.	HENDRICKS.	H. SEYMOUR.	A. JOHNSON.
Alabama	8	8	..	..	..	..	..
Arkansas	5	..	..	..	5	..	..
California	5	..	..	..	5	..	..
Connecticut	6	..	6	..	..	..	..
Delaware	3	3	..	..	..	..	..
Florida	3	..	..	..	3	..	..
Georgia	9	9	..	..	..	..	..
Illinois	16	..	..	..	16	..	..
Indiana	13	..	..	..	13	..	..
Iowa	8	..	..	..	8	..	..
Kansas	3	1	..	..	2	..	..
Kentucky*	11	..	..	..	..	..	..
Louisiana	7	7	..	..	..	..	..
Maine	7	4½	..	..	2½	..	..
Maryland	7	6	..	..	1	..	..
Massachusetts*	12	..	..	..	..	..	..
Michigan	8	..	..	..	8	..	..
Minnesota	4	..	..	..	4	..	..
Mississippi	7	7	..	..	..	..	..
Missouri	11	2	1	..	8	..	..
Nebraska	3	..	..	..	3	..	..
Nevada	3	..	..	..	3	..	..
New Hampshire	5	4½	..	..	½	..	..
New Jersey	7	..	..	..	7	..	..
New York	33	..	..	..	33	..	..
North Carolina	9	..	..	..	9	..	..
Ohio	21	..	..	..	..	21	..
Oregon	3	..	..	..	3	..	..
Pennsylvania	26	26	..	..	..	..	..
Rhode Island	4	..	..	4	..	..	..
South Carolina	6	6	..	..	..	..	..
Tennessee	10	3½	..	..	1½	1	4
Texas	6	6	..	..	..	..	..
Vermont	5	..	..	..	5	..	..
Virginia	10	10	..	..	..	..	..
West Virginia	5	..	..	..	5	..	..
Wisconsin*	8	..	..	..	..	..	..
Total	317	103½	7	4	145½	22	4

* Not voting.

NATIONAL DEMOCRATIC CONVENTION.

Table of Twenty-Second Ballot amended before the vote was announced.

H. SEYMOUR.		H. SEYMOUR.	
Alabama	8	Nebraska	3
Arkansas	5	Nevada	3
California	5	New Hampshire	5
Connecticut	6	New Jersey	7
Delaware	3	New York	33
Florida	3	North Carolina	9
Georgia	9	Ohio	21
Illinois	16	Oregon	3
Indiana	13	Pennsylvania	26
Iowa	8	Rhode Island	4
Kansas	3	South Carolina	6
Kentucky	11	Tennessee	10
Louisiana	7	Texas	6
Maine	7	Vermont	5
Maryland	7	Virginia	10
Massachusetts	12	West Virginia	5
Michigan	8	Wisconsin	8
Minnesota	4		
Mississippi	7	Total	317
Missouri	11	Necessary to a choice	212

Mr. PRESTON of Kentucky. — I believe there is no business before the Convention, and I ask if the nomination of Vice-President is now in order, or whether a resolution to that effect has been adopted. If not, I make the motion.

Mr. CLYMER. — I move that the Convention take a recess of one hour for consultation with regard to Vice-President.

The President *pro tem.* stated the question on the motion of Mr. Preston.

Mr. WOODWARD. — Is it in order now to nominate a candidate for Vice-President?

The PRESIDENT *pro tem.* — Wait until this motion is decided by the Convention.

The motion of Mr. Preston prevailed.

Mr. WOODWARD. — Mr. President —

The SECRETARY. — A resolution was adopted several days ago that in the nominations of President and Vice-President the States shall be first called in order for nominations.

Mr. WOODWARD. — I rose for the purpose of making a nomination; but I understand that the roll is to be called.

The PRESIDENT *pro tem.* — The roll of the States will now be called; any State desiring to nominate a candidate for Vice-President can rise through their Chairman, and make their nomination.

The Secretary called the roll of States as follows, —

Alabama.—The Chairman of the Delegation: Alabama makes no nomination.

Arkansas.— The Chairman of the Delegation: Arkansas makes no nomination.

California. — Mr. BIGLER: California has no nomination to present.

Mr. BOYER, of Pennsylvania. — I move that the Convention take a recess of half an hour for the purpose of consultation.

A DELEGATE. — I move that the resolution of the gentleman from Pennsylvania lie on the table.

The President *pro tem.* put the question, and there were cries of "No, no!"

The question was then taken on ordering a recess of five minutes, which was decided in the negative.

A motion for recess of ten minutes did not prevail.

A DELEGATE from California. — I desire to put in nomination FRANK P. BLAIR. (Loud cheers.)

Mr. BIGLER, of Pennsylvania. — Mr. Chairman, I desire to make a suggestion to the members of the Convention, and that is, that the nomination for Vice-President will be an important part of the coming election. I suggest the propriety and the necessity of a recess for at least half an hour, in order that we may confer upon the subject.

Mr. PRESTON, of Kentucky. — We are on a question of order, — the calling of the States, — and I submit here that no motion to adjourn or for a recess is in order. (Applause.) This will be interminable, if we should go on this way with motions to adjourn and to take a recess while taking a vote on an order.

The PRESIDENT *pro tem.* — The proposition is to adjourn for half an hour.

Mr. PRESTON, of Kentucky. — We are on an order for calling States.

Judge WOODWARD. — I move that the order of the Convention be suspended for the purpose of receiving from the delegation from Pennsylvania a nomination for Vice-President.

The SECRETARY. — The order of the Convention directing the Secretary to call the roll of States for nominations for Vice-President was in progress, and the Secretary was calling the roll of States alphabetically.

Judge WOODWARD. — My motion was that the order be suspended.

The PRESIDENT *pro tem.* — Mr. Woodward moves to suspend the rules by which the Convention ordered nominations to be made, and the Clerk was calling the roll of States.

Mr. PRESTON, of Kentucky. — If you will withdraw it, there will be no difficulty. We will make the nomination unanimously, and then take a recess.

Judge WOODWARD, of Pennsylvania. — I desire to make a nomination for Vice-President. The Pennsylvania delegates together —

The PRESIDENT *pro tem.* — The question is upon suspending the rules as proposed by the gentleman from Pennsylvania.

The question was put and declared lost.

Mr. STUART, of Michigan. — I move to take a recess for one hour.

Mr. MILLER, of Pennsylvania. — Pennsylvania is for General Blair.

The President *pro tem.* put the question on the motion to take a recess for one hour, and declared the motion carried.

The Vice-Presidential Nomination.

After recess, the Convention was called to order at 3.20 o'clock.

The PRESIDENT *pro tem.*, General Price. — The Clerk will proceed with the call of the States for the nominations for Vice-President.

The SECRETARY. — I will state to the Convention that several resolutions have been sent up here, and will remain upon the table to be taken up in their order. The call of the roll was interrupted at Connecticut. We will commence with Delaware.

The States of Delaware, Florida, and Georgia made no nomination.

Illinois.

Mr. SPARKS, of Illinois. — Mr. President: the State of Illinois cast, by the instruction of the State Convention that sent us here, the vote of that State for the greatest man of the West, George H. Pendleton. (Applause.) The State of Illinois through its delegation followed the lead of that distinguished statesman, and voted his particular choice, in voting for the greatest man in this broad Union, — Horatio Seymour. (Applause.) Having voted thus far, I am instructed by the delegation of that State now to present to this Convention as a candidate for Vice-President, the name of one of its own distinguished citizens, mentioning whom I go back to times past, and mention the peer of Clay and Webster, and mention the name rendered distinguished as that of a Major-General in the late war, — a man who, if he did not get the credit for the capture of Vicksburg, possesses the brains that originated its capture. (Applause.) But, holding a subordinate position, the glory was given to a much inferior man. (Applause.) I mean General JOHN A. MCCLERNAND, of Illinois. (Great applause.)

The SECRETARY. — Illinois puts in nomination for Vice-President General John A. McClernand, of Illinois. (Renewed cheers.)

General McClernand withdraws.

General MCCLERNAND, on rising, was greeted with loud applause. He said, —

Mr. President: the State of Illinois, through her delegation in this Convention, has done me the honor to present my name for the high office of Vice-President of the United States. This compliment is far above any merit which I possess. I beg in return to offer my sincerest thanks, and in doing so I beg that the delegates of Illinois will withdraw my name from the consideration of the Convention. (Cries of "No! no!") I am here, Mr. President and gentlemen, seeking no office, but to contribute my humble efforts to liberate the country from the thraldom which now binds her and degrades her. (Applause.) I have given my efforts as a delegate to the Soldiers and Sailors' Convention and in a very humble way in this Convention. As a Democrat and as a citizen I approve the nomination for President which has been made to-day. (Applause.) I can say, on behalf of the numerous and distinguished body of soldiers and sailors assembled in this city a few days since, that the nomination will meet with their hearty response; and the coming election will determine the fact that all the soldiers and sailors of this country are not for a sham hero — a mere fatuity — a mere compromise between abler and better men; that they are not to have a plagiarism of other and better mens' deserts; but that they are to have Horatio Seymour, of New York, an eminent statesman, an orator, and a gentleman, — a man every way qualified to administer the executive office of this country. They will prove, I say, in the approaching election, that one-half, and more than one-half, of the patriotic soldiers and sailors are for Horatio Seymour. (Applause.) And now a word to my friends, against whom I was so lately arrayed in battle. I say to them, by-gones are by-gones. (Cries of " Good!" "good!" and cheers.) Let the dead bury the dead. I stretch to them the hand of fellowship and say to them, let us co-operate to arrest disunion and usurpation. We have a common interest in the country, we have a common stock in it, and unless we do it the government will be overthrown; it is even now a despotism. I have said much more, Mr. President, than I intended to say when I arose. I am in earnest in what I have said, and I ask, I appeal to my delegation to withdraw my name as a candidate before this Convention. (Cries of "No! no!") There are other gentlemen in this Convention whom I had rather support than have my name presented.

Mr. SPARKS, of Illinois. — It is believed, by me at least, that when a gentleman declines a nomination, we ought to consult his wishes. At the request of General McClernand, whom Illinois would take great pleasure in supporting, I now withdraw his name.

Indiana made no nomination.

Hon. Asa C. Dodge nominated.

The State of Iowa being called, Mr. O'NEIL said, —

Mr. President: I am instructed by fifteen of the sixteen members of the Iowa delegation to put a name in nomination for the Vice-Presidency. Although he is not here present in the Convention, I am instructed by my delegation to present the name of a gentleman of irreproachable and stainless private character, of incorruptible integrity, of unswerving devotion to the principles of the Democratic party; a man whose patriotism and fidelity have never been questioned; a man whose reputation is national. I wish to say to this Convention that he has represented the State of Iowa in four different Congresses; that he has been for two terms the representative of that State in the Senate of the United States; that he has been for four years, under the administrations of Mr. Pierce and Buchanan, the American Minister to the Court of Spain. The Iowa delegation puts in nomination for the office of Vice-President, before the Convention, the name of the Hon. A. C. DODGE, of Iowa (Cheers.)

Thomas Ewing, Jr., nominated.

Kansas being called, Mr. Blair of Kansas said, —

Mr. President: I hold in my hand a letter addressed to me by the Executive Committee appointed by the Soldiers and Sailors' Convention recently assembled in this city, which I now forward to the Secretary, with a request that it be read for the information of the delegates, and that it be spread upon the minutes of this Convention as a part of the proceedings thereof. Before it is read, Mr. President, I desire, on behalf of the people of Kansas, to present to the consideration of the Convention the name of one of her most honored citizens in connection with the second office in the gift of the American people. I desire to present to this Convention the name of a man who is celebrated as a judicial officer, and distinguished as a statesman, and whose military career was the very impersonation of chivalric and knightly honor. I desire to present for the consideration of this Convention a name honored alike in the sire and in the son. I desire, sir, on behalf of Kansas, to present for the consideration of this Convention the name of General Thomas Ewing, Jr., of Kansas. (Cheers.)

The Secretary then read the following letter, which was ordered to be placed on the minutes of the Convention, —

NEW YORK, July 8, 1868.

DEAR GENERAL, — At a meeting of the National Executive Committee, appointed by the Soldiers and Sailors' Convention, held this morning, it was voted, unanimously, that their first choice for candidate of your Convention for the Presidency is General Hancock. But in the event of failure to nominate him, and any gentleman not connected with the army should be selected from the East, then our first choice for the second place on the ticket was General Ewing, of Kansas; and if from the West, then our choice would be General Franklin, of Connecticut.

Very truly yours, etc.,

ELI C. BINOLEY,
Member of the National Executive Committee, from Massachusetts.
General CHARLES W. BLAIR, *Chairman Kansas Delegation.*

Kentucky nominates Frank P. Blair.

Kentucky being called, ex-Confederate General PRESTON, of Kentucky, said, —

Mr. President, I am instructed unanimously, by the State of Kentucky, by its delegates here assembled, to place in nomination a gentleman of great distinction in his State, and in the country. One in the prime of manhood; distinguished by his devotion to the Union, having served it both in a civil and in a military capacity with the utmost honor, and obtained a reputation in the army second to no man of his grade. Kentucky feels that this nomination is due to the great West. No Southern State has presented any nominee for any place, as you will observe here; but I feel that it is appropriate — for we have entertained different opinions from him — to state that I am instructed now to nominate him in order to testify that we, the soldiers of the South, stretch forward our hands to the soldiers of the North (Applause), in the spirit of a noble amity that your resolutions have inculcated. (Applause.) It is with that view, sir, after consultation with the Northern delegations, and one of the most powerful, that the duty is devolved upon me of making this nomination. I now have the privilege, therefore, of nominating as a candidate for the Vice-President of the United States, General FRANCIS P. BLAIR, of Missouri. (Applause.)

General JAMES B. STEADMAN, of Louisiana. — Mr. President, I rise, sir, as one of the humble representatives of the United States Army in the late war, holding a seat in the Convention, to second, on behalf of Louisiana, the nomination of my comrade-in-arms, Major-General Frank P. Blair. (Applause.) When this Convention adjourned, I went immediately to the headquarters of the Soldiers and Sailors' Executive Committee, on Union Square. I met there some ten or twelve gentlemen, who were distinguished in the army, and consulted them in regard to their choice for a candidate for Vice-President of the United States; and by a unanimous vote of all who were present, I was requested to say to this Convention, without disparagement to the name of any other soldier that has been presented here, or may be presented, that General Frank P. Blair would be acceptable to the soldiers of the United States Army. (Applause.) The exhibition of magnanimity that has been made in this Convention by the soldiers of the Confederate Army, in coming up and giving a contradiction to the charge of the Radical party that they did not accept sincerely the situation in casting their votes as they did in this Convention, for that distinguished soldier of the United States Army, Major-General Winfield Scott Hancock, is appropriately followed up, and they have given renewed assurances of their devotion to the Union, of their willingness to accept the issues of the war, by presenting to this Convention, through General Preston, — whom I met on the bloody field of Chicamauga, — the name of Major-General Francis P. Blair. (Loud applause.) I therefore feel authorized to say that if General Blair is nominated, his nomination will meet with a response from every brave and true man that fought on either side, who desires to see peace and prosperity restored to our common country. (Applause.)

Maine having been called, the chairman of the delegation said, —

Mr. President, I do not rise to make any nomination, but simply to second the nomination so ably and eloquently made by the gentleman from Kansas, and to present to the Convention a recommendation signed by three of the Executive Committee of the Soldiers and Sailors' Convention, similar to the one heretofore presented by the gentleman from Kansas.

The following paper was read by the Secretary, —

NATIONAL EXECUTIVE COMMITTEE OF SOLDIERS AND SAILORS.
NEW YORK, July 7, 1868.

To the Chairmen of the New England Delegations to the Democratic National Convention now in session:

GENTLEMEN, — While we are desirous that General Hancock may receive the nomination of your Convention for President of the United States, yet deeming it possible that he may not be the choice of your Convention, we respectfully suggest, and urge that if you nominate a civilian from the West, the second place upon your ticket be awarded to General William B. Franklin; and that, if you nominate a civilian from the East, General Thomas Ewing, Jr., may be selected by you for the second place.

[Signed.]   A. W. BRADBURY,
ELI C. KINSLEY,
I. M. DONAHOE,
Chairmen of Delegations for New England to the Soldiers and Sailors' Convention.

The CHAIRMAN of the Maryland Delegation. — Maryland makes no nomination, but heartily concurs in the nomination made by the State of Kentucky. (Applause.)

Massachusetts, Michigan, and Minnesota made no nomination.

The CHAIRMAN of the Minnesota Delegation. — Mr. President, the State of Mississippi makes no nomination, but most cordially seconds the nomination of General Blair.

The CHAIRMAN of the Missouri Delegation. — Missouri makes no nomination, but seconds the nomination of General Blair. (Applause.)

The CHAIRMAN of the Nebraska Delegation. — Nebraska makes no nomination, but seconds the nomination of General Frank P. Blair. (Applause.)

The CHAIRMAN of the Nevada Delegation. — Nevada makes no nomination, but seconds that of Frank P. Blair.

New Hampshire and New Jersey made no nomination.

Mr. TILDEN, of New York. — The delegation from New York desires to be passed for the present.

The CHAIRMAN of the North Carolina Delegation. — Mr. President: North Carolina makes no nomination for Vice-President, but in order to show the people of the United States that we have no prejudice against a gallant soldier, who fought for his section of the country, we desire to second the nomination of General Francis P. Blair. (Applause.)

Ohio made no nomination.

The CHAIRMAN of the Oregon Delegation. — Oregon makes no nomination, but seconds the nomination of General Francis P. Blair.

Mr. WOODWARD. — Mr. President: The State of Pennsylvania makes no nomination, but I am instructed by the Delegation of Pennsylvania to second the nomination of that brave soldier and judicious statesman, General Frank P. Blair. (Applause.)

Rhode Island made no nomination.

Mr. CAMPBELL, of South Carolina. — Mr. Chairman: The State of South Carolina answers her call, not by her Chairman, but by her best beloved son, a soldier, who knows better than I do how to interchange the courtesies which belong to enemies in war and friends in peace. I have the honor to introduce to this Convention, Mr. Wade Hampton. (Loud cheers.)

Speech of Wade Hampton.

MR. CHAIRMAN, — The only reason I can give why my State has done me the honor to ask me to speak for her, on this occasion, is, I suppose, that I met the distinguished gentleman whose name has been presented by Kentucky on more than one field. Our State wishes me to say to the soldiers, and in reply to the remarks of the distinguished soldier from Illinois, that the soldiers of the South cordially, heartily, and cheerfully, accept the right hand of friendship which is extended to them. (Cries of "Good!" and cheers.) We wish to show that we appreciate the kindness and cordiality that have been extended to us by all classes. We wish particularly to make an acknowledgment to the Federal soldiers who have met us in so friendly a manner. It is due to them, I think, that they should have the second place upon the ticket. It is due to that Convention which so cordially approved your platform. It is due to the South; and I, for my State, most heartily second the nomination of General Blair.

Upon the conclusion of his remarks, Mr. Hampton was congratulated, personally, by General McClernand, and General McCook, amid the applause of the Convention and the spectators.

The call of States was then proceeded with.

The CHAIRMAN of the Tennessee Delegation. — Tennessee makes no nomination, but concurs in, and most cordially indorses, the nomination of General Blair. (Cheers.)

Texas and Vermont made no nomination.

GENERAL KEMPER, of Virginia. — As a son of the old Commonwealth of Virginia, I am instructed to strike hands with the soldiers of the Army of the North, and, in the name of Virginia, to accept and ratify, as a token of the perpetuity of this Union, the nomination of Major-General Francis P. Blair, of Missouri. (Applause.)

West Virginia and Wisconsin made no nomination.

Mr. TILDEN, of New York. — The State of New York, following Ohio, and the other great States of the North-west, concurs in the nomination of General Frank P. Blair.

Cries of " Good ! " and cheers.

The Name of Ewing withdrawn.

Mr. CHARLES W. BLAIR, of Kansas. — Mr. Chairman : As I had the honor to present to this Convention the name of Thomas Ewing, Jr., of Kansas, I now desire, on behalf of his friends, and at his instance, to withdraw his name, and move that the nomination of Frank P. Blair be made by acclamation.

The Name of Dodge withdrawn.

Mr. O'NEIL, of Iowa. — In view of the almost unanimous sentiment of this Convention, I beg leave, in the name of the Iowa Delegation, to withdraw the name of General Dodge, and to second the nomination of General Frank P. Blair. (Cheers.)

The Nomination of Blair.

Mr. BIGLER, of Pennsylvania. — As I have understood the ruling of the Chair, it has been that it is required that the States be called, and the ballot cast. I move that the rule be suspended, and that the nomination of Francis P. Blair be made by acclamation.

There being expressions of dissent, Mr. Bigler withdrew his motion.

The Secretary then proceeded with the call of States.

The Chairman of the Alabama Delegation being called, said, —

I take pleasure in casting the votes of my State for that accomplished soldier of the Union Army, General Francis P. Blair.

The CHAIRMAN of the Arkansas Delegation. — Arkansas casts her entire vote for Francis P. Blair.

The CHAIRMAN of the California Delegation. — California having been the first to nominate, now cordially casts her entire vote for Francis P. Blair.

The CHAIRMAN of the Connecticut Delegation. — Connecticut casts her six votes for General Blair.

The CHAIRMAN of the Delaware Delegation. — Delaware casts her three votes for General Blair.

The CHAIRMAN of the Florida Delegation. — Florida casts her three votes for General Francis P. Blair.

The CHAIRMAN of the Georgia Delegation. — Georgia casts her nine votes for General Blair.

The CHAIRMAN of the Illinois Delegation. — Illinois casts her entire vote for Frank P. Blair.

The CHAIRMAN of the Indiana Delegation. — Indiana casts twelve and a half votes for Francis P. Blair, one-half being absent.

Several DELEGATES. — Make it unanimous.

The CHAIRMAN of the Indiana Delegation. — We make it unanimous.

The CHAIRMAN of the Iowa Delegation. — Iowa casts her eight votes for General Blair.

The CHAIRMAN of the Kansas Delegation. — Kansas is for the first time united, and casts her three votes solid for Frank P. Blair. (Laughter.)

The CHAIRMAN of the Kentucky Delegation. — Kentucky gives her entire vote for General Blair.

The CHAIRMAN of the Louisiana Delegation. — Louisiana casts her seven votes for General Blair.

The CHAIRMAN of the Maine Delegation. — Maine casts her seven votes for General Blair.

The CHAIRMAN of the Maryland Convention. — Maryland casts her seven votes for General Frank P. Blair.

The CHAIRMAN of the Massachusetts Delegation. — The State of Massachusetts casts her twelve votes for Frank P. Blair. (Applause.)

The CHAIRMAN of the Michigan Delegation. — The State of Michigan casts her eight votes for Frank P. Blair.

The CHAIRMAN of the Minnesota Delegation. — Minnesota casts her full vote for General Frank P. Blair.

The CHAIRMAN of the Mississippi Delegation. — Mississippi casts her full vote for General Blair.

The CHAIRMAN of the Missouri Delegation. — Missouri casts her eleven votes for General Blair.

The CHAIRMAN of the Nebraska Delegation. — Nebraska casts her vote for General Blair.

The CHAIRMAN of the Nevada Delegation. — Nevada casts her vote for General Blair.

The CHAIRMAN of the New Hampshire Delegation. — New Hampshire casts her vote for General Blair.

Mr. KIERNAN, of New York. — In the absence of the Chairman, I am directed by the delegation to say that New York casts thirty-three votes for General Blair. (Applause.)

The CHAIRMAN of the North Carolina Delegation. — North Carolina casts her vote for General Blair.

The CHAIRMAN of the Ohio Delegation. — Ohio casts twenty-one votes for General Blair.

The CHAIRMAN of the Oregon Delegation. — Oregon casts her three votes for General Francis P. Blair.

The CHAIRMAN of the Pennsylvania Delegation. — Pennsylvania casts her twenty-six votes for General Blair, and proposes, next November, to cast her electoral vote for Seymour and Blair by more than twenty thousand majority. (Applause.)

The CHAIRMAN of the Rhode Island Delegation. — Rhode Island casts her four votes for General Blair.

The CHAIRMAN of the South Carolina Delegation. — South Carolina casts her six votes for General Blair.

The CHAIRMAN of the Tennessee Delegation. — Mr. Chairman: It is the pleasure of the Tennessee delegation that the vote of the State of Tennessee shall be cast by a distinguished Southern soldier, whom I have the honor to present to the Convention, N. B. Forrest. (Great applause.)

General Forrest. — I have the pleasure, sir, to cast the vote of Tennessee for General Blair; and I wish to take this occasion to thank the delegates here for the kind and uniformly courteous treatment that the Southern delegates have received at this Convention. (Great cheering.)

The Chairman of the Texas Delegation. — Mr. President, the Texas delegation desire that a distinguished soldier from that State should respond for it.

General Smith, of Texas. — Mr. President, I esteem it a great honor that I have been requested by the Chairman of the Texas delegation, and the members of that delegation, on this occasion, to cast the six votes of the State of Texas for Major-General Frank P. Blair. It is an evidence that the soldiers of Texas, who fought through the Confederate war, will give, when we come to vote, as warm a reception in the support of General Frank P. Blair, as we gave him on the field of battle from the commencement of the war to the end of it. (Cheers.)

The Chairman of the Vermont Delegation. — Five votes for General Blair.

The Chairman of the Virginia Delegation. — The State of Virginia ends where she begun, and casts ten votes for General Blair.

The Chairman of the West Virginia Delegation. — West Virginia casts her five votes for Francis P. Blair.

The Chairman of the Wisconsin Delegation. — Wisconsin casts her eight votes for General Frank P. Blair, Jr.

The Announcement of the Result.

The Secretary. — The vote stands upon Vice-President, as follows, — Whole vote of the Electoral College, 317, which were given unanimously for Frank P. Blair, of Missouri.

The following is a table of the first ballot for Vice-President, —

	Blair.		Blair.
Alabama	8	Nebraska	3
Arkansas	5	Nevada	3
California	5	New Hampshire	5
Connecticut	6	New Jersey	7
Delaware	3	New York	33
Florida	3	North Carolina	9
Georgia	9	Ohio	21
Illinois	16	Oregon	3
Indiana	3	Pennsylvania	26
Iowa	18	Rhode Island	4
Kansas	3	South Carolina	6
Kentucky	11	Tennessee	10
Louisiana	7	Texas	6
Maine	7	Vermont	5
Maryland	7	Virginia	10
Massachusetts	12	West Virginia	5
Michigan	8	Wisconsin	8
Minnesota	4		
Mississippi	7		
Missouri	11	Total	317

Three hearty cheers greeted this announcement, and another scene of enthusiasm ensued.

The PRESIDENT *pro tem.* — The unanimous vote of the Convention having been cast for Frank P. Blair, Jr., of Missouri, for Vice-President, he is declared the candidate of the Democratic party for Vice-President. (Great cheering.)

Mr. COX, of New York. — I only rise to make a motion. We have made an unanimous declaration of Democratic principles; we have made an unanimous choice of our candidate for President, and I move, sir, that our nomination for Vice-President be made unanimous by both delegations and audience.

A voice in the galleries, " With a will."

Another scene of intense enthusiasm and excitement followed, delegates and audience rising to their feet, and joining in cheer after cheer.

Committee to Wait on the Nominees.

Mr. MCDONALD, of Indiana, offered the following resolution, —

Resolved, That a committee of one from each State be appointed by this Convention to inform the nominees of the action of this Convention, and to tender them the nominations made here to-day; and that the members of the committee be named by the delegations of the several States.

The question was taken, and the resolution adopted.

Mr. WOODWARD, of Pennsylvania, offered the following resolution, —

Resolved, That the proceedings of the Convention be prepared, and published in pamphlet form, by E. O. Perrin, Secretary of the Convention.

The PRESIDENT *pro tem.* — If there be no objection, the resolution will be considered as agreed to.

No objection was made.

The SECRETARY. — I am requested to read the following telegraphic despatch, —

LANCASTER, Pennsylvania, July 9, 1868.

A. J. Steinman, Pennsylvania Delegation, —

The Democratic voters of this city are now firing fifty guns for the nomination of Horatio Seymour, and his nomination is received with the greatest enthusiasm and satisfaction.

GEORGE W. KENDRICK.

Mr. A. A. PURMAN, of Pennsylvania, offered the following, —

Resolved, That the cordial thanks of the delegates of the National Convention are extended to the citizens of the city of New York for their large-hearted courtesy, and generous hospitality, during their session in this metropolis, the only great city which never faltered in her devotion to the Democracy, the Constitution, and the laws. (Cheers.)

The question was taken and the resolution adopted.

Mr. WHITE, of Maryland, offered the following resolution, —

Resolved, That the thanks of this Convention are hereby tendered to the President and other officers of the Convention, for the able, impartial, and most satisfactory manner in which they have discharged their respective duties.

The resolution was adopted with cheers.

Mr. VALLANDIGHAM offered the following resolution, —

Resolved, That this Convention sympathize cordially with the working-men of the United States in their efforts to protect the rights and promote the interests of the laboring classes of the country.

The resolution was adopted.

The PRESIDENT, *pro tem.* — The roll of States will now be called, and the chairmen of delegations will please name each a member of the Committee to wait upon the Candidates for President and Vice-President, and inform them of their nomination.

A delegate moved that the Territories be represented in the committee.

The PRESIDENT, *pro tem.* — Unless there is objection to that proposition, it will be considered agreed to.

No objection was made.

Mr. SANSOM, of Pennsylvania, offered the following resolution, —

Resolved, That the thanks of the delegates of this Convention be tendered to the Tammany Society for the use of their splendid hall, and to the Manhattan Club of this city for their generous hospitality.

The resolution was adopted.

Mr. KERR, of Pennsylvania, offered the following resolution, —

Resolved, That we tender our thanks to the press of New York for its faithful report of the proceedings of this Convention.

The resolution was adopted.

Mr. S. S. COX, of New York. — I wish to suggest that our distinguished Secretary announce that there will be a ratification to-night in Union Square of the nominations of this Convention, at eight o'clock, and that delegations have expressed their hope that Tammany Hall will take charge of it. (Cheers.)

The SECRETARY. — I am requested to announce that there will be a ratification meeting to-night in Union Square at eight o'clock, and that everybody and his wife are expected to be present. (Laughter.)

The Secretary read the list of the Committee appointed to wait on Candidates, and inform them of their Nomination, as follows, —

Committee to inform the Nominees of their Nomination.

Alabama. — Michael J. Bulger.
Arkansas. — P. O. Thweatt.
California. — Joseph Roberts.
Connecticut. — James A. Hovey.
Delaware. — Thomas B. Bradford.
Florida. — Wilkinson Call.
Georgia. — Colonel D. P. Hill.
Illinois. — William C. Gondy.
Indiana. — General Mahlon D. Manson.
Iowa. — Hon. A. C. Dodge.
Kansas. — Isaac Sharpe.
Kentucky. — General William Preston.

Louisiana. — Thomas Allen Clarke.
Maine. — R. B. Rice.
Maryland. — William Pinckney White.
Massachusetts. — J. G. Abbott.
Michigan. — Hon. C. E. Stuart.
Minnesota. — Willis A. Gorman.
Mississippi. — W. H. McCardle.
Missouri. — General Thomas L. Price.
Nebraska. — George L. Miller.
Nevada. — D. E. Buel.
New Hampshire. — Albert W. Hatch.
New Jersey. — Henry S. Little.
New York. — Francis Kernan.
North Carolina. — M. W. Ransom.
Ohio. — General George W. Morgan.
Oregon. — N. R. Bell.
Pennsylvania. — Colonel William C. Patterson.
Rhode Island. — Thomas Steere.
South Carolina. — J. B. Campbell.
Tennessee. — General William D. Bate.
Texas. — F. S. Stockdale.
Vermont. — P. S. Benjamin.
Virginia. — General James L. Kemper.
West Virginia. — John A. Martin.
Wisconsin. — George Reed.
Montana. — General Greene Clay Smith.
Idaho. — Thomas W. Betts.
New Mexico. — Robert B. Mitchell.
Arizona. — Thomas E. Evershed.
Colorado. — General William Craig.

Mr. KERNAN, of New York, offered the following, —

Resolved, That the thanks of the Convention are tendered to Chief Justice Salmon P. Chase for the justice, dignity, and impartiality with which he presided over the Court of Impeachment on the trial of President Andrew Johnson.

Applause and cries, "We have already done that."

The resolution was adopted.

General McCook, of Ohio. — I move, sir, that this Convention, having performed its important duties, do now adjourn *sine die.*

The motion was put by the chair, and carried; and at fifty minutes past three o'clock the Convention adjourned *sine die,* amid enthusiastic cheers for Seymour and Blair.

RECAPITULATION OF ALL THE BALLOTS FOR PRESIDENT.

CANDIDATES.	1.	2.	3.	4.	5.	6.	7.	8.	9.	10.	11.	12.	13.	14.	15.	16.	17.	18.	19.	20.	21.	22.
George H. Pendleton	105	104	119½	118½	122	122½	137½	156½	144	147½	144½	145½	134½	130	129½	107½	70½	56½	..	..	..	..
Andrew Johnson	65	52	34½	32	24	21	12½	6	5½	6	5½	4½	4½	..	5½	5½	6	10	..	..	5	..
W. S. Hancock	33½	40½	45½	43½	46	47	42½	28	34½	34	32½	30	48½	56	79½	113½	137½	144½	135½	142½	135½	..
Sanford E. Church	34	33	33	33	33	33	33	..	..	..	..	..	..	..	..	..	..	..	..	..	..	..
Asa Packer	26	26	26	26	27	27	26	26	26½	27½	26	26	26	26	..	..	..	..	22	..	..	..
Joel Parker	13	15½	13	13	13	13	7	7	7	7	7	7	7	7	7	7	7	3½	..	..	..	..
James E. English	16	12½	7½	7½	7	6	6	6	6	..	..	..	..	..	..	..	..	..	6	16	19	..
James R. Doolittle	13	12½	12	12	15	12	12	12	..	12	12½	12½	13	13	12	12	12	12	12	12	12	..
Reverdy Johnson	8½	8	11	8	..	..	..	..	12	..	..	..	..	..	..	..	..	..	..	..	..	..
Thomas A. Hendricks	2½	2	9½	11½	19½	30	39½	75	80½	82½	88	89	81	84½	82½	70½	80	87	107½	121	132	..
F. P. Blair, Jr.	½	10½	4½	2	9½	5	½	½	½	½	½	½	½	..	..	..	..	..	13½	13	..	..
T. Ewing, Jr.	..	½	1	1	..	..	..	..	..	..	..	..	..	..	..	..	..	..	..	..	..	..
Horatio Seymour	..	..	..	9	..	..	..	..	..	..	..	..	..	..	..	..	..	..	..	..	..	317
J. Q. Adams	..	..	..	..	1	..	..	..	..	..	..	..	..	..	..	..	..	..	..	..	..	..
George B. McClellan	..	..	..	..	..	..	..	..	..	..	..	1	..	..	..	..	..	..	..	..	½	..
Salmon P. Chase	..	..	..	..	..	..	..	..	..	..	..	½	½	..	..	..	½	½	½	..	4	..
Franklin Pierce	..	..	..	..	..	..	..	..	..	..	..	..	1	..	..	..	..	..	..	..	..	..
John T. Hoffman	..	..	..	..	..	..	..	..	..	..	..	..	..	..	..	..	3	3	..	..	½	..
S. J. Field	..	..	..	..	..	..	..	..	..	..	..	..	..	..	..	..	..	..	15	9	8	..
T. H. Seymour	..	..	..	..	..	..	..	..	..	..	..	..	..	..	..	..	..	..	4	2	..	..

National Democratic Committee.

Hon. AUGUST BELMONT, New York, Chairman.
Hon. FREDERICK O. PRINCE, Boston, Mass., Secretary and Treasurer.
Alabama. — JOHN FORSYTH, Mobile.
Arkansas. — JOHN M. HARRELL, Little Rock.
California. — JOHN BIGLER, Sacramento City.
Connecticut. — WILLIAM CONVERSE, Franklin.
Delaware. — SAMUEL TOWNSEND, Newcastle.
Florida. — CHARLES E. DYKE, Tallahassee.
Georgia. — A. H. COLQUITT, Albany.
Illinois. — WILBUR F. STOREY, Chicago.
Indiana. — WILLIAM E. NIBLACK, Vincennes.
Iowa. — DANIEL O. FINCH, Des Moines.
Kansas. — ISAAC E. EATON, Leavenworth City.
Kentucky. — THOMAS C. MCCREARY, Owensboro.
Louisiana. — JAMES MCCLOSKEY, New Orleans.
Maine. — SYLVANUS R. LYMAN, Portland.
Maryland. — ODIN BOWIE, Prince George.
Michigan. — WILLIAM A. MOORE, Detroit.
Minnesota. — CHARLES W. NASH, St. Paul.
Mississippi. — CHARLES E. HOOKER, Jackson.
Missouri. — CHARLES A. MANTZ, St. Louis.
Nebraska. — G. L. MILLER, Omaha.
Nevada. — J. W. MCCORKLE, Virginia City.
New Hampshire. — HARRY BINGHAM, Littleton.
New Jersey. — JOHN MCGREGOR, Newark.
North Carolina. — THOMAS BRAGG, Raleigh.
Ohio. — JOHN G. THOMPSON, Columbus.
Oregon. — J. C. HAWTHORNE, Portland.
Pennsylvania. — ISAAC ESKISTER, Lancaster.
Rhode Island. — GIDEON BRADFORD, Providence.
South Carolina. — CHARLES H. SIMONTON, Charleston.
Tennessee. — JOHN W. LEFTWICH, Memphis.
Texas. — JOHN HANCOCK, Austin.
Vermont. — H. B. SMITH, Milton.
Virginia. — JOHN GOODE, Norfolk.
West Virginia. — JOHN HALL, Port Pleasant.
Wisconsin. — FREDERICK W. HORN, Cedarburg.

Executive Committee.

Hon. AUGUST BELMONT,
" JAMES MCCLOSKEY,
" JOHN FORSYTH,
" JOHN W. LEFTWICH,
" WILBUR F. STOREY,

Hon. JOHN G. THOMPSON,
" ISAAC E. EATON,
" JOHN MCGREGOR,
" WILLIAM M. CONVERSE,
" F. O. PRINCE.

Letter of Acceptance from Hon. Horatio Seymour.

UTICA, August 4.

GENTLEMEN: When, in the city of New York on the 11th of July, in the presence of a vast multitude, on behalf of the National Democratic Convention, you tendered to me its unanimous nomination as its candidate for the office of President of the United States, I stated I had no words "adequate to express my gratitude for the good-will and kindness which that body had shown to me. Its nomination was unsought and unexpected. It was my ambition to take an active part, from which I am now excluded, in the great struggle going on for the restoration of good government, of peace and prosperity to our country. But I have been caught up by the whelming tide which is bearing us on to a great political change, and I find myself unable to resist its pressure. You have also given me a copy of the resolutions put forth by the Convention, showing its position upon all the great questions which now agitate the country. As the presiding officer of that Convention, I am familiar with their scope and import; as one of its members, I am a party to their terms. They are in accord with my views, and I stand upon them in the contest upon which we are now entering, and shall strive to carry them out in future, wherever I may be placed in political or private life."

I then stated that I would send you these words of acceptance in a letter, as is the customary form. I see no reason, upon reflection, to change or qualify the terms of my approval of the resolutions of the Convention.

I have delayed the mere formal act of communicating to you in writing what I thus publicly said, for the purpose of seeing what light the action of Congress would throw upon the interests of the country. Its acts, since the adjournment of the Convention, show an alarm lest a change of political power will give to the people what they ought to have, — a clear statement of what has been done with the money drawn from them during the past eight years. Thoughtful men feel that there have been wrongs in the financial management which have been kept from the public knowledge. The Congressional party has not only allied itself with military power, which is to be brought to bear directly upon the elections in many States, but it also holds itself in perpetual session, with the avowed purpose of making such laws as it shall see fit, in view of the elections which will take place within a few weeks. It did not, therefore, adjourn, but took a recess, to meet again if its partisan interests shall demand its reassembling. Never before in the history of our country has Congress thus taken a menacing attitude towards its electors. Under its influence, some of the States organized by its agents are proposing to deprive the people of the right to vote for Presidential electors, and the first bold steps are taken to destroy the rights of suffrage. It is not strange, therefore, that thoughtful men see in such action the proof that there are with those who shape the policy of the Republican party, motives stronger and deeper than the mere wish to hold political power; that there is a dread of some exposure which drives them on to acts so desperate and impolitic.

Many of the ablest leaders and journals of the Republican party have openly deplored the violence of congressional action, and its tendency to keep up discord in our country. The great interests of our Union demand peace, order, and a return to those industrial pursuits without which we cannot maintain the faith or honor of our government. The minds of business men are perplexed by uncertainties. The hours of toil of our laborers are lengthened by the costs of living made by the direct and indirect exactions of government. Our people are harassed by the heavy and frequent demands of the tax-gatherer. Without distinction of party, there is a strong feeling in favor of that line of action which shall restore order and confidence, and shall lift off the burthens which now hinder and vex the industry of the country. Yet, at this moment, those in power have thrown into the Senate Chamber and Congressional Hall new elements of discord and violence. Men have been admitted as Representatives of some of the Southern States, with the declaration upon their lips that they cannot live in the States they claim to represent, without military protection. These men are to make laws for the North as well as the South. These men, who, a few days since, were seeking as suppliants that Congress would give them power within their respective States are, to-day, the masters and controllers of the actions of those bodies. Entering them with minds filled with passions, their first demands have been that Congress shall look upon the States from which they come as in conditions of civil war; that the majority of their populations, embracing their intelligence, shall be treated as public enemies; that military forces shall be kept up at the cost of the people of the North, and that there shall be no peace and order at the South save that which is made by arbitrary power. Every intelligent man knows that these men owe their seats in Congress to the disorder in the South; every man knows that they not only owe their present positions to disorder, but that every motive springing from the love of power, of gain, of a desire for vengeance, prompts them to keep the South in anarchy. While that exists, they are independent of the wills or wishes of their fellow-citizens. While confusion reigns, they are the dispensers of the profits and the honors which grow out of the government of mere force. These men are now placed in positions where they cannot urge their views of policy, but where they can enforce them. When others shall be admitted in this manner from the remaining Southern States, although they will have, in truth, no constituents, they will have more power in the Senate than a majority of the people of this Union living in nine of the great States. In vain the wisest members of the Republican party protested against the policy that led to this result. While the chiefs of the late rebellion have submitted to the results of the war, and are now quietly engaged in useful pursuits for the support of themselves and their families, and are trying, by the force of their example, to lead back the people of the South to the order and industry, not only essential to their well-being, but to the greatness and prosperity of our common country, we see, that those who, without ability or influence, have been thrown, by the agitations of civil convulsion, into positions of honor and profit, are striving to keep alive the passions to which they owe their elevation. And they clamorously insist that they are the only friends of our Union, — a Union that can only have a sure foundation in fraternal regard, and a common desire to promote the peace, the order, and the happiness of all sections of our land.

Events in Congress, since the adjournment of the Convention, have vastly increased the importance of a political victory by those who are seeking to bring back economy, simplicity, and justice in the administration of our national affairs. Many Republicans have heretofore clung to their party who have regretted the extremes of violence to which it has run. They have cherished a faith that while the action of their political friends has been mistaken, their motives have been good. They must now see that the Republican party is in that condition that it cannot carry out a wise and peaceful policy, whatever its motives may be. It is a misfortune, not only to a country, but to a governing party itself, when its action is unchecked by any form of opposition. It has been the misfortune of the Republican party that the events of the past few years have given it so much power that it has been able to shackle the Executive, to trammel the Judiciary, and to carry out the views of the most unwise and violent of its members. When this state of things exists in any party, it has ever been found that the sober judgments of its ablest leaders do not control. There is hardly an able man who helped to build up the Republican organization, who has not, within the past three years, warned it against its excesses, who has not been borne down and forced to give up his convictions of what the interests of the country called for; or, if too patriotic to do this, who has not been driven from its ranks. If this has been the case heretofore, what will be its action now with this new infusion of men, who, without a decent respect for the views of those who had just given them their positions, begin their legislative career with calls for arms, with demands that their States shall be regarded as in a condition of civil war, and with a declaration that they are ready and anxious to degrade the President of the United States whenever they can persuade or force Congress to bring forward new articles of impeachment?

The Republican party, as well as we, are interested in putting some check upon this violence. It must be clear to every thinking man that a division of political power tends to check the violence of party action, and to assure the peace and good order of society. The election of a Democratic Executive, and a majority of Democratic members to the House of Representatives, would not give to that party organization the power to make sudden or violent changes, but it would serve to check those extreme measures which have been deplored by the best men of both political organizations. The result would most certainly lead to that peaceful restoration of the Union and re-establishment of fraternal relationship, which the country desires. I am sure that the best men of the Republican party deplore, as deeply as I do, the spirit of violence shown by those recently admitted to seats in Congress from the South. The condition of civil war, which they contemplate, must be abhorrent to every right-thinking man.

I have no mere personal wishes which mislead my judgment in regard to the pending election. No man who has weighed and measured the duties of the office of President of the United States can fail to be impressed with the cares and toils of him who is to meet its demands. It is not merely to float with popular currents, without a policy or a purpose. On the contrary, while our Constitution gives just weight to the public will, its distinguishing feature is that it seeks to protect the rights of minorities. Its greatest glory is that it puts restraints upon power. It gives force and form to those maxims and principles of civil liberty for which the martyrs of freedom have struggled through ages. It declares the right of the people "to be secure in their persons, houses, and papers, against unreasonable searches and seizures; that Congress shall make no law respecting an establishment of religion, or the free exercise thereof, or abridging the freedom of speech, or of the press, or the right of the people to petition for redress of grievances." It secures the "right of a speedy and public trial by an impartial jury."

No man can rightfully enter upon the duties of the Presidential office, unless he is not only willing to carry out the wishes of the people, expressed in a constitutional way, but is also prepared to stand up for the rights of minorities. He must be ready to uphold the free exercise of religion. He must denounce measures which would wrong personal or home rights, or the religious conscience of the humblest citizen of the land. He must maintain, without distinction of creed or nationality, all the privileges of American citizenship.

The experience of every public man who has been faithful to his trust teaches him that no one can do the duties of the office of President, unless he is ready not only to undergo the falsehoods and abuse of the bad, but to suffer from the censure of the good, who are misled by prejudices and misrepresentations. There are no attractions in such a position which deceive my judgment, when I say that a great change is going on in the public mind. The mass of the Republican party are more thoughtful, temperate, and just than they were during the excitements which attended the progress and close of the civil war. As the energy of the Democratic party springs from their devotion to their cause and not to their candidates, I may with propriety speak of the fact that never in the political history of our country has the action of any like body been hailed with such universal and wide-spread enthusiasm as that which has been shown in relation to the position of the National Democratic Convention. With this the candidates had nothing to do. Had any others of those named been selected, this spirit would have been, perhaps, more marked. The zeal and energy of the conservative masses spring from a desire to make a change of political policy, and from the confidence that they can carry out their purpose.

In this faith they are strengthened by the co-operation of the great body of those who served in the Union army and navy during the war. Having given nearly sixteen thousand commissions to the officers of that army, I know their views and wishes. They demand the Union for which they fought. The largest meeting of these gallant soldiers which ever assembled was held in New York, and endorsed the action of the National Convention. In words instinct with meaning, they called upon the government to stop in its policy of hate, discord, and disunion, and, in terms of fervid eloquence, they demanded the restoration of the rights and liberties of the American people.

When there is such accord between those who proved themselves brave and self-sacrificing in war, and those who are thoughtful and patriotic in council, I cannot doubt we shall gain a political triumph which will restore our Union, bring back peace and prosperity to our land, and will give us once more the blessings of a wise, economical, and honest government.

I am, gentleman, truly yours, etc.,

HORATIO SEYMOUR.

To Gen. W. G. MORGAN, and others, Committee, etc., etc.

Letter of Acceptance from Gen. Frank P. Blair, Jr.

GENERAL, — I take the earliest opportunity of replying to your letter notifying me of my nomination for Vice-President of the United States, by the National Democratic Convention recently held in the city of New York.

I accept, without hesitation, the nomination tendered in a manner so gratifying, and give you and the Committee my thanks for the very kind and complimentary language in which you have conveyed to me the decision of the Convention.

I have carefully read the resolutions adopted by the Convention, and most cordially concur in every principle and sentiment they announce.

My opinions upon all the questions which discriminate the great contending parties have been freely expressed on all suitable occasions, and I do not deem it necessary at this time to reiterate them.

The issues upon which the contest turns are clear, and cannot be obscured or distorted by the sophistries of our adversaries. They all resolve themselves into the old and ever-recurring struggle of a few men to absorb the political power of the nation. This effort, under every conceivable name and disguise, has always characterized the opponents of the Democratic party, but at no time has the attempt assumed a shape so open and daring as in this contest. The adversaries of free and constitutional government, in defiance of the express language of the Constitution, have erected a military despotism in ten of the States of the Union, have taken from the President the power vested in him by the supreme law, and have deprived the Supreme Court of its jurisdiction. The right of trial by jury, and the great writ of right, the *habeas corpus*, — shields of safety for every citizen, which have descended to us from the earliest traditions of our ancestors, and which our Revolutionary fathers sought to secure to their posterity forever in the fundamental charter of our liberties, — have been ruthlessly trampled under foot by the fragment of a Congress; whole States and communities of people of our race have been attainted, convicted, condemned, and deprived of their rights as citizens, without presentment, or trial, or witnesses, but by congressional enactment of *ex post facto* laws, and in defiance of the constitutional prohibition denying even to a full and loyal Congress the authority to pass any bill of attainder or *ex post facto* law. The same usurping authority has substituted as electors in place of the men of our race, thus illegally attainted and disfranchised, a host of ignorant negroes who are supported in idleness with the public money, and are combined together to strip the white race of their birthright through the management of freedmen's bureaus and emissaries of conspirators in other States. And, to complete the oppression, the military power of the nation has been placed at their disposal, in order to make this barbarism supreme. The military leader, under whose prestige this usurping Congress has taken refuge since the condemnation of their schemes by the free people of the North, in the elections of the last year, and whom they have selected as their candidate, to shield themselves from the result of their own wickedness and crime, has announced his acceptance of the nomination, and his willingness to maintain their usurpations over eight millions of white people at the South, fixed to the earth with his bayonets. He exclaims, "Let us have peace!" "Peace reigns in Warsaw" was the announcement which heralded the doom of the liberties of a nation. "The empire is peace," exclaimed Bonaparte, when freedom and its defenders expired under the sharp edge of his sword. The peace to which Grant invites us is the peace of despotism and death. Those who seek to restore the Constitution by executing the will of the people condemning the reconstruction acts, already pronounced in the elections of last year (and which will, I am convinced, be still more emphatically expressed by the election of the Democratic candidate as President of the United States), are denounced as revolutionists by the partisans of this vindictive Congress. Negro Suffrage (which the popular vote of New York, New Jersey, Pennsylvania, Ohio, Michigan, Connecticut, and other States has condemned as expressly against the letter of the Constitution) must stand, because their Senators and Representatives have willed it. If the people shall again condemn these atrocious measures by the election of the Democratic candidate for President, *they* must not be disturbed! Although decided to be unconstitutional by the Supreme Court, and although the President is sworn to sustain and support the Constitution, the will of a fraction of a Congress, reinforced with its partisan emissaries sent to the South, and supported there by the soldiery, must stand against the will of the people, and the decision of the Supreme Court, and the solemn oath of the President, to maintain and support the Constitution! It is revolutionary to execute the will of the people! It is revolutionary to execute the judgment of the Supreme Court! It is revolutionary in the President to keep inviolate his oath to sustain the Constitution! This false construction of the vital principle of our Government is the last resort of those who would have their arbitrary reconstruction sway and supersede our time-honored institutions. The nation will say that the Constitution must be restored, and the will of the people again prevail. The appeal to the peaceful ballot to attain this end is not war, — is not revolution. They make war and revolution who attempt to arrest this quiet mode of putting aside military despotism and the usurpations of a fragment of a Congress, asserting absolute power over that benign system of regulated liberty left us by our fathers. This must be allowed to take its course. This is the only road to peace. It will come with the election of the Democratic candidate, and not with the election of that mailed warrior, whose bayonets are now at the throats of eight millions of people in the South, to compel them to support him as a candidate for the Presidency, and to submit to the domination of an alien race of semi-barbarous men. No perversion of truth, or audacity of misrepresentation, can exceed that which hails this candidate in arms as an angel of peace.

I am, very respectfully, your most obedient servant,

FRANK P. BLAIR.

To Gen. G. W. MORGAN, and others.

Organization of the National Democratic Committee.

NEW YORK, July 9, 1868.

THE members of the new National Democratic Committee, consisting of one representative from each State, met this day at the rooms of the Committee, in Tammany Hall, New York.

Mr. FREDERICK O. PRINCE, Secretary of the retiring committee, called the meeting to order, and called the roll of members, as follows, —

LIST OF MEMBERS.

Alabama. — JOHN FORSYTH, Mobile.
Arkansas. — JOHN M. HARRELL, Little Rock.
California. — JOHN BIGLER, Sacramento City.
Connecticut. — WILLIAM M. CONVERSE, Franklin.
Delaware. — SAMUEL TOWNSEND, Newcastle.
Florida. — CHARLES E. DYKE, Tallahassee.
Georgia. — A. H. COLQUITT, Albany.
Illinois. — WILBUR F. STOREY, Chicago.
Indiana. — WILLIAM E. NIBLACK, Vincennes.
Iowa. — DANIEL O. FINCH, Des Moines.
Kansas. — ISAAC E. EATON, Leavenworth City.
Kentucky. — THOMAS C. MCCREARY, Owensboro.
Louisiana. — JAMES MCCLOSKEY, New Orleans.
Maine. — SYLVANUS R. LYMAN, Portland.
Maryland. — ODIN BOWIE, Prince George.
Massachusetts. — FREDERICK O. PRINCE, Boston.
Michigan. — WILLIAM A. MOORE, Detroit.
Minnesota. — CHARLES W. NASH, St. Paul.
Mississippi. — CHARLES E. HOOKER, Jackson.
Missouri. — CHARLES A. MANTZ, St. Louis.
Nebraska. — G. L. MILLER, Omaha.
Nevada. — J. W. MCCORKIE, Virginia City.
New Hampshire. — HARRY BINGHAM, Littleton.
New Jersey. — JOHN MCGREGOR, Newark.
New York — AUGUST BELMONT, New York City.
North Carolina. — THOMAS BRAGG, Raleigh.
Ohio. — JOHN G. THOMPSON, Columbus.
Oregon. — J. C. HAWTHORNE, Portland.
Pennsylvania. — ISAAC ESKISTER, Lancaster.
Rhode Island. — GIDEON BRADFORD, Providence.
South Carolina. — CHARLES H. SIMONTON, Charleston.
Tennessee. — JOHN W. LEFTWICH, Memphis.
Texas. — JOHN HANCOCK, Austin.
Vermont. — H. B. SMITH, Milton.
Virginia. — JOHN GOODE, Norfolk.
West Virginia. — JOHN HALL, Port Pleasant.
Wisconsin. — FREDERICK W. HORN, Cedarburg.

THE TEMPORARY ORGANIZATION.

Mr. WILBUR F. STOREY, of Illinois, was unanimously elected temporary Chairman, and

Mr. FREDERICK O. PRINCE, of Massachusetts, was unanimously elected temporary Secretary of the Committee.

THE PERMANENT ORGANIZATION.

It having been moved and voted to proceed to the permanent organization of the Committee, the Hon. AUGUST BELMONT was elected Chairman, and the Hon. FREDERICK O. PRINCE, Secretary of the Committee.

A motion was made to dispense with an Executive Committee, but was not carried.

It was voted that a Committee of five be appointed by the Chairman to select an Executive Committee; and Messrs. Storey of Illinois, Lyman of Maine, Leftwich of Tennessee, McGregor of New Jersey, and McCorkie of Nevada, were appointed to such Committee.

The Committee subsequently reported, recommending the following gentlemen to constitute

THE EXECUTIVE COMMITTEE

AUGUST BELMONT, New York.
JOHN MCGREGOR, Newark, New Jersey.
WILLIAM M. CONVERSE, Franklin, Connecticut.
WILBUR F. STOREY, Chicago, Illinois.
JOHN G. THOMPSON, Columbus, Ohio.
ISAAC E. EATON, Leavenworth City, Kansas.
JAMES MCCLOSKEY, New Orleans, Louisiana.
JOHN FORSYTH, Mobile, Alabama.
JOHN W. LEFTWICH, Memphis, Tennessee.
FREDERICK O. PRINCE, Boston, Massachusetts.

It was voted that Mr. FREDERICK O. PRINCE be the Treasurer of the National Committee.

It was voted that the subject of the appointment of a Congressional Democratic Committee at Washington be referred to the Executive Committee.

CONGRESSIONAL DEMOCRATIC COMMITTEE.

The following gentlemen were appointed as the Congressional Democratic Committee, —

Hon. J. R. DOOLITTLE, U. S. Senator, Wisconsin.
Hon. C. R. BUCKALEW, U. S. Senator, Pennsylvania.
Hon. SAMUEL J. RANDALL, M. C., Pennsylvania.
Hon. JAMES M. HUMPHREY, M. C., New York.
Hon. WM. H. BARNUM, M. C., Connecticut.
Hon. LEWIS W. ROSS, M. C., Illinois.
Hon. LAWRENCE S. TRIMBLE, M. C., Kentucky.
Hon. MONTGOMERY BLAIR, Washington City.
JONAH D. HOOVER, ESQ.,   "   "
CHARLES MASON, ESQ.,   "   "
General THOMAS EWING, Jr.,   "   "

Printed in Dunstable, United Kingdom